Transforming
SUBURBAN
BUSINESS
DISTRICTS

**Urban Land
Institute**

About ULI–the Urban Land Institute

ULI–the Urban Land Institute is a nonprofit education and research institute that is supported by its members. Its mission is to provide responsible leadership in the use of land in order to enhance the total environment.

ULI sponsors education programs and forums to encourage an open international exchange of ideas and sharing of experiences; initiates research that anticipates emerging land use trends and issues and proposes creative solutions based on that research; provides advisory services; and publishes a wide variety of materials to disseminate information on land use and development. Established in 1936, the Institute today has more than 16,000 members and associates from some 60 countries representing the entire spectrum of the land use and development disciplines.

Richard M. Rosan
President

Recommended bibliographic listing:
Booth, Geoffrey, et al. *Transforming Suburban Business Districts.* Washington, D.C.: ULI–the Urban Land Institute, 2001.

ULI Catalog Number: T16
International Standard Book Number: 0-87420-881-5
Library of Congress Control Number: 2001095693

Copyright 2001 by ULI–the Urban Land Institute
1025 Thomas Jefferson Street, N.W.
Suite 500 West
Washington, D.C. 20007-5201

ULI Project Staff

Rachelle L. Levitt
Senior Vice President, Policy and Practice
Publisher

Dean Schwanke
Vice President, Development Trends and Analysis

Geoffrey Booth
Director, Retail Development
Project Director

Nancy H. Stewart
Director, Book Program

Carol E. Soble
Manuscript Editor

Betsy VanBuskirk
Art Director
Cover Design

Helene Y. Redmond
HYR Graphics
Book Design/Layout

Diann Stanley-Austin
Director, Publishing Operations

Cover:
Foreground image: Starwood Urban
Background image: Geoffrey Booth

Acknowledgments

There are many minds that mold a manuscript and many hands that work together to produce a publication. The following people deserve acknowledgment for bringing *Transforming Suburban Business Districts* to print. J. Thomas Black sowed the conceptual seed for this book. Michael Beyard provided assistance and critical comment in refining the book's inception outline. Stephen Blank, Gary Cusumano, Robert Dunphy, Steven Fader, Richard Galehouse, Thomas Lee, Christopher Leinberger, Charles Lockwood, Gregg Logan, Patrick Phillips, David Salvesen, Jantrue Ting, and Richard Ward, as contributing authors, brought the draft manuscript to life. ULI leaders Kenneth Hughes, Christopher Kurz, J. Kevin Lawler, James Todd, and Smedes York each read the complete manuscript at short notice. Their critical and constructive comments were both encouraging and invaluable in refining the book, as were their enthusiasm and commitment to seeing the book published. A task force of 17 development and planning practitioners met in June 2001, using the research work undertaken for this book and the draft manuscript, to devise ULI's ten principles for transforming suburban business districts. Michael Pawlukiewicz coordinated the meeting of the task force.

Ann Oliveri nourished the process with ULI leadership tapes, current books and reviews, and sage advice on whom to consult to focus the book on the needs and aspirations of ULI members in particular and of the U.S. land use and real estate community in general. Lori Hatcher read the manuscript and made the point that a chapter on multifamily housing should be included. Patricia Riggs kept me in touch with national print media journalists, and Karen Schaar and Kristina Kessler provided a continuing diet of excellent and topical articles in *Urban Land.* The research articles delivered by Rick Davis on a weekly basis were invaluable in giving the book sharper focus. Joan Campbell came to my rescue with industry reports and reference citations.

Nancy Stewart's management and guidance of the editorial and production process made clear the ULI way to produce a book. Without her quiet determination and advice this book would have floundered. Carol Soble worked tirelessly and with great skill to smooth the manuscript with a flow and direction that readers will find engaging. Helene Redmond's magic in laying out the book completed the transformation from manuscript to publishable standard. Diann Stanley-Austin coordinated the printing of the book and Betsy VanBuskirk designed the cover. Meg Batdorff, Leslie Holst, Ryan Kommpa, and Clark Mercer provided assistance in case study and photographic image collection. Ronnie Van Alstyne provided me with administrative support throughout the process.

Dean Schwanke gave me constructive comment and support with his determination to see case study material play a stronger role in supporting the book's conclusions and recommendations. His willingness to read the manuscript and share his knowledge and experience constituted the realization of ULI's true collegiate potential. To those colleagues in ULI's Policy and Practice Department, particularly Jo Allen Gause, who willingly shared their thoughts, ideas, research, photographic images, and words of encouragement, I look forward to returning the favor over the years ahead. My mates in Australia, particularly Ross Elliott, chief operating officer of the Property Council of Australia, have provided me with E-mails and letters of encouragement, advice, and support. Rachelle Levitt launched the research and gave me the opportunity to assume principal authorship of this book.

Many other people in public and private practice made important contributions to this book. I hope that everyone associated with this book will be rewarded with an improved standard of real estate development—one that increasingly creates *place.* The place-making dividend is there for the taking in the transformation of suburban business districts.

Geoffrey Booth
Principal Author

Authors and Reviewers

Transforming Suburban Business Districts brings together a wide variety of contributing authors who have studied this subject over several decades. Their work was consolidated and expanded into a manuscript that was critically reviewed by an external panel of ULI members. All five external reviewers have extensive experience in real estate development and finance. They were joined in the review process by ULI's vice president, development trends and analysis. In addition, a 17-member task force of development and planning experts met for two and one-half days in Washington, D.C., in June 2001 to distill ULI's ten principles for transforming suburban business districts, which are outlined in the last chapter of this book.

Principal Author

Geoffrey Booth, an urban planner and real estate developer from Australia, was appointed in January 2000 as director of retail development at the Urban Land Institute in Washington, D.C.

Contributing Authors

Stephen Blank is an investment banker and senior resident fellow, finance, the Urban Land Institute in Washington, D.C.

Gary Cusumano is a real estate developer and recently appointed chair of the Newhall Land and Farming Company in Valencia, California.

Robert Dunphy is a transportation planner and senior resident fellow, transportation and infrastructure, the Urban Land Institute in Washington, D.C.

Steven Fader is an architect and principal of Steven Fader Architect in Los Angeles, California.

Richard Galehouse is an architect, planner, and principal of Sasaki Associates, Inc., in Watertown, Massachusetts.

Thomas Lee is a real estate developer and recently retired chair of the Newhall Land and Farming Company in Valencia, California.

Christopher Leinberger is a real estate developer and founding partner of Arcadia Land Company in Santa Fe, New Mexico.

Charles Lockwood is an author and urban planning commentator based in Los Angeles, California.

Gregg Logan is an urban analyst and managing director of Robert Charles Lesser & Co. in Atlanta, Georgia.

Patrick Phillips is an urban analyst and president of Economics Research Associates (ERA) in Washington, D.C.

David Salvesen is an urban planner and director of the smart growth and new economy program in the Center for Urban and Regional Studies at the University of North Carolina at Chapel Hill, North Carolina.

Jantrue Ting is an urban planner and research associate at Sasaki Associates, Inc., in Watertown, Massachusetts.

Richard Ward is an urban planner and president of Development Strategies, Inc., in St. Louis, Missouri.

Reviewers

Kenneth Hughes is a real estate developer and president of UC Urban in Dallas, Texas. He is a member of ULI's Policy and Practice Committee.

Christopher Kurz is a real estate developer, financier, and president and CEO of Linden Associates Incorporated of Baltimore, Maryland. He is chair emeritus of ULI's Baltimore District Council.

J. Kevin Lawler is a real estate developer and president of J.K. Lawler Associates, Inc., of West Palm Beach, Florida. He is a member of ULI's Policy and Practice Committee.

Dean Schwanke is an urban planner and vice president, development trends and analysis, the Urban Land Institute in Washington, D.C.

James Todd is a real estate developer and president of the Peterson Companies in Fairfax, Virginia. He is a governor of the ULI Foundation, a ULI Trustee, and a member of ULI's Policy and Practice Committee.

Smedes York is a real estate developer and president of York Properties, Inc., in Raleigh, North Carolina. He is a past ULI chair, a governor of the ULI Foundation, and a ULI Trustee.

Task Force

Chair

A. Eugene Kohn—Kohn Pedersen Fox, New York

Members

Laura Aldrete—City and County of Denver, Colorado

Geoffrey Booth—Urban Land Institute, Washington, D.C.

Gary Bowden—RTKL Architects (retired), Baltimore, Maryland

Robert Dunphy—Urban Land Institute, Washington, D.C.

Richard Galehouse—Sasaki Associates, Watertown, Massachusetts

Terry Holzheimer—Arlington County, Virginia

Nicholas Javaras—Shelter Bay Retail Group, Corte Madera, California

David Kitchens—Cooper Carry Architects, Alexandria, Virginia

Bruce Leonard—Starwood Urban, Washing-ton, D.C.

Maureen McAvey—Urban Land Institute, Washington, D.C.

Michael Pawlukiewicz—Urban Land Institute, Washington, D.C.

Patrick Phillips—Economics Research Associates, Washington, D.C.

William Roache—Vanasse Hangen Brustlin, Inc., Watertown, Massachusetts

Ken Voigt—The HNTB Companies, Milwaukee, Wisconsin

Michael Wanchick—City of Richardson, Texas

Richard Ward—Development Strategies, Inc., St. Louis, Missouri

Contents

Transforming
SUBURBAN
BUSINESS
DISTRICTS

chapter 1

What Is the Problem, What Is the Opportunity?

For most of the latter half of the 20th century, Americans lived, worked, and shopped in separate places, availing themselves of the automobile and the best highway system in the world to commute from one place to another. It was a period of relative affluence, high levels of automobile ownership and homeownership, and a suburban lifestyle that typically included two kids, a mortgage, and two working parents to pay for it all. It was a dream come true for real estate developers, financiers, investors, and government: a growing market, an accepted range of real estate products, formulaic developments that worked, and a secure suburban tax base. By the 1990s, the demographics began to undergo a major shift with the growth of new household types and population segments such as

- the aging baby boomers, whose children—the GenXers and Yers—had now left home;
- the GenXers and Yers—or echo boomers;
- the active adults—the parents of the baby boomers; and
- a growing proportion of minority and immigrant communities.

This new demographic profile points to a generally affluent and well traveled population that has developed a heightened appreciation of place. Tired of traffic congestion, many of today's households are looking to trade in their suburban lifestyle for one that gives them greater choice and flexibility. What many are looking for are integrated live-work-shop places that are exciting, aesthetically pleasing, and pedestrian-friendly and that offer a wide choice of transportation options.

Unfortunately, in most of America's suburbs and suburban business districts, such pedestrian-friendly live-work-shop environments are in short supply. While the phrase "suburban business district" suggests parallels with the central business district, the two are markedly different. Most suburban business districts encompass a variety of freestanding uses with little or no integration among uses, a transportation system that is automobile-oriented and often hostile to pedestrians, and an absence of civic identity or sense of place. Thus, though similar to central business districts in that they are strong commercial activity centers, suburban business districts lack fundamental qualities that are increasingly in demand in today's real estate markets.

As the housing, office, retail, and real estate finance markets target today's households, all roads can lead to suburban business districts, but suburban business districts need to be transformed in fundamental ways if they are to serve changing markets. The marrying of market demand and available real estate capital presents the owners and developers of real estate in sub-urban business districts with the opportunity to increase the value of their capital assets. Herein lies the potential for communities, astute real estate developers and investors, and enlightened local governments and their advisers to transform suburban business districts.

Suburban business districts are complex, competitive markets in which space is a commodity and location, quality, and image determine real estate values. Creations of the mid- to late 20th century, suburban business districts evolved as a result of sustained suburban population growth, real estate investment practices, and the fiscal imperatives of local government. As they move into middle age and beyond, aging suburban business districts are providing opportunities for enlightened public policy initiatives and far-sighted real estate development and investment. These opportunities are rich in their potential to deliver highly attractive financial and community-building returns in the form of a place-making dividend.

A place-making dividend is the pride and satisfaction that accrues to the community when districts possess a strong sense of place that in turn results in high levels of repeat visitation and increasing rents, retail sales, leasing demand, and real estate capital value. A place-making dividend occurs when individual real estate projects are so well designed and inter-connected as to work together to create one

© C.J. Walker

integrated place. For the community, the place-making dividend means a special place that the community adopts as its own such that it reaps the benefits of repeat visitation. For the real estate developer and investor, the place-making dividend means repeat patronage or tenant demand, higher rents, and enduring real estate values. This book explains how suburban business districts came into being and identifies how transformation of the districts can cost effectively yield a place-making dividend. This place-making dividend will benefit, in equal measure, both the community and the real estate industry.

Transforming Suburban Business Districts

As locations historically dominated by retail or office use, suburban business districts are changing the structure and use patterns of cities. The building form and layout of most suburban business districts have a fragmentation and separation not found in the traditional central business district. As employment locations, suburban business districts frequently outstrip the down-

town. Access to and within suburban business districts typically requires the automobile, and pedestrian and public park systems are rarely well developed. More often than not, suburban business districts are a collection of geographically proximate but not interconnected property developments—districts rather than centers. The lack of centralization and an environment hostile to pedestrians present a major challenge to public transit, which, oriented to downtown destinations, is unable to serve lower-density and fragmented or dispersed development in a cost-effective manner.

As users demand more of their urban environments, suburban business districts are challenged to improve their access, diversify their land use and tenant mix, and create places that tenants and customers cannot resist. Today, suburban business districts should be encouraged to move beyond automobile-accessible places that are merely places to work and shop. Indeed, they embody the potential to become places where people also reside, build, and celebrate their community. In facing these challenges, owners of real estate assets in suburban business districts can capitalize on the potential to maximize their investment return through the creation of improved suburban business district environments.

Classification of Suburban Business Districts

Is it an urban village core, an edge city, a node, a cluster, or a center? Much of the research into this query has floundered in abstract discussion of competing terminology—urban villages, perimeter cities, edge cities, stealth cities, peripheral centers, satellite cities, suburban activity centers, and technolopoles—to cite just a few. Terms, however, should be used to clarify and advance understanding, not confuse.

The Derivation of the Term "Suburban Business District"

"Suburban" describes the districts' location—in the suburbs, not in the original city center (also called the central business district). Suburban business districts' predominant uses reflect the circumstances of their establishment as business locations, i.e., places typified by shops, offices, hotels, entertainment, technology, educational and administrative service establishments, as well as by some residential properties. In fact, many of the initial developments in suburban business districts took the form of a regional shopping mall or an office complex. Moreover, the individual components or buildings of a development often share geographic proximity but not always pedestrian interconnectivity. Therefore, they are often in the nature of a "district" rather than a center. They are suburban business districts.

The Essence of a Suburban Business District

A suburban business district is more than an ad hoc retail or office building within a residential area or semirural setting or abutting a major road. A suburban business district identifies itself by exhibiting all or most of the following traits:

- a critical mass of floor space—usually more than 5 million square feet in total;

- a land use mix of predominantly office and retail uses, although not necessarily within each building in a given district;
- more jobs than bedrooms;
- a commonly held community perception as a single district; and
- a development form and pattern that was established largely after 1945.[1]

The Three Distinct Types of Suburban Business Districts

While suburban business districts can and have been categorized by age, building form and layout, predominant transportation mode, and land use profile or distance from downtown, this book has adopted the categories of "compact," "fragmented," and "dispersed." Clearly, these three categories of suburban business districts reflect definable spatial characteristics. In all three categories of suburban business districts, real estate assets are generally held in fragmented ownership except for some master-planned centers where the developer has retained ownership of the entire center. Figure 1.1 summarizes the characteristics of the three categories of suburban business districts.

Compact suburban business districts are generally the oldest of the three types of suburban business districts, and they have the great-

Geoffrey Booth

figure 1.1 Categories of Suburban Business Districts

	Compact	Fragmented	Dispersed
Floor/area ratio	2.5 and above	0.5 to 2.5	Up to 0.5
Building coverage	0.5 or more of lot area	0.25 to 0.5 of lot area	Up to 0.25 of lot area
Lot area	Less than one acre	Greater than one acre	Generally exceeds 10 acres
Street layout	Grid	Superblock	Superblock
Land value	High	Medium	Low
Buildings dominate space	Yes, buildings built to street alignment	No, buildings set back from road and separated by surface parking lots	No, buildings set back from road; often one to two stories in height in campus/park setting
Parking	Structured–managed	Surface–managed	Surface–unmanaged
Transportation choice	Wide, frequently includes light- and heavy-rail transit	Limited, usually car and bus	Very limited, usually car with infrequent transit if any
Pedestrian linkages and interconnection of development	Extensive, encourages pedestrian activity	Limited, often no linkages; layout encourages patrons to drive to adjoining developments	Very limited, developments far apart and not within walking distance
Examples	Rosslyn, Arlington County, Virginia	Tysons Corner, Fairfax County, Virginia	College Boulevard–Overland Park, Kansas City, Kansas

Source: Geoffrey Booth, Urban Land Institute, 2001.

est similarity to a central business district. As noted in Figure 1.1, they are characterized by fairly high densities, a grid street layout, transit availability, and a pedestrian environment that is serviceable or even "friendly." As such, in many ways, they are the easiest suburban business districts to tranform, and many already have undergone transformation. Leading examples of such compact suburban business districts that have established a strong sense of place and a pedestrian-friendly environment include Bethesda, Maryland, in the suburbs of Washington, D.C.; Bellevue, Washington, outside Seattle; and Arlington Heights, Illinois, near Chicago.

Fragmented suburban districts are perhaps the most problematic to transform of the three district types. They are characterized by medium densities, superblock configurations, and relatively hostile pedestrian environments. They generally do not contain large parcels of vacant or unused land, although they do contain a good

deal of underused land devoted to parking and other low-intensity uses. In some ways, they are mature in that they are substantially developed and their transportation and land use patterns are somewhat set and difficult to alter. To transform these patterns usually requires strong public intervention, new infrastructure investment, both public and private redevelopment initiatives, and creative infill development, none of which is easy to undertake where property interests are already heavily vested in the current pattern. But the strongest of these suburban business districts, such as Tysons Corner, Virginia, near Washington, D.C., are already experiencing strong growth in demand and thus pressure to redevelop underused land, providing a strong market base for transformation efforts.

Dispersed suburban business districts are the least mature of the three types of districts and are characterized by low densities, superblock configurations, hostile or nonexistent pedestrian environments, and a substantial amount of undeveloped or underused land. They offer greater flexibility in terms of transformation, as land values are relatively low, and transportation and land use patterns are not as strongly established as in the previous two categories. Modest intervention by the public and private sectors can be effective in altering the land use patterns in these districts before they become dysfunctional and congested, allowing more interconnected, diverse, and pedestrian-friendly environments to develop.

Application of this categorization system requires an understanding that some suburban business districts exhibit some but not necessarily all of the elements listed under their respective category. A common-sense, best-fit approach should be adopted in considering the characterization of each suburban business district.

Approach and Objectives

This book has drawn on industry leaders to research and document their understanding of successful suburban business district development, with the objective of providing an explicit understanding of how suburban business districts work, what needs they fulfill, and how the public and private sectors can strengthen them. The book addresses more than matters of design as related to existing suburban business districts. Instead, it offers practical solutions that can enhance suburban business district competitiveness, livability, and the improved satisfaction of community needs. As illustrations of practical analyses and solutions, the book draws examples from both relevant downtown and suburban projects and features case studies of best-practice development projects.

Obviously, not every solution illustrated in the book will be relevant to every type of suburban business district. Nor is there a generic implementation program that will suit all suburban business districts. Rather, community builders willing to learn from the experiences recounted in this book can tailor location-specific solutions that respond to particular needs. As Jane Jacobs said in her introduction to *The Death and Life of Great American Cities,* "Cities are an immense laboratory of trial and error, failure and success in city building and city design."[2] However, some errors can be avoided. By identifying past mistakes and focusing public policy and real estate investment practice on successful community-

In fragmented suburban business districts, like Tysons Corner in Fairfax County, Virginia, buildings can be as tall as those in compact suburban business districts but are constructed on larger lots, often surrounded by surface parking. This makes pedestrian movement unattractive and the provision of public transit less cost-effective. The need to drive to destinations within the fragmented suburban business district generates additional vehicle trips and creates traffic congestion.

Dispersed suburban business districts such as College Boulevard in Kansas City often cover many square miles. Low-density buildings on large lots bear little or no relationship to one another; pedestrian and transit choice is poor to nonexistent.

7

Terrabrook

building initiatives, this book shows how suburban business districts can be transformed to deliver highly attractive financial and place-making dividends.

Rather than simply calling for increases in resource allocation, the book identifies ways in which public and private resources devoted to suburban business districts can be used more effectively and profitably. It is a primary thesis of this work that the nation has reached the tipping point where suburban business districts can fall victim to the same mistakes born of the complacency and inaction that plagued downtowns during the 20th century. However, communities and real estate investors can make a choice. They can either allow suburban business districts to age and decline, or, alternatively, they can become actively involved in transforming these districts from simply automobile-oriented office/commercial districts into diversified central places that offer an attractive public realm, a civic identity, and a sense of place.

This first chapter establishes a definition and classification of suburban business districts and

identifies the purpose of the book—to realize the place-making dividend available to the community and the real estate industry through the transformation of suburban business districts. Chapter two tracks the suburbanization of American cities, reviews the emergence of suburban business districts, and provides an overview of the issues that need to be addressed in their transformation. Chapter three provides insight into the relationship between transportation and the form and structure of suburban business districts. It describes the impact of congestion on real estate values, evaluates the future prospects for each mode of transportation, and looks at how transportation improvements will transform suburban business districts.

While few suburban business districts have yet to integrate multifamily residential development fully into their fabric, chapter four examines the changing nature of American households and the implications for housing choice. It uses three case studies to illustrate how multifamily housing projects are bringing the "live" component to suburban business districts.

Chapter five looks at what office tenants have sought in making location decisions in the 20th century, reviews the distribution and types of office development in contemporary American cities, and uses the examples of three suburban business districts in the U.S. heartland to assess the role that office development and changing tenant needs and demands will play in the transformation of suburban business districts.

Chapter six explores the notion that "it was the shopping center that triggered the initial development of many suburban business districts." It goes on to review how contemporary retail trends are reshaping suburban business districts. Chapter seven makes clear that it is the community that pays the rent, buys the goods, and decides whether to frequent suburban business districts. By drawing on an extensive range of examples throughout the United States, chapter seven distills the essential elements of community that belong in suburban business districts and explains how to foster their development.

Chapter eight defines not only place making but also its value to the community and the real estate industry. It illustrates the essential elements in the creation of place and uses several suburban business district examples to highlight the place-making issues that are critical to the districts' transformation. Chapter nine then examines the eclectic forms of government that administer suburban business districts. It uses a range of examples drawn from both downtowns and the suburbs to demonstrate the issues that need to be addressed in planning, governing, managing, and financing suburban business districts and explains why neither government nor the private sector alone can provide all the needed functions.

Chapter ten highlights the importance of strategic planning in the transformation of suburban business districts. It looks to examples from downtown Chattanooga and the cities that followed that benchmark effort. Using the work-in-progress example of the Cumberland-Galleria suburban business district in Atlanta, chapter ten outlines the elements of a strategic plan necessary to achieve the transformation of a suburban business district. The final chapter stresses the importance of creating place, not just rentable or salable real estate space, in order to capture the place-making dividend. It also distills ULI's ten principles for transforming suburban business districts.

Notes

1. Criteria developed from Joel Garreau, *Edge City: Life on the New Frontier* (New York: Random House, 1992), p. 6.

2. Jane Jacobs, *The Death and Life of Great American Cities* (New York: Random House, 1961), p. 6.

chapter 2

Following The Road to Damascus

"The Road to Damascus" is the new management shorthand for enlightenment—waking up to something to which one had before been blind. It has been a relatively short but instructive road America has taken in creating its suburban business districts. In the 1920s, for the first time in the history of the United States, more than half of the nation's people lived in cities. Despite Thomas Jefferson's vision of a country of yeoman farmers, the United States had become a nation of city dwellers as hundreds of thousands of immigrants swelled the population of American cities. Only five decades later, however, the nation had reversed course. Millions of upper- and middle-class residents fled the crowded conditions of cities for the peace, tranquility, and low-density lifestyle of the suburbs. By 1970, the United States had become a suburban nation, with more people living in the suburbs than in the cities. In fact, as of 1970, 76 million of the nation's 200 million people lived in the suburbs while 64 million lived in central cities, plus another 60 million in nonmetropolitan areas.

Since the nation's founding, Americans have been on the move, always searching for new frontiers to explore, for unspoiled territory in which to begin anew. Perhaps nowhere is this more evident than in U.S. cities, for which the American people have shown deep ambivalence. Americans may be attached to their homes, their families, and their political institutions, but as de Tocqueville observed in 1835, people carelessly leave cities to their own devices.[1]

Over the last 25 years, fragmented and dispersed suburban business districts have been created at the urban fringe, virtually from scratch, to replace traditional downtowns. These suburban business districts are located in every major North American metropolitan area, usually in the form of high-rise office buildings and standalone hotels, condominiums, and shopping malls, all clustered around highway interchanges. Highway interchanges have overtaken waterways and railroad junctions as the preferred location for business and industry. Scattered across the metropolitan landscape, suburban business districts often contain more office and retail space than the central business district. For example, Oakland County, Michigan, outside Detroit has become the dominant business center in that metropolitan area. By 1990, its population had surpassed Detroit's. It now boasts more office space than the Motor City. Yet, despite its youth, Oakland County, as well as several other suburban business districts, is showing signs of aging and needs to address a variety of problems, including obsolete facilities, traffic congestion, and rising crime.

The Suburbanization of American Cities

The movement to the suburbs began well over 100 years ago, before the advent of automobiles, interstate highways, tract homes, and culs-de-sac. In the mid-1800s, American cities were the hub of the nation's commercial activity and civic life. They were compact and scaled for a population that got around mostly on foot. Houses were located close to offices. Shopkeepers lived above their stores. Merchants and the wealthy concentrated around the center, where most business was transacted, while the poor and those of ill-repute lived in shantytowns on the periphery. In stark contrast to today's cities, income and social status declined with distance from the center, although not all poor people were banished to the edge of town. The working poor lived among those who were better off—whether in attics, basements, or back-alley apartments.

Between 1845 and 1855, nearly 3 million Irish and Germans sailed to America. As immigrants poured into the United States, they stretched existing cities to the breaking point. In the annals of American history, the mid-1840s immigration accounted for the greatest single wave of newcomers relative to the size of the population.[2] Cities became overcrowded and living conditions intolerable. The wealthy began leaving for pastoral country estates on the outskirts of town. Exclusive retreats for the well-to-do grew up along rail lines just outside cities, in places such as Llewellyn Park, New Jersey, and Riverside, Illinois. These early suburbs provided bucolic retreats from the stresses of city life. In fact, they were the antithesis of cities, offering features that would later become the hallmarks of suburban design: winding roads, minimum setbacks, detached houses, and income segregation.

Llewellyn Park, built in the mid-1850s, was one of the first planned suburbs in the United States. Designed by architect Alexander Jackson Davis and located in the foothills of New Jersey's Orange Mountains, the community afforded magnificent views of Manhattan, about 12 miles away. The 400-acre subdivision featured three-acre lots along curvilinear roads surrounding 50 acres of natural open space known as the Ramble. Llewellyn Park's developer, wealthy pharmaceutical merchant Llewellyn S. Haskell, sought to create "a retreat for a man to exercise his own rights and privileges."[3] From its inception, Llewellyn Park attracted wealthy businessmen and professionals who could afford the

community's quiet seclusion. Thomas Edison made his home there, as did Davis. According to Kenneth Jackson, author of *Crabgrass Frontier*, Llewellyn Park immediately became fashionable among the well-heeled, and it has retained its exclusive ambience to this day.[4]

The Railroad Suburbs

A decade later, Frederick Law Olmsted and his partner Calvert Vaux, designers of Manhattan's Central Park, were busy drafting plans for an exclusive railroad suburb outside Chicago. The project, known as Riverside, was located on a 1,600-acre site along the Des Plaines River, about ten miles from the city. Olmsted did not see Riverside as an escape from the city but rather as a harmonious blending of man and nature, of town and country. Its design was meant to "suggest and imply leisure, contemplativeness and happy tranquility,"[5] he wrote.

Like Llewellyn Park, Riverside was distinguished by curving, tree-lined roads, spacious homes on large lots, and a landscaped public park. Its plan required homes to be set well back from the road and mandated that homeowners maintain a minimum number of healthy trees on their lots. Unlike Llewellyn Park, however, Riverside struggled financially. Sales were sluggish, and the developer, the Riverside Improvement Company, went bankrupt in 1873.

These early planned suburbs were not getaways for the masses. Few could afford a country home, let alone the train fare to the city. Not until electric streetcars emerged in the 1880s were the suburbs within financial reach of the middle class. Before then, mass transit, such as it was, consisted of electric trolleys, similar to those operating today in San Francisco, and horse-pulled cars. But horsecars were slow, especially when negotiating hills. They were also cramped and unreliable, and the stench and public health risks posed by the endless stream of manure and dead horses presented yet other challenges. Overworked horses often dropped dead on the spot and were left to rot on city streets. Trolleys, while an improvement over horse-powered vehicles, were inefficient and expensive to operate. Streetcars were more

In the late 1800s, American cities such as Philadelphia became congested, fueling citizen desires to escape to the country.

dependable and faster than both, with average operating speeds of about ten to 15 miles per hour. They were also inexpensive; most companies charged passengers a nominal flat fee—five cents—thus making long commutes affordable.

The Streetcar Suburbs

Electric streetcars quickly became the preferred mode of transit. In 1890, the United States counted an estimated 5,700 miles of track for vehicles operated by animal power, 500 miles of track for cable cars, and 1,260 miles of electrified track. By 1902, electrified track had expanded to 22,000 miles while that of horse railways had dwindled to 250 miles.[6]

Cities began to spread out as streetcar lines extended into undeveloped countryside. Speculators purchased and subdivided vacant farmland and built streetcar lines that linked newly developed land with the city, thus increasing by several fold the value of their outlying landholdings. In many cases, selling real estate was the primary purpose of streetcar construction and operation. In fact, it was not uncommon for streetcar lines to run at a loss, with the deficits more than offset by the profits from real estate.[7] Yet, streetcar systems' low-priced flat rates, along with cheap land and advances in wood-

frame construction, made suburban living affordable to the common man. Not that all streetcar suburbs were for working class "stiffs." Some, such as Chevy Chase outside Washington, D.C., were and remain upscale neighborhoods of large, expensive homes. Built in 1893, Chevy Chase was virtually assured of becoming an upper-class settlement through its requirements for large minimum lot sizes, generous setbacks, restrictive land covenants, and even a minimum price for homes, all of which excluded low- and middle-class buyers.

In the late 1800s and early 1900s, streetcar lines pushed development farther into previously inaccessible areas, changing the traditional pattern of urban growth. Instead of slowly expanding the urban edge incrementally, in concentric rings out from the center, streetcar suburbs radiated from the central hub like spokes on a wheel. New suburbs and villages clung to the streetcar lines for the simple reason that homes had to be constructed within walking distance—less than a mile—of transit stops. Thus, the new developments were compact, although not nearly as dense as central cities, and almost exclusively residential.

Gradually, as more and more people moved their place of residence farther out from downtown, businesses followed. Grocery stores, banks,

Parks and Transit Spelled Real Estate Profit

In 1888, U.S. Senator Francis Newlands's Chevy Chase Land Company received a charter to run a trolley line along Connecticut Avenue from the District of Columbia into Maryland. With support from Newlands's fellow stockholder Senator William Morris Stewart and their associates, the Chevy Chase Land Company purchased 1,712 acres of farmland along the proposed route. They also arranged for the creation of Rock Creek Park because "[n]ot only did the presence of the park raise the value of nearby properties owned so largely by the Land Company, but at the same time, as Stewart so candidly expressed it, the action took '2,000 acres out of the market.'"

Landowners who failed to sell to the land company were bypassed by a shift in the direction of the road and the trolley, which explains why Connecticut Avenue changes direction at Chevy Chase Circle. Once the land purchases were complete, Newlands laid out and built the 150-foot-wide right-of-way and then deeded Connecticut Avenue to Maryland and the District of Columbia. Chevy Chase was a totally planned residential area in which the first lots went on sale in 1893. Lots sold with the understanding that no home on Connecticut Avenue could cost less than $5,000 and no dwelling on a side street for less than $3,000. Newlands well understood how the provision of transit and surrounding parkland dramatically enhanced real estate value.

The integration of transit and land use for the sole purpose of creating real estate value stands in stark contrast to transit development in the second half of the 20th century. Although the later examples of transit development were masterpieces of engineering design, they were built on existing rights-of-way to minimize initial capital construction costs. And, remote from people and land use activities, the resulting transit systems did not promote transit ridership or create real estate profit. •

Source: Adapted in part from Kenneth T. Jackson, *Crabgrass Frontier: The Suburbanization of the United States* (New York: Oxford University Press, 1985), p. 123.

---

saloons, and other enterprises gathered around rail stations and near busy intersections, foreshadowing the emergence of office and retail clusters at interstate highway interchanges 100 years later. It was this locational shift that eventually prompted department stores to leave their downtown strongholds and provide the suburban anchors for regional malls. Manufacturers began to leave as well. In his 1915 book *Satellite Cities,* Graham Taylor described how "huge industrial plants are uprooting themselves bodily from cities. With households, small stores, saloons, lodges, churches, and schools clinging to them like living tendrils, they set themselves down ten miles away in the open."[8]

Industrial Decentralization

All across the industrial belt, from St. Louis to New York, manufacturers in search of cheap land, lower taxes, and room for growth abandoned their traditional locations in central cities for less crowded sites along rail lines just outside the city limits. Warehouses and distribution facilities soon followed. In Manhattan, industries such as food processing, textiles, and met- alworking left their cramped quarters for more spacious accommodations in Brooklyn, Queens, and the Bronx as well as for the satellite towns of Newark and Passaic, New Jersey. In St. Louis, manufacturers hopped the Mississippi River to what is now East St. Louis, Illinois. Working-class neighborhoods developed nearby. As early as 1899, suburban business and industrial districts accounted for almost a third of metropolitan employment.[9]

The turn of the 20th century was the period of the company town, when companies secured their labor force by providing a complete live-work urban settlement. In the early 1900s, the United States Steel Corporation built a massive steel plant in Gary, Indiana, along the rolling sand dunes of Lake Michigan. Gary started out as a satellite city of Chicago, largely dependent on the Windy City for workers and railway facilities. However, it quickly evolved into an independent industrial city in its own right, with "15 miles of paved streets, 25 miles of cement sidewalks, two million dollars' worth of residences completed and occupied, a sewer system, water and gas plants, electric lighting, a national and state bank, six hotels, three dailies and one weekly newspaper, two public schoolhouses, several churches and many well-appointed stores."[10]

By the early 1900s, two main types of suburbs had emerged. The first type was the residential suburb for the wealthy or middle class. The second was the industrial suburb, which housed the working class. Both grew rapidly, although company towns such as Tacony outside Philadelphia and Pullman in Chicago became more common. Suburbs developed around every major city. For example, of 71 new towns incorporated in Illinois, Missouri, and Michigan in the 1920s, two-thirds were located in the suburbs of metropolitan Chicago, St. Louis, and Detroit. Examples are Elmwood Park outside Chicago and Grosse Pointe near Detroit.[11] By the onset of the Great Depression in the late 1920s, the growth rate of suburbs exceeded that of the cities around which they were developing. At that time, suburban development was largely limited to a one-mile radius around rail stations. Areas beyond a reasonable walking distance remained off limits until the debut of the automobile.

The Advent of the Automobile and Affordable Housing

Early in the 20th century, the advent of private cars freed development from the strict confines of rail lines and turned vast tracts of previously undevelopable land into prime real estate. Early on, relatively few people could afford to own a car. However, Henry Ford's mass-produced Model T, unveiled in 1908, made cars affordable to the common man and ushered in the age of the automobile. In 1905, there were 77,400 registered automobiles in the United States. Ten years later, the number jumped to over 2.3 million. In 1927, the 15 millionth Model T, the Tin Lizzie, rolled off Ford's assembly line.[12]

Despite the remarkable growth in automobile ownership, before World War II most workers either walked to their jobs or took public transit in the form of a bus, trolley, or streetcar. After World War II, returning veterans and families, eager to escape the deplorable living conditions of cities, created enormous pent-up demand for suburban housing. Ten years of economic depression and a world war had taken its toll on

In the 1920s, as shown in this photograph of downtown Los Angeles, the automobile and the streetcar shared the use of the roadway.

the nation's cities. Homebuilders across the country began producing subdivisions of nearly identical ranch or split-level homes. The building industry, dominated by small operators, could scarcely keep up with demand until one builder revolutionized homebuilding by introducing mass production techniques that rivaled those of Ford's assembly lines.

In 1947, Abraham Levitt and his sons William and Alfred began constructing tract homes on what were previously potato fields in Nassau County, New York, about 25 miles east of Manhattan. The company turned homebuilding into a science. At precise intervals, trucks dropped off building materials, many of which were prefabricated in off-site factories. Construction crews were specialized, with separate crews for pouring the concrete slab floor, framing the walls, tiling the floors, painting the walls, installing the roof shingles, and performing over a dozen other tasks. Power tools sped construction.

In four years, Levitt and Sons built over 17,000 single-family houses on the 4,000-acre site. At its peak, the company completed over 30 homes a day. The project, aptly named Levittown, was enormously successful. Levitt and Sons subsequently built two more Levittowns, one in New Jersey and another in Pennsylvania. Selling for less than $10,000, Levitt's

simple, uniform, mass-produced tract homes—cookie-cutter Cape Cods—made suburban life a reality for the working masses. Soon, subdivisions resembling Levittown, though not as large, began to be developed across America.

Critics assailed the monotony and homogeneity of suburban tract developments such as Levittown. Gone was the diversity of housing types, the mix of land uses, and, in many cases, the dominance of the pedestrian. Other critics bemoaned the loss of farmland and natural areas, the exclusion of minorities, and the complete separation of uses that makes owning an automobile a necessity for suburban living. Despite the suburbs' shortcomings, the American people overwhelmingly embraced the suburban lifestyle, which liberated thousands of people from cramped quarters in the central city and gave them a small but sacred slice of "American pie"—a detached, single-family home on a quarter-acre lot.

Downtowns and Inner Cities in Decline

Between 1950 and 1970, the population growth of suburbs outpaced that of central cities. American central cities grew by 10 million people while their suburbs increased by 85 million.[13] From 1970 to 1980, employment followed its

figure 2.1 Top 10 Most Populous Cities in 1970 and 2000

Top 10 in 1970	1970 Population	Top 10 in 2000	2000 Population
New York	7,894,851	New York	8,008,278
Chicago	3,362,825	Los Angeles	3,694,820
Los Angeles	2,816,111	Chicago	2,896,016
Philadelphia	1,948,609	Houston	1,953,631
Detroit	1,511,336	Philadelphia	1,517,550
Houston	1,232,407	Phoenix	1,321,045
Baltimore	905,759	San Diego	1,223,400
Dallas	844,189	Dallas	1,188,580
Washington, D.C.	756,510	San Antonio	1,144,646
Cleveland	751,046	Detroit	951,270

Source: *The State of the Cities 2000* (Washington, D.C.: U.S. Department of Housing and Urban Development, 2000) and Bureau of the Census.

workers to suburban locations, with 95 percent of job growth in metropolitan areas occurring in the suburbs. In this period, an additional 1.6 million manufacturing jobs were created in the suburbs as the inner cities lost over 400,000 jobs.[14] Today, the share of both job and population growth in the suburbs continues to outpace that of traditional downtowns and inner-city neighborhoods; however, the trend is starting to slow and is even showing signs of reversal.

Since the 1970s, cities in the South and West have gained population while those in the Midwest and Northeast have shown large losses. Many cities, such as Baltimore, St. Louis, and Cleveland, continue to lose population, but the rate is slowing. Of the 30 largest cities as of 1970, half are still losing population.[15] By 2000, only six of the 1970s ten largest cities remained in the top ten (see Figure 2.1).

Federal Government Policy

The fantastic growth of the suburbs did not happen by accident. It was facilitated by federal government policies that relaxed residential lending practices and by national expenditure priorities that favored highway construction. For example, to jump-start the ailing homebuilding industry, the Roosevelt Administration created the Federal Housing Authority (FHA), which guaranteed private mortgage loans with the full backing of the U.S. Treasury. The guarantee substantially reduced risks to lenders, who were still reeling from the losses suffered during the Great Depression. In turn, lenders were able to offer loans at attractive terms by, for example, stretching the payback period from ten to 30 years. In addition, after World War II, the Veterans Administration (VA) offered returning veterans mortgages with low interest and little or no downpayment. FHA policies heavily favored single-family detached homes in the suburbs at the expense of investments in the inner city, particularly in minority neighborhoods. Race played a significant part in the flight of white middle-class residents to the suburbs. Some observers have argued that federal mortgage programs were openly racist and accelerated the suburbanization process.[16]

In 1956, Congress enacted the Interstate Highway Act, which called for the construction of 41,000 miles of expressways. It was one of the largest public works projects ever undertaken in the United States. By the late 1970s, new multi-lane highways encircled cities, sliced through inner-city neighborhoods, and generally hastened the exodus of businesses and residents to the suburbs. Businesses converged on beltways, which, contrary to their primary purpose of diverting traffic around cities, became the main streets of suburban business districts and acted as magnets for new growth. Freeways made it possible for people to live in far-flung areas, where housing was cheaper, yet still commute by car to the city. Indeed, one of the goals of the highway act was to "disperse our factories, our stores, our people; in short, to create a revolution in living habits." A revolution it was. As Henry Ford predicted years before, "We shall solve the city problem by leaving the city."[17] Public transit systems deteriorated, unable to compete with the convenience of the private automobile.

The combination of FHA and VA loan programs, along with the deduction of mortgage interest from federal taxes, meant that owning a home in the suburbs was often cheaper than renting an apartment in the city. Interstate highways made the commute to the city a breeze, at least initially. The result was predictable. People

In the period after World War II, owning a house in the suburbs became an affordable American dream as shown in this photograph of a typical FHA-financed subdivision in San Diego, circa 1964.

Country Club Plaza in Kansas City was one of the first shopping centers in the American suburbs.

abandoned the city in droves. By the 1960s, bedroom communities crowded the periphery of nearly every city. However, the vast majority of suburban residents still depended on downtowns for services, jobs, shops, recreation, and entertainment. Every weekday morning, commuters left the suburbs for their jobs in the central business district, only to reverse the process in the evening. Suburbanites shopped in downtown department stores, went to the movies at downtown cinemas, and ate in downtown restaurants. But, gradually, businesses and industries followed their customers to the suburbs. Shopping centers, office buildings, and industrial parks developed along freeways and interstate highway interchanges, dramatically altering commuting patterns and threatening, as H.G. Wells[18] predicted, to make traditional cities obsolete. In his 1900 essay, "The Probable Diffusion of Great Cities," Wells prophesied that the forces that drew people and resources to cities would reverse course and lead to the creation of decentralized "urban regions" that would render cities "as obsolete as [the] mailcoach."[19]

Retailing and Employment Relocate to the Suburbs

When Jesse Clyde Nichols, the father of shopping centers, developed Country Club Plaza out-side Kansas City in 1922, the shopping center arrived in the American suburbs. Then came Highland Park Shopping Village in Dallas in 1931. Unlike previous shopping centers and in contrast to main street retailers, Highland Park's storefronts faced inward, away from the streets. This revolutionary design, which allowed designers to isolate shoppers from the world outside, proved extremely successful and was copied by mall designers across the country.

The first standalone shopping malls appeared in the mid-1950s, starting with Northland Center outside Detroit and Southdale Center outside Minneapolis in Edina, Minnesota. Southdale, which opened in 1956, was the first fully enclosed, comfort-controlled, two-level mall. Standalone, fully enclosed shopping malls sought to emulate the ambience and retail mix of downtown shopping districts but without the problems of crime, panhandling, inclement weather, and parking restrictions. In relatively short order, suburbanites abandoned downtown retailers for the comfort, safety, and convenience of suburban malls. Some downtowns never recovered.

Since the 1960s, the growth in the number of shopping centers has been nothing short of phenomenal. In 1960, there were about 3,000 shopping centers in the United States. By 1970, the figure had climbed to over 12,000. Today, the United States claims more than 44,000 shopping

The Essence of Real Estate

Real estate is no more than cash flow packaged in buildings or land and, in most cases, both. It is a tangible asset, yet it is not its tangibility that creates its value. Rather, it is the lease or contract to purchase the real estate that establishes the asset's financial value. Most buildings and land development projects comprising today's cities owe their existence not to the contribution they make to civic architecture and community building but rather to their ability to provide investors with a sound financial return. The extent to which real estate investment projects combine community building and financial success indicates the relative skill of the development teams that deliver such projects.

The first blueprint of any real estate project is a financial analysis of its estimated costs and returns. As Carol Willis's *Form Follows Finance* illustrates, even New York's Empire State Building was, in its initial incarnation, a financial rather than an architectural construct. "From acquisition of the property in May 1929 until the formation of Empire State, Inc., in September, all plans had been entirely financial not architectural. The different schemes were designed only in numbers—stories, cubic feet, operating costs and projected income."[1]

The value of real estate is derived from its intensity of use. It is the human traffic or number of occupants that generates the property's income, either as rents or revenues from sales. To determine a project's capital value on completion, net annual income from the project is capitalized in accordance with the yields of comparable real estate. When the total development cost of the project does not exceed its projected capital value, the project is seen as profitable, provided, of course, that it can be sold for a price at or above its appraised value. If, at the feasibility stage, the projected development profit fails to meet the hurdle rate or desired threshold return,

then the project is deemed too risky and incapable of attracting a lender. In such a case, the developer abandons the project before design or construction commences.

Form Follows Finance

The essential ingredient in most suburban business district developments is the net rental income paid to the owner by a building's tenants. To attract and retain tenants, a real estate development must meet the needs of its occupants. In the commercial and retail context of suburban business district development in the latter half of the 20th century, these needs were reduced to three overriding considerations: access, competitive rents, and an abundance of free parking. How these needs were met has had a major impact on urban form, city structure, and community development.

The net result has been

- the development of comparatively inexpensive greenfield sites at the interchanges of the new interstate and freeway systems;
- the simplification of building design and removal of most architectural fenestration to reduce both cost and duration of construction, thus minimizing interest and holding costs and allowing suburban business district projects to be delivered ahead of their downtown competitors; and
- the adoption of a proven site development layout whereby buildings took the form of standalone boxes surrounded by surface parking lots because neither tenants nor customers wanted to walk great distances from their cars.

With each real estate project standing on its own site without the complications of interconnectivity or dependence on adjoining sites, it was easy to market and manage properties. For tenants and invest-

ors, the new suburban business district projects were simple to understand—what you saw was what you got. Fortuitously, the formula was well suited to both the shopping mall and the office park. As discrete packages, the investment markets found these projects easy to finance and digest. Further, with the growing number of comparable developments, appraisers could readily determine projects' capital value. Interestingly, standalone projects also reflected a compartmentalization of community life in that modern Americans worked, shopped, and lived in separate places, relying on the automobile and the best highway system in the world to commute from one location to another. Zoning laws recognized and enforced the separation of uses and protected communities from what was believed to be the inadvisability of mixing uses and developing projects at medium to high densities.

Finance Follows the Market

There are some who contend that "the market" is an alien entity that stands apart from the needs and aspirations of the community. In fact, the market is the result of choices and decisions made by every individual, the effect of which creates an economy in aggregate and builds a community. It is that community's allocation of finance and investment that creates and shapes the market. We make the market. When we decide to change the way we live and reshape our communities, *we* change the market. ●

[1]Carol Willis, *Form Follows Finance* (New York: Princeton Architectural Press, 1995), p. 95.

Large enclosed shopping centers, like Southlake Center near Minneapolis that opened in 1956, became the catalyst developments for suburban business districts.

centers. Most are strip centers serving nearby subdivisions. Super regional malls, such as the 1.5 million-square-foot Galleria outside Houston, emerged in the 1970s, and malls have grown in size ever since. The granddaddy of all malls is West Edmonton Mall in Alberta, Canada, which encompasses 5.3 million square feet, ten times the size of the original Southdale Center.

Malls became magnets for growth, attracting offices, apartments, hotels, corporate headquarters, and even hospitals. Northland Center attracted apartment and office buildings, a hotel, hospital, research laboratories, and other businesses. It was the first experiment in metronucleation planned around a shopping mall, writes William Kowinski, author of *The Malling of America.*[20]

American City Structure Revolutionized

By the 1970s, the suburbs were no longer just bedroom communities but also offered many of the same features of traditional downtowns— offices, shops, housing, and recreation—in a decentralized setting connected by a vast network of roads. Downtowns became increasingly irrelevant as suburbanites could live, work, shop, and play without setting foot outside the suburbs. Commuting patterns changed dramatically. Workers no longer commuted simply from suburb to downtown but also from suburb to suburb and within suburbs. As a result, mass transit became increasingly infeasible.

The classic notion of a dense central business district surrounded by a ring of dependent suburbs, with density declining with movement outward from the center, was turned on its head. Multicentered agglomerations of office, retail, and residential uses began to develop in suburban locations. These clusters were independent of both downtown and other suburban business districts. It was as if someone had lifted many of the functions of the city's central business district and deposited them along highway interchanges on the metropolitan fringe.

The Emergence of Suburban Business Districts

The emergence of suburban business districts did not go unnoticed. In a 1986 article in the *Atlantic Monthly,* "How Business is Reshaping America," Christopher Leinberger and Charles Lockwood observed that our ". . . cities are becoming groups of interdependent 'urban villages,' which are business, retail, housing, and entertainment focal points amid low-density cityscape."[21] The next year, historian Robert Fishman described in *Bourgeois Utopias* how the suburban landscape had become "a hopeless jumble"[22] of housing, industry, commerce, and even agricultural uses. He asserted that the massive rebuilding that began in 1945 represents not the culmination of the long history of suburbia but rather its end. Indeed, this massive change is not suburbanization at all; instead, it represents the creation of a new type of city, the "techno-city," containing all the economic and technological dynamism of central business districts and renewing the link between work and residence that had been separated in the traditional suburbs.

Washington Post writer Joel Garreau profiled many of these suburban business districts, which he called edge cities. His book, entitled *Edge City: Life on the New Frontier,* chronicled the proliferation of satellite cities across the suburban landscape and challenged traditional notions of what constitutes a city. Our older, central cities were "relics of a time past,"[23] he claimed. Garreau profiled places such as Tysons Corner, Virginia, which was typical of suburban business districts in terms of type, scale, and pace of growth. In 1970, Tysons Corner was little more than a hamlet, a crossroads in the countryside not far from the nation's capital. By 1990, however, it had become one of the dominant locations in the Washington, D.C., region with respect to office and retail space.

According to Garreau, edge cities were places that

- had more than 5 million square feet of office space (about as much as a good-sized downtown);
- had over 600,000 square feet of retail space (the equivalent of a large regional shopping mall);
- had more jobs than bedrooms, with the population increasing at 9:00 a.m. and decreasing after 5:00 p.m. on weekdays;
- were known as regional destinations that "had it all" (jobs, shopping, and entertainment); and
- were nothing like a "city" of 30 years ago.

In 1991, Garreau used the above criteria to identify 123 places as existing edge cities and 83 places as emerging edge cities around the country. Many are known by awkward-sounding names that reflect the malls, highways, or airports they are associated with, such as the Cumberland-Galleria area in Atlanta, the Massachusetts Turnpike and 128 area outside Boston, the Greenspoint-North Beltway-I-45 area of Houston, or the John Wayne Airport area of Los Angeles. Garreau's list included two dozen edge cities or those in progress in greater Los Angeles alone, 23 in metropolitan Washington, D.C., and 21 in the New York City metropolitan region.

Despite their predominately suburban characteristics, some edge cities featured particularly unsuburbanlike housing. For example, in 19 edge cities, a majority of residents lived in buildings with ten or more housing units, including Crystal City, Virginia; the mid–Wilshire area of Los Angeles; the Houston Galleria area; and Las Colinas in Dallas.[24]

The Waves of Suburban Business District Development

The development of suburban business districts occurred in four overlapping periods or waves, as summarized in Figure 2.2. The first wave started during the 1960s, when retail and then office uses followed the lead of residents and relocated to the suburbs. These emerging suburban business districts tended to evolve

figure 2.2 Four Waves of Suburban Business District Development

Wave (when started)	Characteristics	Examples
First (1960s)	First major move of retail uses to the suburbs. Beginning of suburban office development toward the favored quarter. First-class office and hotel space developed outside downtown.	Clayton (St. Louis), Bala Cynwyd (Philadelphia), White Plains (New York)
Second (1970s)	Continued development of office and retail clusters at somewhat lower densities, close to executive housing. Generous surface parking, with ratios of 5–7 spaces per 1,000 square feet of retail space and 4 spaces per 1,000 square feet of office space.	Bellevue (Seattle), Camelback (Phoenix), Hunt Valley (Baltimore), King of Prussia (Philadelphia), Perimeter Center (Atlanta), Tysons Corner (Washington, D.C.)
Third (1980s)	Located farther out (4–8 miles) in the favored quarter and built at lower densities than the first and second waves. Mostly strung along freeways in a more campuslike setting.	Georgia 400 and Gwinnett County (Atlanta), Plano (Dallas), Fair Oaks and Reston (Washington, D.C.), Valencia (Los Angeles), Redmond (Seattle)
Fourth (1990s)	Located still farther out (4–8 miles from the third wave). Even more spread out and campuslike. Some evidence of the end of the favored-quarter model.	Alliance Airport (Dallas/Fort Worth), Ventura County (Los Angeles)

With each successive wave of suburban business district development, density has decreased and buildings have become more dispersed.

close to high-end housing, areas Leinberger and Lockwood dubbed the "favored quarter"—an approximate 90-degree arc starting downtown and expanding in the direction of the executive housing concentration. For example, 94 percent of executive housing in the Phoenix metropolitan area is located to the northeast of the city. In the Kansas City region, 75 percent of executive housing is located to the south. In both cases, these housing concentrations also happen to be the locations of suburban business districts. Indeed, a close correlation between the location of executive housing and suburban business districts can be found in metropolitan areas across the country. The reason is simple. Companies tend to locate close to the boss's house, which typically is situated in the high-end executive housing area. Some large metropolitan areas, such as New York, Los Angeles, Chicago, San Francisco, and Miami, have more than one favored quarter due to their size and geographic peculiarities.

During the 1970s, the second wave took place, typified by the continuing development of suburban office and retail clusters in the favored quarter. These clusters developed at lower densities than those of the first wave and catered almost exclusively to the automobile. Freestanding office or retail structures surrounded by plentiful parking was the norm. The third wave occurred during the 1980s real estate boom and was characterized by low-density office buildings in campuslike settings strung along highways

four to eight miles farther out in the favored quarter. Today, the freeways connecting second- and third-wave suburban business districts are congested in both directions during rush hour. Typically, the third-wave suburban business districts were built at even lower densities than those of the second wave. Finally, the fourth wave began in the 1990s, with the construction of office and retail buildings still farther out on the suburban fringe. Development during the most recent wave of development consists primarily of a loose collection of isolated, extremely low-density buildings but has also included a new breed of projects that are more mixed-use and pedestrian-friendly in nature.

The Transformation of Suburban Business Districts

Many suburban business districts were built on a foundation of comparatively inexpensive land, easy highway access, and a ready supply of low-wage workers for retail, entertainment, and personal services jobs. However, as suburban business districts age, these resources are in increasingly short supply. Ironically, many suburban business districts now suffer from the same types of ills previously associated with the downtowns they replaced, such as crime, noise, poor air quality, disinvestment, and intractable traffic congestion. Such conditions raise questions about the sustainability of suburban business districts, even in a rapidly growing region.[25] All, then, is not entirely well in America's suburban business districts. Some first-wave suburban business districts in Nassau County, New York; DuPage County, Illinois; and Orange County, California, are showing signs of wear and tear. According to Jon Teaford, author of *Post Suburbia,* these pioneers are facing competition from newer suburban business districts located farther from the central business district.[26]

Clearly, the geographic spread of cities is being slowed by the tyranny of distance, which extends business supply lines to the point where a location becomes remote and therefore less economic than one closer to existing markets and labor pools. The tyranny of distance has been brought into focus by programs such as ULI's Smart Growth Initiative, which is helping businesses rediscover first- and second-wave suburban business districts that offer diverse services and offices within walking distance of home or a transit stop. Worsening traffic congestion and the dull sameness of most suburban business districts—the same chain restaurants, same malls, same uninspiring low-rise office buildings, and same sterile parking lots—

are driving residents and businesses alike to consider compact, convenient locations more like the traditional downtown; that is, compact suburban business districts such as Buckhead and Midtown in Atlanta and Ballston and Bethesda outside Washington, D.C.

It is becoming evident that to continue to thrive, suburban business districts will have to become more urban—more compact, pedestrian-friendly, and accessible by mass transit. Suburban business districts can and must become the center of their spheres of influence. However, at present, most lack a management structure, and most have no public space that functions as an identifying focal point and gathering spot. True, suburban business districts contain virtually all the same functions of downtowns, but most lack a pedestrian-friendly atmosphere. Many aging suburban business districts are experiencing an identity crisis as the sum of their parts fails to add up to a community. Their current configuration and design prevent it.

Great civilizations, like great cities, writes Ray Oldenburg in *The Great Good Place,*[27] share a common feature: distinctive, informal public gathering places or what he dubbed "third places"

Geoffrey Booth

Distinctive, informal gathering places within the public realm— the "third place"— outside home and work are sorely lacking in most suburban business districts.

Phillips Place–SouthPark Suburban Business District

Phillips Place is a suburban mixed-use development featuring 130,000 square feet of retail space, 402 residential units, 124 hotel rooms, and a multiplex cinema. Located 20 minutes south of downtown Charlotte, North Carolina, the project includes a pedestrian-scaled main street within a traditional low-density suburban area. The three-story buildings on the main street feature ground-level retail uses with apartments above. The classically influenced architecture and the significant emphasis on high-quality streetscape design and lighting combine to create a pleasant and safe pedestrian experience.

The 32-acre site is located approximately 15 to 20 minutes from Charlotte's airport and outer loop beltway in the rapidly developing SouthPark suburban business district. It was the last remaining site with retail potential in the area. SouthPark itself is home to the Carolinas' largest subur-

ban business district. The challenge of the project was to develop a thriving, mixed-use town center for a traditionally low-density suburban business district. The developer—the Harris Company—sought to achieve this goal by creating a main street with a 124-room hotel anchoring one end and a multiplex cinema anchoring the other, apartments built over retail space on one side of the street, and several separate apartment buildings behind the main street. Commercial tenants include Dean & Deluca, Via Veneto Fashion Shoes, Restoration Hardware, and Palm Restaurant.

The Harris Group partnered with Post Properties of Atlanta to construct and manage the over-the-shop apartments as well as the separate apartment buildings nearby. It chose the Charlotte-based Panos Hotel Group as a hotel partner and operator. A single construction company handled the

retail, hotel, and cinema development, eliminating numerous coordination issues. Construction began in November 1995 and was completed in March 1998.

Town Center

Phillips Place combines specialty retail uses, entertainment venues, townhomes, apartments, and a hotel, all organized around a main street. It provides an important urban gathering place for the surrounding low-density suburban community and illustrates how a relatively dense mix of a variety of uses can create a sense of community in the heart of suburbia.

Pedestrian-Oriented Design

The project was designed to create a pedestrian-scaled town center by internalizing the main street, thereby providing a slower, more controlled environment than the fast-moving, automobile-oriented environments of the surrounding areas. Designers emphasized landscaped features, including two courtyards that terminate at the east/west axis of the main street, streetscaping (including brick sidewalks and outdoor seating), and pleasant lighting to encourage pedestrian mobility throughout the site.

Regulatory Barriers

To build a mixed-use development, the property had to be rezoned. The South District Plan recommended the site for multifamily housing at a density of 22 units per acre that would have permitted 800 units on the site, generating significant traffic during peak hours. The Harris Group argued successfully that it could reduce peak-hour traffic by adding nonresidential uses. The developer also argued that the project's retail and public spaces would serve as valuable community amenities. Complicating the rezoning approval process was

The shop-lined main street at Phillips Place in Charlotte, North Carolina, links the hotel to the cinemas, encouraging residents and pedestrians to stroll and enjoy the place.

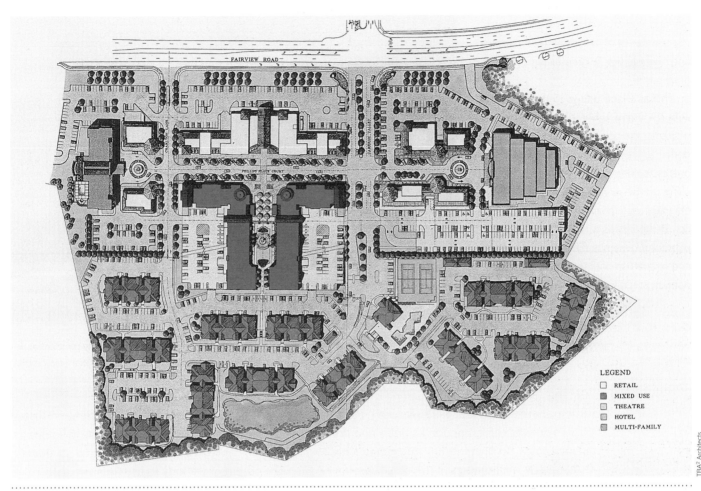

LEGEND

☐ RETAIL
■ MIXED USE
☐ THEATRE
▨ HOTEL
▨ MULTI-FAMILY

TBA² Architects

A critical component of the Phillips Place plan was the integration of the main street with the multifamily residential apartments, which are arranged in separate courtyards as well as above the ground-floor retail uses on the main street.

the fact that the county lacked a mixed-use zoning class. To address this impediment, the Harris Group worked closely with the city's planning staff to create a new zoning category that would allow the integration of retail and residential uses.

Site Constraints

Among the site's several constraints to development were high-tension power lines located at the front of the property (along the arterial frontage) and terrain that slopes from north to south. But the greatest constraint was the site's limited access. Though the site has substantial frontage on Fairview Road (southeast Charlotte's

major east/west thoroughfare), it is not served by any other adjacent street and thus limited the developers' and designers' ability to connect the project to its surroundings.

Public Opposition

Concerns over increased traffic, especially additional traffic flowing through adjacent neighborhoods, made it impossible for the developer to connect the main street to the surrounding neighborhoods with either vehicle or pedestrian linkages. While the site is separated from the adjacent residential neighborhoods by fences, several neighborhood groups—impressed with the

quality and design of the final project—are considering ways to connect their neighborhoods to Phillips Place. Even though the project remains a suburban development accessible primarily by car, original connections to the adjacent neighborhoods would have helped integrate the site into the community and reduce automobile trips.

Lessons Learned

Phillips Place demonstrates how a mixed-use town center can be successfully developed in a fast-growing suburban business district. The project provides an important *continued on next page* "urban" gathering place for the community and illustrates how a relatively dense mix of a variety of uses can create synergy and a whole that is greater than the sum of its parts.

Phillips Place brings to the Charlotte suburbs a new urban element, giving its residents the opportunity to walk to many conveniences and providing visitors and nearby residents and workers with an exciting combination of dining, shopping, and entertainment choices in one location. Phillips Place makes a major contribution to suburban business district place-making and pedestrian-oriented, mixed-use development standards. ●

Source: David J. O'Neill, *The Smart Growth Tool Kit* (Washington, D.C.: ULI–the Urban Land Institute, 2000), p. 93.

Phillips Place creates a critical mass of retail, entertainment, and multifamily residential development in a pedestrian-friendly town center for the SouthPark suburban business district.

after home (first) and work (second). Paris has its sidewalk cafés, London its pubs, and Rome its *piazzas.* To say that the United States has its shopping malls strikes at the very reason why Americans are keen to redefine themselves and their suburban business districts to incorporate the community facilities and place-making excellence that distinguishes third places.

The essence of a downtown is that it promotes and nourishes human contact, not just during the day but also after the evening rush hour. This is what distinguishes a downtown from a shopping mall or an office park, and it is what people crave as the pace of their lives accelerates. Fragmented and dispersed suburban business districts, through their separation of uses and buildings and their lack of public spaces, tend to isolate people rather than bring them together.

Some suburban business districts have begun to remedy the fragmentation of uses by creating town centers. For example, Schaumburg (population 74,000), located about ten miles northwest of Chicago's O'Hare Airport, is developing a town square that is bordered by a supermar-

ket, a variety of small stores, and a library. Townhouses and a handful of single-family homes will be constructed nearby, allowing residents the option of walking to the square.

The trend toward lower- and lower-density suburban business districts located farther and farther out from the central business district has started to reverse itself. As they did immediately after World War II, Americans are beginning to express a change of heart about their metropolitan areas. Residents and businesses are looking to rediscover community centers by transforming their suburban business districts into live-work-shop environments that are pedestrian-oriented, offer a variety of uses, and are transit-linked.

Notes

1. Witold Rybczynski, *City Life* (New York: Touchstone, 1995), p. 109.

2. William Leach, *A Country of Exiles: The Destruction of Place in American Life* (New York: Vintage Books, 2000), p. 10.

3. Kenneth T. Jackson, *Crabgrass Frontier: The Suburbanization of the United States* (New York: Oxford University Press, 1985), p. 77.

4. Ibid., p. 78.

5. Ibid., p. 80.

6. Howard Chudacoff and Judith Smith, *The Evolution of American Urban Society* (Saddle River, N.J.: Prentice Hall, 2000), p. 91.

7. Jackson, *Crabgrass Frontier,* p. 121.

8. Graham Taylor, *Satellite Cities: A Study of Industrial Suburbs* (New York: Arno Press, 1915), p. 1.

9. Richard Harris and Peter Larkham, eds., *Changing Suburbs: Foundation, Form and Function* (New York: Routledge, 1999), p. 148.

10. Taylor, *Satellite Cities,* p. 166.

11. Chudacoff and Smith, *The Evolution,* p. 218.

12. *World Almanac and Book of Facts, 2000* (Mahwah, N.J.: World Almanac Books, 2000), p. 715.

13. Robert Fishman, *Bourgeois Utopias: The Rise and Fall of Suburbia* (New York: Basic Books, 1987), p. 182.

14. *State of the Cities* (Washington, D.C.: U.S. Department of Housing and Urban Development, 1999).

15. *The State of the Cities* (Washington, D.C.: U.S. Department of Housing and Urban Development, 2000), p. 28.

16. Ray Suarez, *The Old Neighborhood* (New York: The Free Press, 1999), p. 111.

17. Mitchell Gordon, *Sick Cities: Psychology and Pathology of American Urban Life* (Baltimore: Viking Penguin, 1965), p. 13.

18. H.G. Wells, *The Works of H.G. Wells, Atlantic Edition, Volume IV: Anticipations and Other Papers* (London: T. Fisher Unwin, Ltd., 1924).

19. Fishman, *Bourgeois Utopias,* p. 186.

20. William Kowinski, *The Malling of America* (New York: William Morrow and Company, 1985), pp. 117–118.

21. Christopher Leinberger and Charles Lockwood, "How Business Is Reshaping America," *Atlantic Monthly,* October 1986, pp. 43–52.

22. Fishman, *Bourgeois Utopias,* p. 190.

23. Joel Garreau, *Edge City: Life on the New Frontier* (New York: Anchor Books, 1991).

24. Joel Garreau, "Edge Cities in Profile," *American Demographics,* February 1994.

25. Andrew Jonas, "Making Edge City: Post-Suburban Development and Life on the Frontier in Southern California," in *Changing Suburbs: Foundation, Form and Function,* Richard Harris and Peter Larkham, eds. (New York: Routledge, 1999), p. 218.

26. Jon C. Teaford, *Post-Suburbia: Government and Politics in the Edge Cities* (Baltimore and London: Johns Hopkins University Press, 1997), p. 5.

27. Ray Oldenburg, *The Great Good Place* (New York: Marlowe & Company, 1999).

chapter 3

Enhancing Real Estate Value with Transportation Improvements

When a transportation system makes one place more accessible than other locations, that place becomes and remains the focus of economic activity and real estate investment. Real estate value is underpinned by the access provided by the local transportation system to the services and markets demanded by customers and tenants. In effect, access facilitates an increased intensity of use in the form of human traffic.

Increased use generates both higher rents and growth in revenues from sales. As the density of development increases, real estate capital values grow, stimulating further investment and, over time, the creation of a deep real estate market that converts a given place into a location with critical mass—a business district.

With more people using the business district, density of development increases to the threshold necessary to provide cost-effective transit. When a choice among transportation options is available, access to the business district further improves, which in turn increases the district's competitive advantage and associated real estate values. However, unless the capacity of the transportation system keeps pace with the demand for access, congestion will result.

Just as the access provided by a transportation system can create an attractive real estate market, congestion or merely the perception of congestion can undermine the value of that market. Even the perception of congestion can motivate new and existing development to locate in more accessible locations, initially to where the transportation system is less burdened but ultimately to where a choice in transportation options is available.

Lessons Not Learned

Nowhere is the relationship between transportation and direction of growth more evident than in the 20th-century development of North America's metropolitan areas. In 1900, the central business districts of American cities were not only the focus of the transportation system but also the primary locus of employment and commerce. These central business district powerhouses drove the expansion of the public transit system. " . . . [T]he extraordinary prosperity and vitality of most central business districts between 1890 and 1950 cannot be understood without reference to the street car systems . . . the routes invariably led downtown. . . . the practical effect was to force almost anyone using public transportation to rely on the downtown . . . radiating outward from the city center, the tracks opened up a vast suburban ring."[1]

The growth of the suburbs produced an even greater dependence on the mechanized transportation system. There was now an "origin"—the suburbs where people lived that were far removed from the "destination"—the central business district where the same people worked and shopped. It was no longer possible to walk or ride a bicycle or horse between the origin and the destination. Thus, the seeds of decline in downtown real estate values were sown, although at the time no one knew it, and anyone suggesting such an occurrence would have been dismissed as a lunatic.

Meanwhile, automobile use exploded. "During the years 1910–1930, the nation's auto registrations rose from 458,000 to nearly 22 million, or from one car per 201 persons to one car per 5.3 persons. . . . [The] automobile had a dramatic impact on the urban fabric and infrastructure. It greatly accelerated the process of deconcentration initiated by the streetcar, caused a vast increase in the flow of commuter traffic between the downtown and suburban residential areas, and sharply increased congestion in the downtown."[2] In the period from 1917 to 1929, automobile use in downtown Pittsburgh, for example, increased by 587 percent, truck use by 251 percent, and the number of streetcars by 81 percent. The pattern was repeated in downtowns across the United States. Downtown business groups called for urgent solutions to congestion as well as for more parking. However, due to the lag between cause and effect, real estate values, rents, and sale turnovers continued to escalate and drive new development. The result was the con-

Geoffrey Booth

tinued exacerbation of congestion and increased demand for more arterial road capacity and downtown parking.

The expansion of road capacity was achieved by eliminating the streetcar and constructing inner-city freeways. Ironically, it was with the support of downtown Los Angeles department stores that the Arroyo Seco Parkway, first envisaged in 1911, was built. Later, the roadway would become part of the most extensive freeway system in the world. In the end, however, it was the issue of parking that ultimately undermined downtown real estate values and dictated the form and structure of suburban business districts.

Despite pressure from the public to provide new roads, cities and counties lacked the financial capacity to build highways to the extent demanded. Clearly, the solution lay in a national program. The Federal-Aid Highway Act of 1944 provided for a 50-50 matching grant for highway construction; however, in 1956, Congress enacted the Interstate Highway Act under which the federal government assumed 90 percent of highway construction costs, with gasoline tax revenues deposited in a Highway Trust Fund to underwrite the program. Retired General Lucius D. Clay chaired the Advisory Committee on a National Highway Program, which recommended the rapid construction of the 41,000-mile highway network on the basis that it would significantly contribute to national security and the health of the economy.[3] The intent of the interstate highway system was to provide high-speed and high-capacity surface transportation routes for through traffic. Its purpose was *not* to provide access to suburban business districts or isolated commercial real estate developments so as to undermine the economic viability of downtowns. However, this is exactly what it has done, and so successfully that the capacity of the interstate system is no longer adequate to serve both through traffic and traffic circulating within fragmented and dispersed suburban business districts.

The Delayed Impact on Downtown Real Estate Value

The department store had been the mainstay of downtown retailing and real estate values. When department stores saw their customers relocating to the suburbs, they decided to relocate with them in order to remain accessible and convenient to their clientele. It started when ". . . Robert E. Wood, Sears's vice president in charge of factories and retail stores . . . a student of population trends . . . decided in 1925 that motor-vehicle registrations had outstripped the parking space available in the metropolitan cores, and he insisted that Sears's new 'A' stores (their other retail outlets were much smaller) be located in low-density areas which would offer the advantage of lower rentals and yet, because of the automobile, be within reach of potential customers. . . . Wood's dictum of ample free parking was rigorously followed throughout the United States."[4] This experiment, begun just before the Great Depression, developed into a real estate tsunami that lasted from the 1950s through the 1960s and into the 1970s. By the 1980s, the department store exodus from downtown was largely complete.

The new breed of enclosed climate-controlled shopping malls and strip centers surrounded by acres of surface parking developed at the intersections of interstates and freeways for one reason—the land was cheap and enjoyed excellent transportation access. The logic was simple. If the malls were conveniently located for their customers, why would anyone drive past them to shop downtown and pay to park or pay for public transit? With the demise of downtown retailing and the substantially improved retail offerings in the suburbs, many downtown and inner-city residents followed those who had already located to the suburbs. As a consequence, the retail sales of the remaining downtown stores declined further. The housing stock left behind was gradually taken up by immigrants and minorities. The post–World War II flight to the suburbs had begun in earnest. The suburban population of U.S. cities grew from 36 million in 1950 to 74 million in 1970, with 83 percent of the nation's total growth over the 20-year period taking place in the suburbs.

The relocation of offices from downtown to the suburbs gained momentum in the 1950s. In 1954, the General Foods Corporation was one of the first large American companies to move from a downtown location—Manhattan—to a suburban location—White Plains in New York's Westchester County. The new headquarters complex featured ample surface parking, abundant open space, and easily accessible highways. The same criteria continue to be important today, although recent studies have also concluded that one of the most important variables determining the relocation decision is proximity to the corporate executives' residences and the neighborhoods in which they spend their leisure hours—what Christopher Leinberger has referred to as the "favored quarter."[5] Other reasons for corporate relocation include a reduction in office occupancy costs over the life of a lease, free parking for employees, easy access to interstates and highways, a college campus–style working environment, landscaped gardens, on-site employee facilities such as gymnasiums, saunas, and child care, and a high level of security.

A study undertaken for the Brookings Institution[6] by Robert Lang found that in 13 of the largest U.S. metropolitan real estate markets, the percentage distribution of office space in 1999 was as follows:

- 37.7 percent in central business districts;
- 6 percent in compact suburban business districts;
- 19.8 percent in fragmented and dispersed suburban business districts encompassing more than 5 million square feet; and
- 36.5 percent in fragmented and dispersed suburban business districts and standalone office developments encompassing less than 5 million square feet.

The study also found that office space in the suburbs of the 13 metropolitan areas had grown from 235.5 million square feet in 1979

Most metropolitan office space is now in fragmented and dispersed suburban business districts like this isolated pod of office buildings in North Bethesda, Maryland.

to 1.12 billion square feet in 1999—an increase of 305 percent. By comparison, central city office space grew from 676 million square feet to 1.57 billion square feet—an increase of 112 percent. Of particular interest was the finding that ". . . 38 percent of all metropolitan office space in 1999 was located in the traditional downtowns while nearly the same amount, 37 percent, was found in highly dispersed, 'edgeless' locations lacking well-defined boundaries and extending over tens if not hundreds of square miles of urban space."[7] It is in these "edgeless locations" (comprising fragmented and dispersed suburban business districts and isolated, standalone real estate developments with less than 5 million square feet of office space) that it is extremely difficult to provide freedom of choice in transportation options.

For families, relocation to the suburbs meant realization of their share of the American dream, something for which many Americans had fought in World War II. Downtown and central city locations were no longer considered suitable residential areas. With the new suburban lifestyle, families either ignored the cost of operating cars or considered such cost to be offset to some degree by home mortgage income tax deductibility and the cachet of owning a new home in the suburbs.

The net result of the flight to the suburbs was a significant decline in the patronage of downtown transit systems. Public transit ridership peaked at just under 25 billion passengers per year in the mid- to late 1940s and steadily decreased to just under 7 billion passengers per year in 1972.[8] At the same time, downtowns throughout the United States experienced serious economic decline as evidenced by the collapse of central city real estate values and the associated tax base. For the patron and the tenant, downtown no longer offered access to a wide range of high-quality retailing. Commercial services and the transit system were no longer considered safe or desirable. It would take several decades and the injection of billions of dollars of taxpayer funds to restart development in these once-robust central business districts.

Lower Development Density Creates Congestion

Compact business districts are the product of either preautomobile-era plats and street layouts or post–1920s developments that called for master-planned town centers intentionally designed with the pedestrian and transit service in mind. By comparison, fragmented and dispersed suburban business districts are the result of universal car ownership, suburban housing affordability, a supply of cheap gasoline, and an unprecedented highway construction program. Figure 3.1 sets out a summary of the development form and attributes of different types of suburban business districts.

The form and structure of fragmented and dispersed suburban business districts follow a standard real estate development formula. The districts consist of individual self-contained real estate developments that are geographically proximate but not interconnected. Often preleased or built to suit a particular tenant, they give no consideration to how they could leverage added value by integrating with neighboring developments.

The predominant mode of transportation to and from fragmented and dispersed suburban business districts is the automobile. It is also the predominant mode of transportation for

Geoffrey Booth

figure 3.1 Development Form and Attributes of Business Districts

Business District Type	Central Business District	Compact Suburban Business District	Fragmented Suburban Business District	Dispersed Suburban Business District
Development density	High	Medium	Low	Very low
Spatial separation between buildings	Very low	Low	High	Very high
Parking cost	Subject to charge	Subject to charge	Free	Free
Dominant parking type	Garages (restricted access)	Garages (restricted access)	Surface parking (restricted access)	Surface parking (unrestricted access)
Quality of transit service	Citywide Frequent	District-centric Less frequent	Local Infrequent	Local Very infrequent
Pedestrian orientation	Very strong	Strong	Weak	Very weak
Dependence on cars for access	Low	Moderate	High	Very high
Choice in mode of transit	Very good	Good	Poor	Very poor

Source: Geoffrey Booth, Urban Land Institute, 2001.

trips within the districts. Such dependence on the car increases the number of vehicle trips, road widths, and the parking areas required for each development. Shared parking is not possible as each development stands alone and is independent.

The case of San Diego's projected growth gives an indication of the extent of land consumed by parking and its impact on development density. As a result of the dispersed, standalone nature of San Diego's development, five parking spaces currently exist for every car. Assuming continuation of current patterns of automobile use, San Diego's projected 1 million increase in population will demand the provision of an additional 685,000 parking spaces over the next 20 years, or 37 square miles of parking lots.[9]

The space required for vehicle circulation and parking in suburban business districts dramatically increases the space between buildings to the point where walking between premises is not practical. Nor is it an attractive proposition. Typically, public open space is absent in suburban business districts. Originally, the omission of open space was linked to fears that open spaces would generate the security problems associated with downtowns. To some extent, this perception persists, encouraging greater use of the

automobile and reducing interaction between uses located in the same business district. This increased use of the automobile contributes to the growing problem of congestion.

As congestion builds on roads in and around many fragmented and dispersed suburban business districts, not to mention around isolated, standalone commercial real estate developments, customers and tenants will see more accessible business districts as a better deal.[10] After all, Americans still make their transportation decisions on the basis of convenience, comfort, and safety. However, in light of growing congestion, they are also factoring in issues of cost and their right to a choice.

Perhaps it is for that reason that the recently released Census 2000 reveals an initial population shift back to downtowns with a well-developed transit system.[11] It is evident that many downtowns are using their transit systems and compact urban form to reestablish a competitive advantage. Similarly, suburban business districts that can offer choice in transportation options, both to and within their centers, will prove more sustainable over time and will offer more attractive real estate investments. The original tenet of real estate development was "location, location, location," to which was added,

33

Americans are constantly reminded about traffic congestion through experiences like this morning commute on I-495 in suburban Washington, D.C.

"timing, timing, timing." However, there is a third leg of the tripod without which investment value will decline—"access, access, access."

The Impact of Congestion

Historically, Americans have followed a predictable pattern of response when their roads become more and more congested. First, as access to their jobs, homes, and services is slowly compromised, they begin to perceive the existence of traffic congestion. Next, they accept the reality of the problem over a significant period of resignation and growing irritation. Finally, however, they spring into action—and what action. Fed up with congested downtowns, post–World War II Americans from all over the nation voted with their feet and changed their residential locations, their employment locations, and, interestingly, their mode of transportation.

This same pattern of behavior has significance for today's suburban business district. Again, the perception of gridlock and parking problems is becoming a major political issue in the United States. Few political issues touch more Americans' daily lives than traffic. The cost of traffic congestion is further reinforced by a steady stream of reports and articles in the popular press. A recent article entitled "American Gridlock" in *U.S. News & World Report*[12] stated, "Since 1982, while the U.S. population has grown nearly 20 percent, the time Americans spend in traffic has jumped an amazing 236 percent. In major American cities, the length of the combined

morning-evening rush hour has doubled, from under three hours in 1982 to almost six hours today. The result? The average driver now spends the equivalent of nearly a full workweek each year stuck in traffic. . . . Congestion costs Americans $78 billion a year in wasted fuel and lost time—up 39 percent since 1990."

Responses to Congestion

Many metropolitan roads are now at or near capacity, particularly those serving suburban business districts that must accommodate both through traffic and traffic circulating within the districts. Given the historic pattern of Americans' response to reduced access, there is little doubt that growing congestion on metropolitan roads will have serious repercussions for suburban business districts. Customers and tenants will move beyond irritation and resignation and leave congested suburban business districts for more accessible locations. The real estate left behind will not only decline in value but also will create dead spots and urban blight. Indeed, this pattern is already identifiable. However, there is a bright spot on the horizon. As mentioned earlier, Americans have demonstrated a willingness to change their residential location and employment locations as well as their mode of transportation. This is significant. Locations that provide a choice of transportation mode will undoubtedly be perceived as more attractive than those that provide a single mode, i.e., the car. Therefore, suburban business districts —as with downtowns—that offer a choice of transportation mode will have a competitive advantage over those that do not.

According to the latest in a series of studies by the Texas Transportation Institute, traffic congestion is growing in American metropolitan areas of every size. "All of the size categories showed more severe congestion that lasts a longer period of time and affects more of the transportation network in 1999 than in 1982. The average annual delay per person climbed from 11 hours in 1982 to 36 hours in 1999. And delay over the same period quintupled in areas with less than 1 million people. The total congestion bill for the 68 areas surveyed in 1999 came to $78 billion, which was the value of 4.5 billion hours of delay and 6.8 billion gallons of excess fuel consumed."[13] The report posed the question, Can more roads solve all of the problem? It answered the question as follows: "In many of the nation's most congested corridors there doesn't seem to be the space, money, and public approval to add enough road space to create an acceptable condition. Only about half of the new roads needed to address congestion . . . were added between 1982 and 1999. And the percentage is actually slightly smaller in the smallest areas—where one might expect roads to top a shorter list of improvements than in larger and more diverse urban areas."[14]

Smart Growth and Funding

The solution to traffic congestion is not simply to build more roads. At a time when Congress has passed a $1.35 trillion tax cut, available federal highway funds will be subject to greater fiscal scrutiny. In this climate, dramatic cost escalations in major new projects such as Boston's "Big Dig" (the Central Artery/Ted Williams Tunnel whose cost has escalated from an initial $2.3 billion to $13.6 billion) and the Springfield (Virginia) Interchange (whose cost has escalated since the start of construction from $350 million to currently $540 million) will draw critical public reaction. The comment made by Fairfax

County Board of Supervisors Chair Katherine K. Hanley, in relation to the Springfield Interchange, expressed the public's concern about "putting all the eggs in one basket" to relieve congestion by building more roads. "That interchange is a giant sucking sound on funding. . . . When you count it in, at whatever the current estimate is, of course you will have a lot of money going to northern Virginia. But a lot is going to only one place."[15]

As public policy moves to embrace the lessons of smart growth, transportation budgets will increasingly reflect greater balance among road, transit, pedestrian, and bike path construction so as to provide the community with an enhanced level of services and a greater range of transportation options. Choice reduces congestion and contributes to the livability of high-density human settlements, as demonstrated by London, New York, and Paris. It is these higher development densities that make transit cost-effective.

The Maryland Department of Transportation has adopted a new approach of "thinking beyond the pavement." The department now considers roads as magnets for suburban sprawl and is placing increased emphasis on the provision of choice in transportation options. Governor Parris N. Glendening's smart growth program "in seeking to focus state transportation spending on established communities in designated growth

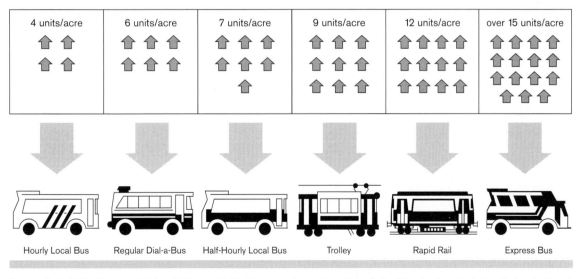

4 units/acre	6 units/acre	7 units/acre	9 units/acre	12 units/acre	over 15 units/acre
Hourly Local Bus	Regular Dial-a-Bus	Half-Hourly Local Bus	Trolley	Rapid Rail	Express Bus

Higher densities make transit more cost- and energy-efficient. Average figures vary with suburban business district size and distances, but minimum densities are generally as shown below.

Source: Boris S. Pushkarev and Jeffrey M. Zupan, *Public Transportation and Land Use Policy* (Ontario, Canada: Indiana University Press/ Bloomington and London, 1977).

areas, hopes to lure developers, businesses and home buyers back from the ex-urban frontier where new subdivisions devour farmland and cough more cars onto the state's crowded roads." Maryland's Highway Design Engineer Robert Douglas summarized the change in approach by stating, "Ten years ago, the whole highway industry had two goals: mobility and efficiency. . . . the interstate system is probably the greatest example in the world of that kind of approach to transportation. . . . (but today) the interstate era is over." Maryland's highway planners are now encouraged to take as much pride in a finely wrought cross walk as they once found in the vast lanes of I-270.[16]

In November 2000, constituents in cities and counties in various parts of the United States went to the polls to vote on proposals to increase taxes to fund 22 new public transit programs estimated to cost in excess of $7 billion. Of these, voters passed 19, including the proposed extension of San Francisco's BART transit system to San Jose, and narrowly defeated three.[17] In a recent national survey on growth and development, 75 percent of respondents called for either improving mass transit or developing less automobile-dependent communities. Only 21 percent called for building new roads.[18] In its companion analysis of the Texas Transportation Institute's 2001 *Urban Mobility Report,* the

Washington-based Surface Transportation Policy Project reported, "An alternative way to address congestion is to give people a way to avoid driving in it . . . analysis of the travel data from the Federal Transit Administration, and the U.S. Census found that in metro areas that offer more transportation choices, (such as more efficient bus and train service), a smaller portion of the population is directly affected by congestion."[19]

These trends bode well for transportation investment in existing suburban business districts. More balanced government transportation spending will enhance the accessibility of existing community and real estate assets rather than providing, as it has to date, the means to abandon existing congested locations for greener pastures on the urban fringe and beyond. Those suburban business districts that fail to balance good automobile access with improved pedestrian and transit access will be putting their future patronage, attractiveness, and capital value at risk.

Suburban Business District Travel Patterns

Even in those fragmented and dispersed suburban business districts with a full range of civic, corporate, retail, and residential uses, it is virtually impossible to go from one building to

Geoffrey Booth

figure 3.2 Employee Midday Mode Shares: Metropolitan Washington, D.C., Business Districts

	Central Business District	Compact Suburban Business District	Fragmented Suburban Business District	Dispersed Suburban Business District
Automobile–driver	5.6%	23.3%	80.5%	84.0%
Automobile–passenger	1.7%	3.2%	9.3%	5.3%
Transit	8.6%	6.2%	0.0%	0.7%
Walk	80.5%	67.3%	10.2%	8.5%
Other	3.6%	0.0%	0.0%	1.6%
Total	100.0%	100.0%	100.0%	100.0%

Source: Data from G. Bruce Douglas et al., "Urban Design, Urban Form, and Employee Travel Behavior" in *TRB Transportation Planning Applications Conference Papers* (Washington, D.C.: U.S. Department of Transportation, 1997). Note: business district categories developed by ULI–the Urban Land Institute.

figure 3.3 Employee Midday Tripmaking: Metropolitan Washington, D.C., Business Districts

	Central Business District	Compact Suburban Business District	Fragmented Suburban Business District	Dispersed Suburban Business District
Midday trips per employee	1.4	1.3	1.2	0.9
Midday vehicle trips per employee	0.1	0.3	1.1	0.8
Midday vehicle miles traveled per employee	0.9	3.5	6.4	12.7
Midday trips per employee versus central business district	1	0.9	0.9	0.6
Vehicle trips per employee versus central business district	1	3.3	11.1	7.8
Vehicle miles traveled per employee versus central business district	1	4	7.5	14.9

Source: Data from G. Bruce Douglas et al., "Urban Design, Urban Form, and Employee Travel Behavior" in *TRB Transportation Planning Applications Conference Papers* (Washington, D.C.: U.S. Department of Transportation, 1997). Note: business district categories developed by ULI–the Urban Land Institute.

another without driving. The total amount of traffic generated by a single district becomes the sum of that generated by individual buildings, with no economies of scale.

In 1997, Bruce Douglas compared workers' daily trips by drawing on four different types of business districts in metropolitan Washington, D.C., as follows:[20]

- downtown Washington, D.C. (a central business district served by several Metro rail stations and Metro bus transit);
- Bethesda, Maryland (a compact suburban business district served by one Metro rail station and Metro and county bus transit);
- Rock Spring Park, Maryland (a fragmented suburban business district served by county bus transit, with the nearest Metro rail station two miles away); and
- Gaithersburg Office Park, Maryland (a dispersed suburban business district served in part by county bus transit, with the nearest Metro rail station one to three miles away).

The causal relationships between development form and density and vehicle trip generation and congestion are clearly evident in Figures 3.2 and 3.3. A similar survey of other U.S. metropolitan business districts is likely to yield the same results.

Geoffrey Booth

Significant Differences in Transportation Mode

According to Douglas, in the central business district, pedestrians accounted for 80 percent of all midday trips. As the density and compactness of development dropped in each suburban business district, the percentage of midday trips made by pedestrians likewise declined—by 67 percent in compact suburban business districts, 10 percent in fragmented suburban business districts, and 8.5 percent in dispersed suburban business districts. Clearly, higher-density and more compact business districts provide greater choices and reasons to walk within a business district. The lack of good connectivity within fragmented and dispersed suburban business districts is a strong disincentive to pedestrian and transit modes—if they even exist—because of the excessively long routes required to reach desired destinations. The use of anything other than an automobile in these circumstances is neither time- nor cost-effective.

Increased Number and Distance of Vehicle Trips

With increasing use of the automobile comes an increase in both distance and the number of midday trips made by employees. While Douglas found that central business district employees made more midday trips per employee than their counterparts in dispersed suburban business districts, fewer made automobile trips, and

the average length of trip per employee was 0.9 miles for the central business district employee but 12.7 miles for employees in suburban business districts. In fact, the average employee in a dispersed suburban business district drove more miles at midday than the average central business district employee drove to work. Development density and compactness of form clearly have a major impact not only on the number of midday trips generated per employee but also on the distance of those trips—a major contributor to traffic growth and highway congestion.

The Quality of Working Lives in Suburban Business Districts

In summary, Douglas found that

- greater density, mix, and size (central business districts and compact suburban business districts) lead to more total trips, more pedestrian trips, more transit trips, fewer automobile trips, and more eating/shopping trips during midday; and
- lower density, mix, and size (fragmented and dispersed suburban business districts) lead to much higher vehicular traffic vehicle miles traveled per employee.

"The quality of daytime life for workers in the central business district seems better than for the suburban workers. More people are able to leave the building at midday, and they more often leave for nonwork activities. These midday trips are often accomplished by walking. In the suburban office settings most people eat at their desks (63 percent in the dispersed business district). When they do leave the building it is usually on assignment, and it is usually in an automobile . . . [there are] dramatic differences in the travel patterns of employees with similar jobs and incomes depending on the urban character of the work place (including mix of land uses)."[21]

The Competitive Advantage of Mixed Uses in Suburban Business Districts

In a 1989 survey of six U.S. shopping centers located within suburban business districts,[22]

figure 3.4 Origin of Trips to Malls in Suburban Business Districts

Shopping Mall	Percent from within Suburban Business District	
	Midday	Evening
Prestonwood Town Center, Dallas	68	57
Perimeter Mall, Atlanta	50	18
Parkway Center, Dallas	47	41
Bellevue Square, Seattle	32	21
Southdale Mall, Minneapolis	30	15
Tysons Corner Center, Fairfax County, Virginia	22	7
South Coast Plaza, Los Angeles	7	7
Overall average	37	24

Source: K.G. Hooper, *Travel Characteristics at Large-Scale Suburban Activity Centers*, NCHRP Report 323 (Washington, D.C.: Transportation Research Board, National Academy of Sciences, October 1989).

K.G. Hooper found that a significant share of total midday and evening trips came from within the suburban business district. The survey results as shown in Figures 3.4 and 3.5 reveal that the shopping mall within a suburban business district generates significant trip making among suburban business district employees. These trips are most pronounced during the midday and in the evening and demonstrate that shopping malls account for significant visitation by employees from the suburban business district of which the malls form a part. The exception is South Coast Plaza, which draws from a comparatively small surrounding office employment population and is, by the nature of its retail mix, a high-end shopping mall with a particularly extensive trade area; in fact, South Coast Plaza is often referred to as the Fifth Avenue of the West Coast.

In many suburban business districts, the interior of the shopping mall–like Tysons Corner Center shown here–is the only pedestrian-friendly environment to be found.

figure 3.5 Characteristics of Trips Made by Suburban Business District Employees

	Bellevue Square	South Coast Plaza	Parkway Center	Perimeter Center	Tysons Corner	Southdale Mall
Trip to Work						
Proportion of employees who stop	34%	23%	21%	17%	17%	17%
Proportion who stop within suburban business district	15%	8%	9%	12%	9%	7%
Average number of stops per trip	1.4	1.2	1.2	1.2	1.2	1.2
Midday Trips						
Proportion of employees who make a midday trip	55%	59%	45%	46%	55%	42%
Proportion who make a midday trip within the suburban business district	29%	22%	20%	33%	32%	23%
Average number of stops per trip	1.7	1.9	1.6	1.6	1.6	1.6
Trip from Work						
Proportion of employees who stop	66%	40%	37%	35%	36%	36%
Proportion who stop within suburban business district	14%	6%	9%	16%	10%	13%
Average number of stops per trip	1.7	1	1.1	1.2	1.5	1.5

Source: K.G. Hooper, *Travel Characteristics at Large-Scale Suburban Activity Centers*, NCHRP Report 323 (Washington, D.C.: Transportation Research Board, National Academy of Sciences, October 1989).

Figure 3.5 summarizes the behavior of suburban business district employees in each of the surveyed shopping malls.

Hooper reported that despite their geographic proximity to a shopping mall, most suburban business district residents and employees drove to the mall because of poor-quality pedestrian interconnectivity. Only Parkway Center enjoyed significant pedestrian access—17 percent. In that case, office development was located close to the shopping mall.

Comparatively few customers traveled to the shopping malls by transit largely because most malls were not well served by public transportation. While dependence on transit to patronize shopping malls is less significant than in the case of other transportation modes, those customers who did rely on transit often spent more per shopping trip than other customers. This finding is at odds with the general perception held by many retailers and shopping center managers.

The Metropolitan Transit Development Board in San Diego surveyed bus riders at seven shopping malls in 1994 and found that 51 percent of transit riders shopped at one or more of the malls and spent an average $56 per trip. In its December 1997 survey, the board found that riders at trolley stations near two regional malls constituted an even higher percentage of shoppers—79 percent—and spent an average of $79 per trip.

The extensive volume of travel generated by suburban business districts points to the need for good access via all transportation modes. But how do you manage congestion, provide better transit connections, and deliver an improved, pedestrian-friendly environment in suburban business districts?

Managing Travel Demand

As the capacity of the road system has failed to keep pace with traffic growth, federal and state transportation agencies have increasingly turned to travel demand management (TDM) to maximize the transportation capacity of the existing highway infrastructure. TDM techniques often call for

- shifting peak-hour trips to other times of the day;
- encouraging more people to work at home;
- restricting the days on which owners can use their vehicles;
- encouraging ridesharing;
- providing express lanes for high-occupancy vehicles (HOV) on arterial roads and highways;
- raising the cost of reliance on private automobiles;
- increasing the cost of parking;
- encouraging greater use of public transit for work trips; and
- using intelligent vehicle highway systems.[23]

The most direct method of reducing traffic congestion is to decrease the length of essential vehicle trips and eliminate extraneous trips. Suburban business districts can achieve the necessary reductions by offering a compact form and a rich mix of land uses. The inclusion of residential development, retail uses, and entertainment venues in a convenient and accessible town center within a suburban business district reduces vehicle trip generation, spreads peak-hour flows on arterial roads, makes transit provision more cost-effective, and allows more people to live closer to their place of employment. To achieve these travel demand management initiatives, federal and state agencies must work with the cities and counties that control land use and development form.

Providing Transportation Choice

The types of transportation needed to improve access to and circulation within a suburban business district, as well as accommodate projected growth, cover a range of options—from providing

The inclusion of mixed-use development lining a pedestrian linkage, as demonstrated at Downtown Disney in California, can reduce trip generation, spread peak-hour flows on arterial roads, make transit provision more cost-effective, and allow more people the option of living closer to their place of employment.

Geoffrey Booth

A free bus shuttle, which connects the Walnut Creek, California, business district, downtown shopping area, and BART station, is one way of mitigating the separation of land uses in fragmented and dispersed suburban business districts.

Buses with character can be used as major place-making elements in suburban business districts.

new transit services to strategically locating and configuring parking, creating pedestrian-friendly environments, and providing cycling paths. Admittedly, suburban business districts have developed around automobile access, and, for most districts, the automobile will continue to be the dominant means of transportation. However, several strategies can improve transportation connections and help a district offer greater freedom of choice in transportation mode.

Providing New Transit Services

A transit center or interchange developed as part of a suburban business district's town center is an important element in improving transit access and increasing real estate values. If properly located and configured with other uses, a transit center will generate pedestrian traffic and create well-traveled pedestrian linkages within a suburban business district. Local transit buses, shuttle buses, light rail, and trolleys can serve the suburban business district and link it to the regional rail systems beyond the immediate reach of the suburban business district. Local transit systems successfully serve Walnut Creek, California, and White Flint and Rockville Pike in Bethesda, Maryland. In fact, some shuttle services can become significant place-making elements in their own right, such as the cable cars and historic trolleys still operated by Muni Metro in San Francisco.

The largest suburban business district in the Washington, D.C., area is Tysons Corner, Virginia, which was developed at the intersection of three major roads. The original plan for Washington's Metro rail system did not provide for service to Tysons Corner. Thus, to retrofit this vibrant suburban business district with rail transit service, current proposals call for up to six stations that will involve not only a significant cost but also impose a substantial time penalty on those traveling directly to downtown Washington from Washington Dulles Airport or beyond. Accordingly, the need for improved transit service to both Tysons Corner and Dulles has led to a two-stage proposal: a bus rapid transit system (BRT) that will use the Dulles access road on an interim basis (estimated cost at $280 million) to be followed by a longer-term extension of the Metro rail system (estimated cost at $2.2 billion). In suburban business districts without the scale or critical mass of a Tysons Corner, the O-Bahn bus system in Adelaide, South Australia, provides a cost-effective transit alternative.

Managing Transit Provision

Generally, a regional transit operator provides transit services over several county and city

The Adelaide O-Bahn

The world's longest and fastest guided busway is the Adelaide O-Bahn. Offering an unparalleled level of speed, comfort, and safety, this unique system combines the best attributes of bus transportation with the benefits of rail-type track. Requiring significantly less space than conventional busways, the O-Bahn's construction is simple and its operation cost-effective. Operating in a narrow landscaped corridor from the central business district to the South Australian capital's northeastern suburbs, the O-Bahn opened in 1986 to meet the transit needs of the city's growing population.

Flexibility is the key to the O-Bahn system. Where many transit systems work on a network of bus-rail connections, the O-Bahn provides both in one vehicle. Although O-Bahn buses travel at high speeds on a separate concrete track, they also travel on roads. Each bus has a special "guide wheel" by the front wheels that allows the bus to transfer from road to track in one smooth, easy movement. With the guide wheels directly connected to the vehicle's steering mechanism, the track effectively steers the bus once the wheels are locked in place.

Because O-Bahn passengers are not required to transfer to a different vehicle, O-Bahn traveling times are shorter. With speeds of up to 60 miles per hour, the Adelaide O-Bahn completes its 7.2-mile journey in only ten minutes. In addition, the system allows a high frequency of service. Buses are able to travel safely on the corridor at 20-second intervals. Owing to the system's versatility, the passenger service area has proved significantly larger than that of rail.

Safety on the O-Bahn is unparalleled. The mechanical excellence of the O-Bahn buses has resulted in few breakdowns, although special maintenance and recovery vehicles equipped with guide wheels can be used for bus maintenance and recovery. In the event of a mechanical problem, buses traveling the O-Bahn even at speeds of up to 60 miles per hour can stop in a distance of less than two bus lengths. If tire damage should occur on the front axle, the wheels are equipped with a metal inner tire to prevent full deflation, allowing a loaded bus to travel at a speed of 30 miles per hour for 9.6 miles.

The engineering excellence of the O-Bahn extends to the busway itself, with special consideration given to aesthetics, economy, and efficiency throughout the design process. Extensive landscaping along the busway complements the well-designed infrastructure and offers Adelaide commuters pleasant surroundings.

Fast Facts

- At 7.2 miles long, the Adelaide O-Bahn is the longest and fastest guided bus service in the world.
- More than 7 million passengers a year, including local, interstate, and overseas visitors, use the O-Bahn. The system can move 18,000 people per hour in each direction.
- The busway consists of 5,800 sleepers, 5,600 pylons drilled to a depth of ten feet, 4,200 track pieces, 25 bridges, eight pedestrian overpasses, and a 200-foot-long tunnel.
- Compared with equivalent rail systems, the O-Bahn is almost 50 percent cheaper to operate while providing faster, more flexible service than many other transit systems.
- At the time of its building, the entire O-Bahn project (including the bus fleet) cost approximately US $73.5 million. ●

Source: Adelaide Metro, Passenger Transit Board, South Australia, http://www.adelaidemetro.com.au/guides/obahn.html.

---

areas—in the case of the Washington Metropolitan Area Transit Authority (Metro), over two states and the District of Columbia—and draws its capital funding from all levels of government. In some cases, a regional system operates multitransit modes—rail, light rail, bus, and/or ferries; in other cases, it operates only a single transit mode. In addition, a wide array of private transportation companies, counties, and cities operate local bus and shuttle services.

Because of their location astride regional travel corridors, many suburban business districts are situated near transit routes. The problem is that transit often does not provide direct access to the districts. For example, freeway bus routes normally transport passengers downtown, and an extra stop at a suburban business district would inconvenience other users, as it generally takes significant time to leave and reenter a freeway system at peak hours. In the case of transit services on an arterial road, bus stops are often located too far away from passengers' final destinations, and the walk to those destinations is often fraught with traffic hazards.

Transit services can, however, be extended to serve newly developing areas, although such extensions are best accomplished as part of a regional transportation strategy. Fortunately,

Geoffrey Booth

recent years have seen growing recognition of the importance of transit to suburban business districts. Regional plans now emphasize the clustering of growth and the provision of sound transit connections. In the Puget Sound region, all 21 suburban business districts identified in the regional growth plan have bus service, 14 include current or planned transit centers, and 17 were designated for stations in the planned regional light-rail system.[24]

Reconfiguring Internal Roads and Parking

The superblock plat and the associated dominance of a limited number of high-capacity roads in fragmented and dispersed suburban business districts contrast with the more intimate grid plat and larger number of narrower

The Dividend from Transportation Mode Choice

Bellevue, Washington, is the third-largest suburban business district in the Seattle region. It is located on the east side of Lake Washington, 12 miles from downtown Seattle, at the crossroads of two radial freeways, I-90 and State 520, and a major north/south route, I-405. In the 1970s, concern over a proposal to build a shopping mall outside Bellevue prompted property owners to establish the Downtown Bellevue Association and to work with the city council to make this compact suburban business district a financial and business hub. At the same time, the vision expressed in Bellevue's Downtown Subarea Plan called for the creation of a major retail focus, the location of a major office development to complement the district's retail activities, and the development of high-density housing. The city offered density bonuses to developers to encourage the provision of pedestrian and other amenities. A design review initiative ensured that all proposals were well conceptualized in furtherance of plan implemen-

tation. To provide the suburban business district with a choice in transportation modes and a premium level of access, decision makers recognized that it was imperative to create a pedestrian focus and critical mass of activity by undertaking three essential actions as follows:

- major improvements in transit service;
- management of employee parking; and
- an effective travel demand management (TDM) program.

Establishing a critical mass of activity for the improved transit service was an important element of the Downtown Subarea Plan. However, the transit proposal faced the typical "Catch-22." It was hard to justify significant levels of transit service without higher employment densities. Yet, if the transit service were not of a sufficiently high standard at the outset, people would not support it with repeat patronage. Eventually, the city worked out an innovative incentive agreement with Seattle Metro (the regional transit operator) to ease the front-

end shortfall in cash flow. Bellevue also established a transit terminal in the heart of the suburban business district, thereby creating an important symbol and focal point for future development. Simultaneously, Seattle Metro restructured the route system from the typical suburb-to-downtown run to a route that served Bellevue as a major hub by providing reliable and timely connections. Transit-based commuting has since grown from negligible levels to about 13 percent of all commuters. To encourage increased use of transit, the city has worked to raise parking charges and has constructed new road links within the business district to enhance transit access and pedestrian circulation.

Bellevue is slated for several stations in a planned rail system. Interestingly, an important part of the transit agreement with Seattle Metro was the requirement for increased parking charges. To enhance transit access and operation and pedestrian movement within the business district, the sixth north/south road in the suburban busi-

streets found in compact suburban districts and central business districts. The grid plat and its narrow streets allow better transit circulation, create a more pedestrian-friendly atmosphere, accommodate shared parking rather than each development's provision of its own parking, reduce the physical separation of development, decrease vehicle trip generation within the suburban business district, and provide for greater freedom of choice in transportation mode.

Providing More Minor Roads

Patterned on a superblock street network with no street grid, Uptown Houston is typical of a suburban business district that developed with limited interconnectivity among its component parts. One block of Post Oak Boulevard, one of the district's main streets, stretches for 3,400 feet

Geoffrey Booth

Fragmented and dispersed development, as illustrated by this suburban business district in Wheaton, Maryland, does not achieve the needed critical mass of activity, and walking long distances between buildings is inefficient.

ness district's new grid was completed in April 2001, ahead of schedule. It cost less than its budgeted $3.1 million. The suburban business district's new grid layout is now taking shape and is replacing the superblocks that were a significant barrier to pedestrian and transit access.

Transportation access to the suburban business district is being improved through the addition of extra lanes on the interstate and the provision of a bus rapid transit line.

In recognition that transit would not be cost-effective in the face of abundant free parking, the city reduced the parking requirements for new development. Specifically, Seattle Metro wanted the price of parking to at least equal the cost of a two-zone bus pass. Accordingly, the city agreed to reduce its parking requirements from a previous minimum of five spaces per 1,000 square feet to a maximum of 3.3 spaces. The city has since lowered the ratio to 2.7 spaces per 1,000 square feet. In addition to making driving less attractive, the parking reductions increased the

financial return on those parking spaces developers were allowed to provide. Real estate returns rose and, with them, capital values. As a result, parking rates increased from $2 per day in 1979, when most parking was limited to surface lots, to $13 per day by 2000. Retail parking is still free, but, where managed by individual retailers or shopping centers, it is not shared parking; patrons are required to move their car when they shop at another center. This requirement will make transit increasingly attractive as the desired mode of transportation.

Bellevue began operating TDM programs in the late 1970s. With the support of downtown property owners, the city established a transportation management association (TMA) in the 1980s; major members included U.S. West, PACCAR, and Puget Power. The city made $100,000 available in matching funds for employers that provided discounts for transit users. Developers and employers offered participants rideshare matching, van pooling,

cycling facilities, and Guaranteed Ride Home programs. The city's integrated policy approach to the encouragement of transit use has played a major role in the transformation of the Bellevue suburban business district throughout the 1990s. In the ten years following 1990, more than 1,000 new residential units were constructed in Bellevue, attracting rents on the order of $900 per month for single-family units. Office rents cleared $30 per square foot per year, and vacancy rates fell despite a 2.1 million-square-foot increase in office space. Entertainment facilities retain many of the 35,000 daytime workers after 5:00 p.m., creating a vibrant retail market and spreading the evening peak. Bellevue's strategy shows how various common-sense transportation and land use initiatives can work together to rebuild community and increase real estate values in a suburban business district. ●

Source: Adapted in part from ULI Advisory Services Report, *Downtown Bellevue, Washington,* 1996, and *Puget Sound Business Journal,* February 19, 1999.

without east/west public access. A Local Mobility Improvement Program, however, calls for the construction of 15 miles of streets to create a secondary street network that will improve local access, redistribute traffic across a larger number of streets, and reduce congestion at major intersections. It will also create real estate development opportunities by providing transportation access to development sites previously used as surface parking lots landlocked by the superblocks.[25]

Increasingly, planners and developers are coming to appreciate the advantages of a better-connected street network—traffic relief on main streets and at major intersections and the provision of more direct travel between different parts of the suburban business district. Improved connections are essential to facilitating pedestrian and transit travel. A good secondary street network, such as that proposed in Uptown Houston, allows shorter trip distances and faster trips. It also removes trips from an already overburdened arterial network whose major purpose is to provide access to the district, not circulation within it. Addison Circle in Addison, Texas, and Legacy Town Center in Plano, Texas, are following a similar approach and breaking up their superblocks to improve interconnectivity and circulation.

An opportunity for a similar retrofit often occurs with the redevelopment of older malls. In San Diego, for example, a Sears store was rebuilt as a convenience center, with higher-density housing connected to the original street grid. Englewood Town Center in Colorado, a suburban business district outside Denver, contains a failed mall that is undergoing redevelopment along a main street grid, with improved connections and a light-rail station that opened in 2000. As an indication of how new connections can improve the density of blocks per square mile, a suburban business district in the Seattle area's Federal Way plans to add several new streets that will raise the block density from 24 to 73, thereby increasing interconnectivity within the center.[26]

Better connections can facilitate the potential for public transit by providing opportunities for more door-to-door–type service. At the same time, clustering activities along a reasonably direct transit route will improve access for transit users without establishing an unnecessarily inconvenient or circuitous route. One of the greatest impediments to the use of transit is the perception of waiting time, which typically seems two to three times longer than it is in actuality. For that reason, frequent transit service is needed, and stops are best located where activities occupy the traveler and make the waiting time seem shorter.

Rethinking Parking Use and Configuration

Free parking is the symbol of fragmented and dispersed suburban business districts just as

The Uptown Houston Local Mobility Improvement Program includes the creation of 15 miles of new streets to improve vehicular and pedestrian access within the suburban business district.

Source: Barton Smith, Vinson & Ellis et al., *Project Plan and Reinvestment Zone Financing Plan* (Houston: City of Houston, 1999).

Using the ground floor of a parking garage to accommodate restaurants and shops can provide additional cash flow as well as an active streetfront in suburban business districts. Photograph taken in Walnut Creek, California.

the single-family home is the symbol of the suburban lifestyle. Businesses are often attracted to fragmented and dispersed suburban business districts because of the appeal of free parking for their employees. However, just because parking is free does not mean that it is cheap. Someone must pay for construction and maintenance of the facilities, whether surface or structured. Moreover, parking involves an opportunity cost, which is the forgone cost of the land that could be put to more productive uses. In fragmented and dispersed suburban business districts, developers build more space for parking than for buildings. The vast spaces needed for parking lots constrain project design and work against more innovative street forms, which, over the long term, would benefit the district, the tenant, and nearby residents. When combined with municipal setback codes, which often prescribe the distance of a building from the adjacent street, conventional suburban parking standards undermine interconnectivity and produce a pattern of buildings surrounded by parking and so far removed from the street that the only access is by automobile.

In compact suburban business districts, shared parking is possible because vehicle trips can be multipurpose trips. The creation of town centers with critical mass and their own transit terminals can achieve some of the economies of scale associated with multipurpose trips, thus reducing the amount of land required for parking. Economies of scale arise when each property owner is not required to provide its own on-site parking but rather takes advantage of a shared facility that is centrally located. Such an arrangement averts trip generation that results from driving from one parking area to another within fragmented and dispersed suburban business districts.

Municipal funding or underwriting is often required to cover the difference in construction cost between surface parking lots and parking garages. Federal Realty Investment Trust's Bethesda Row project in Bethesda, Maryland, depended on Montgomery County's funding of the parking garage to make the project viable. The initial capital investment in a parking garage can be offset in some measure by charging nominal parking fees or requiring new developments to buy or lease existing centrally located parking garage spaces from the municipality. Rental income from shops and entertainment venues located on the ground floor of parking

Sidewalks along major arterials with little separation from moving vehicles feel unsafe and are less likely to be used.

Sidewalks can be separated from traffic and parking by trees and landscaped mounds.

garages can also be used to offset the cost of construction.

The city of Walnut Creek, California, used the ground floor of one parking garage to accommodate streetfront cafés. In Mizner Park in Boca Raton, Florida, residential apartments were developed along the streetfront of the parking garage to offset the cost of structured parking. The strategic location of shared parking facilities can also create well-traveled pedestrian linkages that can be lined with shops. Enticing patrons along shop-lined pedestrian linkages, which connect the parking facility to the primary entertainment destination or anchor store, creates place and generates retail sales. It is this concentration of pedestrian flow that drives the success of retail outlets in Downtown Disney

and Universal CityWalk in Los Angeles. When parking facilities are strategically located and configured within suburban business districts, they generate retail sales, reduce vehicle trips, promote pedestrian and place-making activity, and increase real estate value.

To create a pedestrian-friendly environment, suburban business districts must establish a grid of direct connections in a pleasant walking environment. In Bellevue, Washington, a ULI Advisory Services panel suggested the city build "green" streets that feature landscaping, lower speed limits, and on-street parking as opposed to the urban streets that provide general access and accommodate efficient traffic movement.[27] Beyond efforts to create street types, it is also important to orient destinations toward potential walking trips. Compact rather than spread-out forms and connected rather than "pod" clusters create greater opportunities for walking, which is most desirable for distances of about one-quarter mile or less. It is easier to encourage walking trips in a developing rather than in an already developed center because the overall character of development can be established as a project unfolds.

Upgrading an older center requires special attention to pedestrians. In the case of Kendall, a highly successful retail and office center outside Miami, Florida, the Downtown Kendall Master Plan calls for creating a true downtown and making pedestrians the top priority. As an alternative to the intimidating journey required under Kendall's current configuration, the plan calls for shading pedestrians from sun and rain and clustering buildings along the streetfront to add interest.[28]

Sidewalks

The development of sidewalks is normally the responsibility of the developer or property owner. Accordingly, full interconnectivity depends on the completion of all planned development. Nonetheless, in low-density fragmented and dispersed suburban business districts, interconnectivity remains a problem; in compact suburban districts, on the other hand, it is less of an issue because of much higher densities.

One indicator of a district's density is the number of street blocks per square mile. Among the districts identified in the Puget Sound region, for example, the downtowns registered a large number of street blocks per square mile, which is indicative of an older, pedestrian-oriented community and is similar to the conditions that typify compact business districts. In contrast, fragmented and dispersed suburban business districts, which are primarily made up of office parks and shopping malls, exhibited a much lower density of street blocks per square mile. Thus, it is likely to take many years and higher densities than currently exist before continuous sidewalks are provided in fragmented and dispersed suburban business districts.

Pedestrian and Bicycle Access

Development of a system of effective pedestrian and bicycle circulation requires a fine-grained, interconnected street pattern. Where a grid street network does not exist, pedestrian linkages should maintain walking continuity via pedestrian cut-throughs of culs-de-sac. Large-lot commercial developments should be encouraged to provide numerous linkages to surrounding residential areas and between office buildings, nearby restaurants, and shops.[29]

A block pattern scaled to pedestrians, with buildings oriented to the street, can go a long way to create attractive walking opportunities. Within suburban business districts, pedestrian linkages represent one of the most cost-effective and successful means of decreasing the number of vehicles using the roads and the number of required parking spaces. Significant pedestrian linkages should be supported with pedestrian facilities that

- directly connect trip generators;
- provide shelter or other appropriate amenities;
- offer visual interest; and
- limit conflicts with vehicles.

In the core of the South Coast Metro center, a network of pedestrian paths separated from automobile traffic connects buildings. In turn,

This landscaped pedestrian bridge provides access above the arterial roads and parking lots to the South Coast Plaza shopping centers and adjoining office and cultural precincts. Its construction would not have been required had the suburban business district established a pedestrian-friendly integration of uses as a priority in the district's initial design.

Geoffrey Booth

One of the pedestrian bridges at South Coast Plaza showing the third-floor connection and clearance above the parking lots and access road. That stairs or an escalator must be used to reach the bridge plus the fact that the bridge is not lined with retail uses make it less appealing to pedestrians than a main street town center.

the pedestrian network is connected to the mall by two long pedestrian bridges. The developer constructed the network as a traffic mitigation measure to eliminate pedestrian crossings and reduce car trips within the suburban business district. Many workers use the bridges to reach the mall at lunch time.[30]

Improving pedestrian access gives users of a suburban business district a transportation choice for internal circulation other than the automobile. Furthermore, pedestrian improvements are inexpensive compared with major transportation improvements. In the South Coast Metro area of Orange County, California, all the

pieces were in place—offices, residential development, and world-class shopping—and relatively proximate to one another. The problem was that the only way to navigate between the various uses was to get into a car and add to the traffic, just to buy lunch. In Atlanta, the major office developments at Perimeter Center are separated from the shopping mall by an arterial road that is both unsafe and uninviting to cross. The result is that most office workers get in their cars, drive out of their office parking lots to cross the arterial road, and park at Perimeter Mall. After shopping, they return to their cars and reverse the journey—little wonder the roads are congested.

In the Glendale/Cherry Creek area, an older suburban business district in Denver, the transportation management association created a site design committee that implemented sidewalk improvements in one year simply by photographing problems and convincing property owners to remedy them. Uptown Houston in Texas experienced a similar problem because of the lack of pedestrian connections to areas within both the suburban business district itself and the adjoining residential neighborhoods. The Uptown Houston business partnership identified pedestrian deficiencies and developed an improvement plan.

It is important and cost-effective to provide bike trails that deliver cyclists safely to suburban

To promote bicycle use to and from transit stations, secured bicycle parking–like these lockers at the Grosvenor Metro station in Maryland–should be provided.

business districts. Riparian areas and disused rail rights-of-way are especially well suited to accommodating bike trails. In Washington, D.C., a bike trail follows Rock Creek all the way from the Potomac River in downtown Washington to Montgomery County, across the state line in Maryland. The Iron Horse Trail, an old railroad right–of-way in San Ramon County, California, has been converted to a bike trail linking the dispersed suburban business district, Bishop Ranch, to surrounding residential areas. The suburban business districts of Addison Circle and Legacy Town Center, Texas, have devoted special attention to the provision of bike trails and bicycle storage facilities. In an environment where active adults want to combine their journey to work with an aerobic workout or period of quiet reflection, the provision of bike trails to increase access both to and within suburban business districts gives a community a competitive advantage.

Putting the Car in Its Proper Place

It is significant that a large share of the traffic traversing suburban business districts represents through trips. Therefore, particularly along retail strips, it is important to balance the de-

mands of through traffic with the need to provide access to local destinations. Traffic must be tamed and managed so that the goose that laid the golden egg is not killed.[31] While conventional transportation strategies have long called for increasing speeds and reducing congestion, it may make sense in some circumstances to slow things down. "Putting the car in its place" is an important part of the implementation concept in the plan for downtown Kendall, Florida. Given that excessively wide roads and large turning radii encourage speeding, Kendall's planners encouraged the Florida Department of Transportation to reduce both the number of lanes and lane widths, expand the median, and add on-street parking.[32]

Better management of traffic can also involve transportation management programs that encourage transit and carpooling by keeping employees informed of their transportation options. Such programs can reduce the level of automobile use and promote the availability of a range of transportation choices. The largest suburban center in Atlanta, Perimeter Center, has been struggling with how to provide the transportation capacity needed to serve its growth. An assessment of all planned highway and transit improvements, including stations on the Metropolitan Atlanta Rapid Transit Authority (MARTA)

Integrating bicycle parking and trails linking to the suburban business district promotes additional transportation mode choice in suburban business districts, as shown in Walnut Creek, California.

Geoffrey Booth

51

rail system, found that the improvements would still fail to satisfy expected growth. Consequently, the Metro Atlanta Chamber of Commerce suggested an aggressive program of travel demand management techniques aimed at achieving a 50 percent reduction in vehicle trips per employee. Techniques called for car pool and van pool incentives, feeder buses to new MARTA stations, and cycling and walking strategies.[33] Access has become a particularly sensitive issue at Perimeter Center since Hewlett Packard announced the delay of its planned expansion because of employee complaints about traffic congestion.

Aligning Land Use and Transportation

In properly aligning the transportation system with land use, the age-old question remains, Which should follow which? Should all development be concentrated around transit (transit-oriented development (TOD)), or should transit be extended to serve existing and new suburban business districts that currently lack transit service? The answer varies according to local circumstances and needs.

The TOD approach encourages suburban business district development around existing or new transit stations. Arlington County in Northern Virginia—just outside Washington, D.C.—has adopted a policy to concentrate growth near transit in order to encourage job creation and expand the county's tax base. By the time Metro rail planning began in the late 1960s, the intensive revitalization of the Rosslyn section of Arlington, directly across the river from downtown Washington, was well underway. In response, the county prudently opted for a transit route to the west along Rosslyn's aging commercial corridor rather than along nearby I-66.

A 1972 plan emphasized intensive development around the five stations along the one-mile Rosslyn/Ballston corridor. Another corridor was planned to the south, toward the city of Alexandria. The county has enjoyed immense success, concentrating virtually all new office development along the Rosslyn/Ballston and Jefferson Davis corridors—a total of 35 million

square feet of office space by 1999, with an additional 5 million square feet under construction or approved. Arlington County has succeeded so well that development has largely clustered in two sectors of the county, leaving the rest of Arlington as primarily single-family neighborhoods and fattening the county's tax coffers. Without doubt, Arlington County has leveraged its investment in the Metro rail system by aligning development with rail transit. Arlington's experience stands in sharp contrast to the option of routing transit down the middle of an existing freeway corridor where the opportunity to align land use and transit is highly constrained. The latter approach does nothing to consolidate and expand the tax base.

Using a Transportation Management Association

Many suburban business districts have established business associations or public/private organizations to deal with various development issues, the most prominent of which is traffic. Examples include the following:

- the Hacienda Park Business Association, which manages significant car pool matching and transit services in a major suburban business district in San Ramon, California;
- the BWI Business Partnership, a collaboration among real estate developers, businesses, the Maryland Aviation Authority, and federal agencies located near the Baltimore/Washington International Airport; and
- TYTRANS, the Tysons Corner Transportation Association, a 501(c)4 nonprofit corporation that is one of the nation's oldest TMAs, dating from 1981. Representing 10,000 employees and more than 40 corporations, it operates a car pool and van pool matching program, provides commuter advice on timetables and tax-free concessions, and negotiates with government on transportation infrastructure upgrading.

A single owner can manage an office park or shopping center, whereas a business district with many owners requires a city council or business improvement district to perform the

Transit stations in suburban business districts can provide an opportunity to develop mixed-use projects like this example at Mockingbird Station in Dallas, Texas, in which shared parking is provided and rail users are major patrons of the shops.

management function. The privatization of many traditional urban design, traffic, and parking functions allows the creation of a suburban "park" setting that can function without external management, often in an unincorporated area. However, transportation strategies suited to compact and fragmented suburban business districts usually entail the promotion of shared parking, car pooling, traffic signage, traffic signal management, subsidy schemes, integrated transit (new routes, shuttles within the district and between buildings and connecting to the rail or bus station), and the construction of integrated bike paths and pedestrian facilities. A privately (or publicly) sponsored TMA, a business improvement district, or even a new approach to municipal management can perform these functions. One other option is the creation of an ad hoc group—without the benefit of a corporate structure—to address pressing transportation issues in a given suburban business district. With the right people and agency support, such groups can be as effective as more formal organizations.

There are many ways to finesse the management issue. Effectively managed ad hoc groups may be able to deliver the needed public services in support of accessibility improvements

for a suburban business district. One recent success story concerns southeast Denver, where a business partnership has addressed several transportation issues of concern to the future of the suburban business district. In suburban Denver, as in many other areas, traffic congestion is a major issue, causing numerous complaints from employees and drawing unfavorable media coverage. In response, the partnership established a transportation committee that conducted surveys and reviewed plans. The result was major transportation improvements: an expansion of the light-rail system and an expansion of I-270, the latter occurring after the partnership successfully made its case to state and regional transportation agencies. The partnership followed its local advocacy effort with a lobbying campaign in Washington, D.C., and eventually secured the necessary funding for the $1.6 billion transportation improvement program known as T-Rex.

Funding Transportation through Local Taxation

The Uptown Houston suburban business district recognized in the late 1990s that it was under serious competitive pressure from emerging business districts and that it would slip into decline without further investment. It adopted an innovative approach and decided to fund its transportation and access improvement program by raising funds from within the suburban business district. The city created a tax-increment reinvestment zone and developed a program of local mobility improvements totaling $144 million for major streets, local streets, and pedestrian and parking enhancements.[34] In addition, the city worked with the Texas Department of Transportation to reconstruct an adjacent freeway to the tune of $140 million and supported a new $320 million toll road to serve the area. Finally, the city is negotiating with the transit authority to secure $232 million in local transit improvements. Uptown Houston's example clearly demonstrates that, with sufficient creativity and influence, a suburban business district can finance the initial investment needed to leverage transportation and access improvements.

Ensuring the Future Value of Suburban Business Districts

Tony Pangaro, a principal of real estate developer Millennium Partners of Boston, says, "Today, good development sites around transit are like the highway exits used to be in the 1960s. . . . Back then, if you knew where the highway exit was going to be, you bought and built. Much the same is happening today with transit systems."[35] Congestion is causing Americans to rethink where they live, where they work, and their mode of transportation. They have done it before, demonstrating a determination to abandon their once-vibrant downtowns for less congested and more accessible locations. Suburban business districts that act decisively to reinvent their development configuration, density, use mix, and transportation choices will reap dividends in the form of enhanced real estate values and community building. The precise strategy for each suburban business district must necessarily vary according to local circumstances and needs. For those that ignore the opportunity, the future holds less promise.

Notes

1. Kenneth T. Jackson, *Crabgrass Frontier* (New York: Oxford University Press, 1985), p. 113.

2. Royce Hanson, ed., *Perspectives on Urban Infrastructure* (Washington, D.C.: National Academy Press, 1984), p. 35.

3. Ibid., p. 46.

4. Jackson, *Crabgrass Frontier,* p. 257.

5. Christopher Leinberger, "The Connection between Sustainability and Economic Development," in Douglas R. Porter et al., *The Practice of Sustainable Development* (Washington, D.C.: ULI–the Urban Land Institute, 2000), p. 56.

6. Robert E. Lang, *Office Sprawl: The Evolving Geography of Business* (Washington, D.C.: The Brookings Institution, 2000).

7. Ibid., p. 5.

8. Robert Dunphy et al., *Transportation Management through Partnerships* (Washington, D.C.: ULI–the Urban Land Institute, 1990), p. 27.

9. Phillip J. Longman, "American Gridlock," *U.S. News & World Report,* May 28, 2001, p. 22.

10. Surface Transportation Policy Project, *Easing the Burden—A Companion Analysis of the Texas Transportation Institute's Congestion Study* (Washington, D.C.: Surface Transportation Policy Project, 2001), p. 1.

11. Rebecca R. Sohmer et al., *Downtown Rebound* (Washington, D.C.: Fannie Mae Foundation and The Brookings Institution, 2001), p. 9, and Roger L. Galatas et al., *Charlotte, North Carolina, South Corridor Advisory Services Panel Report* (Washington, D.C.: ULI–the Urban Land Institute, 2000), p. 19.

12. Longman, "American Gridlock," p. 16.

13. David Schrank et al., *The 2001 Urban Mobility Report* (College Station, Texas: Texas Transportation Institute, 2001), p. 1.

14. Ibid., p. 2.

15. Alan Sipress, "Plan Boosts Northern Virginia Highway Funds," *Washington Post,* September 21, 2000, p. B3.

16. Lori Montgomery, "Md. Going 'Beyond the Pavement'—State Shifting Focus from Roads to Pedestrians and Transit," *Washington Post,* September 15, 2000, p. A1.

17. Phyllis Myers et al., *Growth at the Ballot Box: Electing the Shape of Communities in November, 2000* (Washington, D.C.: The Brookings Institution, 2001), p. 18.

18. Belden, Russonello, and Stewart, *National Survey on Growth and Land Development September 2000* (Washington, D.C.: Smart Growth America, 2000), p. 3.

19. Surface Transportation Policy Project, *Easing the Burden,* p. 5.

20. G. Bruce Douglas III et al., "Urban Design, Urban Form, and Employee Travel Behavior" in *TRB Transportation Planning Applications Conference Papers* (Washington, D.C.: U.S. Department of Transportation, 1997), p. 298.

21. Ibid., p. 306.

22. K.G. Hooper, *Travel Characteristics at Large-Scale Suburban Activity Centers,* NCHRP Report 323 (Washington, D.C.: Transportation Research Board, National Academy of Sciences, October 1989), p. 37.

23. Anthony Downs, *Stuck in Traffic—Coping with Peak-Hour Traffic Congestion* (Washington, D.C.: The Brookings Institution, 1992), p. 61.

24. Puget Sound Regional Council, *Urban Centers in the Central Puget Sound Region,* PSRC, 1997, p. 46.

25. Barton Smith, Vinson & Ellis et al., *Project Plan and Reinvestment Zone Financing Plan* (Houston: City of Houston, 1999), p. 20.

26. Puget Sound Regional Council, *Urban Centers,* p. 42.

27. ULI, *Downtown Bellevue, Washington: An Evaluation of Development Potential and Recommendations for Strategies to Shape a Vibrant Central Business District* (Washington, D.C.: ULI–the Urban Land Institute, 1996), p. 42.

28. Downtown Kendall Master Plan, Results of a Design Charrette, ChamberSOUTH, Miami, June 5–12, 1998.

29. Jennifer O'Toole and Bettina Zimny, "Bicycle and Pedestrian Facilities," *Transportation Planning Handbook* (Washington, D.C.: Institute of Transportation Engineers, 1999), p. 640.

30. Calthorpe Associates, *Design for Efficient SAC's: Phase I Report March 1997* (Washington, D.C.: Federal Transit Administration, March 1997), pp. 126, 127.

31. Michael Beyard and Michael Pawlukiewicz, *Ten Principles for Reinventing America's Retail Strips* (Washington, D.C.: ULI–the Urban Land Institute, 2001).

32. Downtown Kendall Master Plan, Results of a Design Charrette.

33. Metro Atlanta Chamber of Commerce, "Street Smarts, Perimeter Center CID Study," 1998, pp. 2, 43.

34. Barton Smith, *Project Plan,* p. 29.

35. Jim Miara, "On Route—Evidence Clearly Shows That Transit Lines Stimulate Development," *Urban Land,* May 2001, p. 85.

chapter 4

Housing for America's New Demographic Profile

Humans spend their lives in places—in real estate products such as homes, offices, shops, and a wide variety of other buildings and spaces all connected to land. The choices people make about how and where to live their lives determine the types of places they desire and need. Real estate development is the art of creating income streams and property values by matching built forms and spaces to growing or changing market demands. While the detached house in the suburbs may have been perfect for the U.S. demographic profile of the 1950s, the new century is already witnessing demand for a much wider range of housing choices. Today, the traditional family accounts for only 24 percent of all households and, by 2020, will represent only one in five households. "Since the driving demographic force for the future is the age-based growth of households that have largely completed child-rearing, the residential future of cities may well depend on how they appeal to people in life's later years."[1]

According to Professor Edward Glaeser of Harvard University, the cities that will thrive are those that evolve into attractive and exciting places for people to live—remade consumer cities that offer a rich variety of services, a vibrant social and cultural environment, and excellent access to public amenities. "The future of the city depends on the continued advantages of density. . . . The dominant urban form of the future, almost unquestionably, will be the edge city [the suburban business district as defined by ULI] with its moderate density levels."[2] No longer is the top-rated prime-time television program set in a detached house in the suburbs complete with monogamous parents, their kids, and extended family. Now, it is all about the "forever young" and "young at heart" who, without kids, live an exciting life "doing the restaurants, coffee houses, and cultural attractions" of a live-work-shop place. Rental apartment living allows the forever young to enjoy the freedom to travel and explore the pleasures of life.

In his book *Servicescapes,* John F. Sherry makes the point that Americans, though priding themselves on individualism and freedom of choice, actually take many of their cultural and behavioral cues from the media. "People today consume symbols and environments along with goods and services. For the most part, this commercial universe melds seamlessly with the mediascape of popular culture programming on TV and in magazines, advertising, Hollywood films, and the rock music industry. . . themed environments can be explained as. . . an engineered extension of mass advertising and mass media."[3] Subliminal cues and the increasing affluence of America's new demographic profile will continue to drive the explosion of choices in housing and housing location. The housing industry is now very much focused on developing and tailoring housing products to specific demographic and market segments, including a diverse

multifamily sector. As America's multifamily housing developers struggle to find development sites and consumers demand new choices,[4] the transformation of suburban business districts constitutes a major real estate opportunity.

Trends in U.S. Household Demographics[5]

In 1950, there was one dominant and socially acceptable way for adults to live their lives—the ideal family was composed of a homemaker-wife, a breadwinner-father, and two or more children. Americans shared a common image of what a family should look like and how mothers, fathers, and children should move through the lifecycle. Families either lived or aspired to live in a detached house in the suburbs. In the second half of the 20th century, however, America's changed family values and attitudes manifested themselves in a transformed demographic profile. Figure 4.2 shows the major changes in the U.S. household structure that occurred between 1960 and 2000.

Several factors influenced household formation in the United States during the latter half of the 20th century, including delayed marriage, shifting attitudes toward monogamy, greater social tolerance, rising educational standards, the liberation of women and unprecedented entry of women into the labor force, increasing life expectancies, declining fertility, and in-

a birth may occur before marriage (increasing the formation of single-parent households).

Changed Attitude toward Monogamy

The second half of the 20th century saw American society become more accepting of divorce, cohabitation, and sex outside marriage. Society became more open-minded about a variety of living arrangements, family configurations, and lifestyles. The development of effective contraception and the legalization of abortion reduced the fertility rate. More households formed as an increasing divorce rate fueled the demand for housing. In large measure, a new ideology that stressed personal freedom, self-fulfillment, and individual choice in living arrangements and family commitments replaced old societal values.

A More Tolerant Society

America is demonstrating increasing tolerance and acceptance of homosexual households. Homosexual households are better educated, more likely than heterosexual households to rent, and show a strong preference for urban locations. For the nation as a whole, 60 percent of gays and 45 percent of lesbians reside in 20 U.S. cities that account for about 26 percent of the total U.S. population. Yet, only 22 percent of lesbian-couple households and 5 percent of gay-couple households have children compared with 59 percent of married-couple households. Accordingly, homosexual households are less likely to require a detached dwelling in a suburban location. Indeed, multifamily housing in suburban business districts would afford gay and lesbian households greater choice in residential location given their preference for urban living environments rich with social, cultural, and educational opportunities.

Educational Standards and the Liberation of Women

The nation's shift from a manufacturing-based to a services-based economy has meant that a college education is necessary to acquire the work skills required of higher-paying jobs. From

Mutifamily housing in suburban business districts provides housing choice to America's new demographic profile.

creased immigration and ethnic diversity. The interplay of all these factors has increased household numbers but decreased household size. The ramifications are important for the prospects of integrating multifamily residential development into suburban business districts—in short, it is these factors that are creating the demand that will sustain the market.

Delayed Marriage

In 1956, the median age at first marriage was 20 years for women and 23 years for men. In 2000, 40 percent of women and 52 percent of men between ages 25 and 29 had never married. This trend allows young adults to experiment with alternative living arrangements before they settle down (increasing the demand for rental housing) and/or to cohabitate before marriage (and simply move out if the relationship fails). It also lengthens the period before entry into adult roles and stable relationships and delays parenthood while increasing the chances that

Well-Located Multifamily Housing Minimizes Traffic Congestion

A prevailing misconception is that multifamily housing contributes to a community's traffic problem. In fact, the opposite is true. When affordable multifamily housing near job centers is in short supply, workers must live in distant suburbs. The result is not only long, uncomfortable, and expensive commutes but also increased traffic congestion. As more cars traverse the community from distant homes to employment centers, commuters consume more fuel, exacerbate already unacceptable levels of air pollution, and experience increased frustration. Multifamily housing located in suburban business districts, however, allows more people to live in housing that they can afford and that is located near their place of employment. Moreover, when multifamily housing is integrated into suburban business districts, it makes public transit more

cost-effective. Transit is not cost-effective in serving low-density development because it must navigate great distances to benefit comparatively few people. As demonstrated in Figure 4.1, the Institute of Transportation Engineers estimates that a single-family home is likely to generate ten automobile trips per weekday compared with six trips for an apartment or condominium.

Residents of multifamily housing tend to own fewer cars and use them less often. Higher-density housing developments within multiuse suburban business districts allow more people to enjoy pedestrian or transit access to employment, shopping, services, and leisure activities, thereby reducing dependence on the automobile. •

Source: Diane R. Suchman, *The Case for Multifamily Housing* (Washington, D.C.: ULI–the Urban Land Institute, 1991).

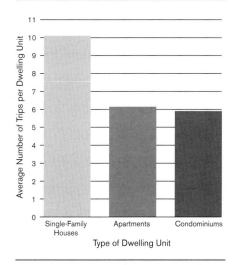

figure 4.1 Weekday Vehicle Trip Generation for Residential Areas

Source: Wolfgang S. Homburger et al., *Residential Street Design and Traffic Control* (Washington, D.C.: Institute of Transportation Engineers, 1989).

1969 to 1996, the percentage of college graduates earning income grew from 5 to 11 percent in households at or below median income and from 16 to 33 percent in households above median income. Both men and women are remaining single longer and are more likely to leave home to pursue a college education, to live with a partner, and to launch a career before assuming the responsibility of a family of their own. In the interim, rental accommodation within suburban business districts that provide a live-work-shop place would prove highly attractive to this demographic group.

The entry of women into the labor force has allowed the productive expansion of the U.S economy and has made a major contribution to real per capita income growth. In the 20 years from 1979 to 1999, the percentage of women in full-time employment between the prime "work and family" ages of 25 to 54 years grew from 32 to 50 percent; part- or full-time employment for this cohort grew from 66 to 79 percent in the same period. The dramatic entry of women into the labor force has created a major demand for

child care facilities; in fact, the number of preschool children in such facilities rose from 7 percent in 1965 to 29 percent in 1994. Females now

figure 4.2 Trends in U.S. Households, 1960 to 2000

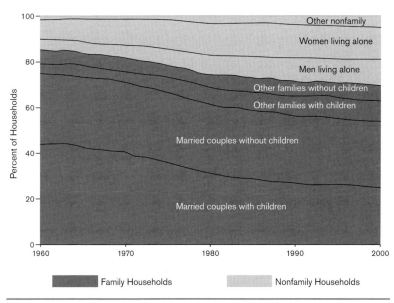

Source: Suzanne M. Bianchi et al. *American Families* (Washington, D.C.: Population Reference Bureau, 2001), p. 1.

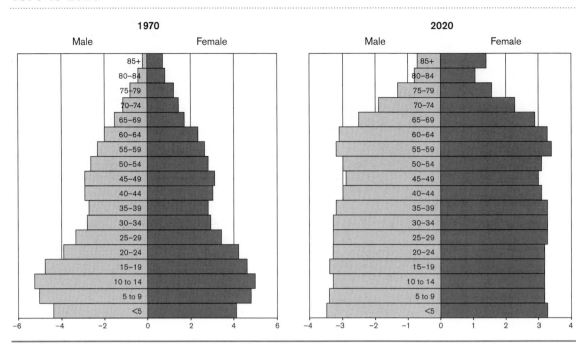

Source: Martha Farnsworth Riche, *The Implications of Changing U.S. Demographics for Housing Choice and Location in Cities* (Washington, D.C.: The Brookings Institution, 2001), p. 5.

exercise a financial role in the selection of housing type and location that is influenced by proximity to work and child care.

Living a Longer and Healthier Active Life

An American born in 1900 had an average life expectancy of just below 50 years. Significant advances in medical science, the emergence of the health care industry, the changing nature of work, and rising per capita income contributed to an average U.S. life expectancy at birth of 77 years as of 1998. Figure 4.3 shows the transformation of America's demographic profile from that of a pyramid (where the younger age groups are in the majority) to a pillar (where each age group is of similar size).

Not only do Americans now live longer lives, they also live more of their life in a healthy and active state. Today, parents and children spend nearly two-thirds of their years together as adults —parents devote a smaller portion of their lives parenting young children and caring for aged parents at home. Older Americans are now more likely to spend their later years with their

spouse or living alone than with adult children. Multifamily housing in suburban business districts would allow older Americans to live close to their children while releasing them from the responsibilities of keeping up a single-family dwelling.

Between 1970 and 2000, per capita income in the United States grew in constant dollar terms by 69 percent.[6] With not only the money but now also with time on their hands, Americans are traveling abroad extensively and experiencing new living environments previously not available to them at home. Both the exposure to ideas gained from overseas travel and the cultural practices introduced by the nation's growing immigrant population are predisposing Americans to consider a wide range of choices in housing type, size, and location.

Declining Fertility

The fertility rate of American women in the early part of the 20th century prompted fears of overpopulation, but the rate dropped as a result of the Great Depression, then rose again in the post–World War II period, and

figure 4.4 Projected Population Distribution by Age of Whites and Minorities in 2020

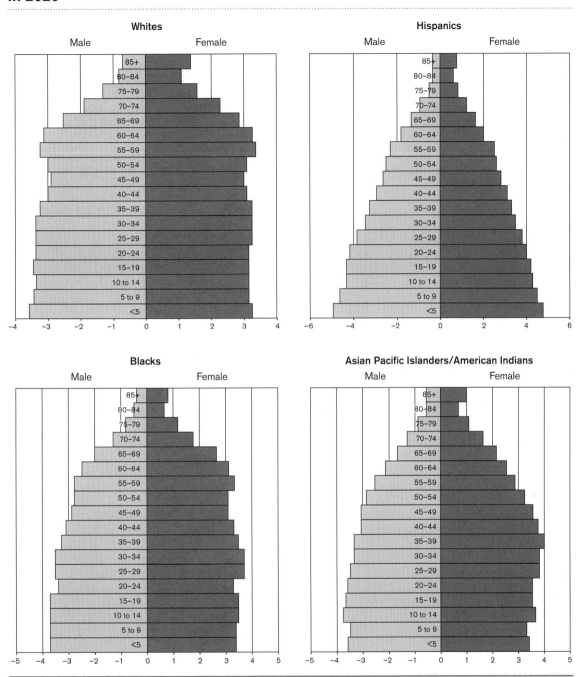

Source: Martha Farnsworth Riche, *The Implications of Changing U.S. Demographics for Housing Choice and Location in Cities* (Washington, D.C.: The Brookings Institution, 2001), p. 13.

now has again fallen to around two children per female. The 3.9 million births in 1998 were still below the number of annual births during most of the 1950s, when there were at least 20 million fewer women in the child-bearing age groups than today. The average number of children per family in a minority household is greater than that of white households.

Figure 4.4 shows that in 2020 Hispanic Americans will be the only population group to retain the traditional pyramid structure in terms of age distribution.

A fertility rate of two children per female allows for replacement of the existing population; however, in such circumstances, net population growth is reliant on immigration.

figure 4.5 Growth in U.S. Population, Households, and Per Capita Income, 1970 to 2000

	1970	2000	Increase
U.S. population	203 million	281 million	38%
U.S. households	64 million	105 million	64%
U.S. per capita income	$13,000	$22,000	69%

Source: Bureau of the Census, various years.

figure 4.6 Projected Growth in U.S. Households by Race, 2000 to 2020

Households	2000	2020	Increase
Whites	79,400	87,893	11%
Blacks	12,697	17,409	37%
Hispanics	9,380	16,887	80%
Asian/Other	4,053	7,146	76%
Total	105,530	129,335	23%

Source: Joint Center for Housing Studies, *State of the Nation's Housing 2001* (Cambridge: Harvard University, 2001), p. 34.

The Increasing Importance of Immigration and Growing Ethnic Diversity

The 1970 U.S. Census revealed that almost 5 percent of the American population had been born overseas, a figure that increased to 8 percent in 1990 and 11 percent in 2000. Asian Americans increased from 6.9 million in 1990 to 10.5 million in 2000, with about 60 percent of that cohort foreign born. One of the greatest surprises of Census 2000 was the dramatic increase in the U.S. Hispanic population from 22 million in 1990 to 35 million in 2000, with 60 percent of U.S. Hispanics of Mexican origin. The African American population increased faster than the non–Hispanic white majority but lacked the additional push from immigration to keep pace with the Hispanic or Asian American growth rates. Significantly, the Joint Center for Housing Studies at Harvard University found in its *State of the Nation's Housing 2001* that ". . . losses among the elderly will disproportionately dampen white household growth over the next 10 years. Hispanics, Asians, and blacks are thus expected to account for nearly 80 percent of

population growth and 65 percent of household growth in each of the first two decades of the 21st century."[7]

In its recent study *City Growth and the 2000 Census,* the Brookings Institution concluded that immigrants were more likely to choose more urban housing locations. "The basic pattern is one in which cities with more foreign-born residents, as of 1990, grew more quickly than cities with fewer foreign-born residents."[8] Many of these immigrants choose to rent multifamily accommodation because it is not feasible or desirable to purchase a house or condominium given their financial resources, lifestyle preferences, or the interval before they move. Many Hispanic and Asian immigrants prefer the greater sense of community and access to facilities and services provided by more urban locations.

Decreasing Household Size Drives Housing Demand

The most important drivers of housing demand are the number of households and the growth in real per capita income. Figure 4.5 shows that the United States experienced particularly robust growth in population, household formation, and real per capita income between 1970 and 2000.

Figure 4.6 illustrates the projected growth of households between 2000 and 2020 and suggests that the demand for housing production will remain strong and may even exceed the levels of the 1990s. As the children of the baby boomers reach adulthood in the next ten years, they will demand apartments and starter homes. At the same time, baby boomers still in their peak earning years and looking to decrease the time and dollar costs of maintaining large suburban homes will invest in apartments in live-work-shop places as well as in new and second homes.

With the ongoing arrival of immigrants and higher rate of natural increase among immigrant groups, the minority share of U.S. households is projected to grow from 25 percent in 2000 to 29 percent in 2010. Given their lower average incomes and lower levels of accumulated wealth, many minority households will face particularly difficult challenges in paying increasingly higher rents and achieving homeownership. The Joint Center for Housing Studies reports that many low-income married couples now rely on both spouses' incomes to afford rental housing and homeownership. The need for labor force housing in and around live-work-shop places will become increasingly vital.

The Existing Housing Inventory

In 1997, America counted just over 112 million housing units, of which just under 100 million were occupied; two-thirds were owner-occupied and 34 percent renter-occupied. Census 2000 found that the number of housing units had increased to just under 116 million, of which 105.5 million were occupied. The ratio of owner occupation to rental occupation remained the same as in 1997. In that year, approximately 60 percent of the housing stock was single-family detached houses, with townhouses accounting for 6 percent of the national housing stock, manufactured or mobile homes for 8 percent, and the balance in multiunit buildings (one-third in two- to four-unit buildings). Of the 112 housing units that existed in 1997, 34 million units were located in the central cities, 51 million in the suburbs, and 27 million outside metropolitan

Using Inclusionary Zoning to Provide Affordable Housing

In 1973, Montgomery County, Maryland, adopted the nation's first inclusionary zoning law. The Moderately Priced Dwelling Unit (MPDU) ordinance mandated that, in any new housing development of 50 or more units, at least 15 percent of the housing units must be affordable to the lowest one-third of the county's households. As compensation, developers can receive a density bonus of up to 22 percent, and, by law, the county can buy one-third of the affordable units. The mandatory program does not permit payments of fees in lieu of construction. In the decades since the ordinance's adoption, for-profit homebuilders have produced just under 11,000 moderately priced dwelling units—two-thirds of which have been purchased by teachers, police officers, and retail and service workers. In *Inside Game/Outside Game*, David

Rusk concludes that the program is a model for the nation as it avoids the further concentration of the poor and underprivileged in central ghettos. Moreover, a scattered-site approach to inclusionary housing tends to avert "not-in-my-backyard" opposition, sparing the local housing commission controversy in its use of public funds to subsidize units.

A program such as the Montgomery County effort helps satisfy the problem of a growing lack of affordable housing located in proximity to employment centers and, at the same time, ensures the community's social and economic integration. With the production burden on the developer, the Montgomery County program represents a highly effective approach to making affordable housing cost-efficient and attractive at the same time. As a consequence

of its program, Montgomery County has become one of America's more racially and economically integrated communities. Ensuring housing for a diversified labor force has also been essential to the successful diversification of the county's job base. For suburban business districts to remain competitive, they must be capable of attracting a diversified labor force. In addition, the provision of affordable housing within a suburban business district not only reduces traffic congestion (workers would otherwise be forced to live far from their place of employment) but also offers workers the opportunity to contribute to the economic and social well-being of the suburban business district. •

Source: Adapted in part from Robert Burchell et al., "Inclusionary Zoning," *New Century Housing*, October 2000.

areas. Over 55 percent of the housing units have three or more bedrooms.[9]

Given declining household size, for many Americans, the prestige value of owning a large, underused detached suburban dwelling will likely give way to the common sense of downsizing to reduce maintenance costs and free up time and money for recreational, cultural, and travel pursuits. A shift in housing preferences will prove itself a strong driver of multifamily housing development in suburban business districts, allowing aging baby boomers all the advantages of a suburban location but at reduced cost and with greater access to civic, retail, entertainment, and community facilities and amenities.

Demographic Impacts on Housing Choice and Product

The *State of the Nation's Housing 2001* reported several major findings relevant to the provi-

sion of multifamily housing in suburban business districts.

- Suburban locations are continuing to outperform central cities. For every three households that moved to the central cities in 1999, five departed. The imbalance is especially noticeable among households earning $70,000 per year—for every one household that headed to the central cities, more than three left. It has been minority population growth—spurred by natural increase and immigration—that prevented central cities from losing population in the 1990s.
- Parents of the baby boomers are driving the demand for housing types that allow them to age close to their families while providing for a later transition to assisted-living and continuing-care communities.
- The stock of multifamily rental property tightened significantly during the 1990s. The removal of 1.25 units from the market offset

The Residential Market Outlook

The *ULI 2001 Real Estate Forecast* reported that with continuing low interest rates, a dramatic change in demographics, and a shift in renter and buyer preferences for live-work-shop transit-rich environments, the residential sector was the most favored real estate market for investment in income-producing property. *The Real Estate Report–First Quarter 2001* released by the Real Estate Research Corporation of Chicago summarized the position in the following terms: "The numbers tell the story as people in the age group of 18 to 34 years are projected to increase by over 5 million between 2000 and 2010. This is significant as this category of the population typically rents before owning a home. Another factor affecting demand is the number of immigrants flowing into the United States, also a heavy renter population . . . over 30 percent of all renters are doing so by choice rather than out of economic necessity according to

Fannie Mae's Annual Housing Survey. The renter-by-choice attitude is one that will fuel the sector in 2001. The bottom line is that time-pressed professionals do not want to have to deal with the stress of long commutes and homeownership. They want to be entertained and have all their needs within arm's reach. This attitude has aided the resurgence of the CBD as a place of residence and has 24-hour cities striving to meet growing demand. This trend has fueled the demand for high-rise apartment living as well as loft-style and condominium living."

Renters are looking for all the amenities—high-speed Internet access, a garage, a local coffee shop and bookstore, a gymnasium, and entertainment and convenience facilities—and they will find them in today's live-work-shop environments, which is the type of milieu enlightened corporations will seek out when looking to provide attractive housing for their staff. Peter Ratcliffe, presi-

dent of Princess Cruises, recently moved his 1,500-employee headquarters from Los Angeles to Valencia, California, because the latter's town center offers all the built-in amenities: restaurants, shops, hotel, clubs, entertainment, health clubs, and in-town housing clustered together in a pedestrian-friendly environment. According to Ratcliffe, "It's in our best interest to have our people happy where they work." Suburban business districts that recognize the strategic advantage of evolving into pedestrian- and transit-friendly live-work-shop places will meet the unsatisfied needs and demands of America's new demographic profile and, in so doing, reap a major place-making dividend. ●

Source: Adapted in part from Dean Schwanke, *ULI 2001 Real Estate Forecast* (Washington D.C.: ULI–the Urban Land Institute, 2001) and Jules A. Marling, ed., *Real Estate Report–First Quarter 2001* (Chicago: Real Estate Research Corporation, 2001).

figure 4.7 Projections of U.S. Population by Age

	2000 Population (in millions)	2020 Population (in millions)	Population Change	Percent Change
Under 10 years	38.9	43.5	+4.6	+11.8
10 to 19 years	39.9	42.7	+2.8	+7.0
20 to 29 years	36.0	42.9	+6.9	+19.2
30 to 39 years	41.7	41.9	+0.2	+0.5
40 to 49 years	42.3	37.4	−4.9	−11.6
50 to 59 years	30.5	40.5	+10.0	+32.8
60 to 69 years	20.1	38.1	+18.0	+89.6
70 to 79 years	16.1	23.3	+7.2	+44.7
80 years and older	9.2	12.4	+3.2	+34.8

Source: Martha Farnsworth Riche, *The Implications of Changing U.S. Demographics for Housing Choice and Location in Cities* (Washington, D.C.: The Brookings Institution, 2001), p. 5.

the construction of 1.6 million new rental units. Multifamily developers confirm that a lack of sites has driven up land prices to the point where the development of rental units for moderate-income families is barely profitable.[10]

- Substantial numbers of higher-income households now rent rather than own their homes. In 1999, 2.6 million households earning at least 20 percent more than the area median income lived in single-family rentals and another 2.6 million in multifamily rentals. For some types of households—young adults, frequent movers, recent immigrants, senior citizens, and divorced individuals—ownership is neither feasible nor otherwise preferred. Many people are finding that renting is a better financial choice in that it permits them to forgo the high transaction costs of buying and selling and eliminates the risk of losing money over short holding periods.
- Given the growing shortage of multifamily rental accommodation, single-family homes now make up more than 37 percent of the rental stock compared with 33 percent in 1993. When this reality is combined with the growth of employment in the suburbs and the lack of affordable multifamily housing in suburban locations, the result is a powerful push for low-density suburban growth and

all its associated impacts. Multifamily housing in suburban business districts could redirect some of this growth.

The integration of multifamily housing into suburban business districts can cost effectively convert surface parking lots and other underused land into valuable live-work-shop places. These places can meet the increasing demand for accommodation from the following demographic groups, all of which are growing and demanding choices in other than central city locations:

- 20- to 29-year-olds in the premarriage and pre–child-bearing years;
- 50- to 70-year-olds in the post–child-rearing years;
- 70-year-olds and over in need of housing units integrated with medical facilities and assisted-living and continuing-care communities;
- single-person, single-parent, and gay and lesbian households; and
- employees in suburban business districts, including those requiring affordable housing.

Figure 4.7 quantifies the projected growth between 2000 and 2020 among the demographic groups likely to find multifamily accommodation in suburban business districts well suited to their needs and aspirations.

Housing as the Missing Ingredient

Until the 1990s, the integration of housing into the suburban business district's mix of uses received little consideration. In fact, the housing developed over the last five years in suburban business districts is far more urban in character than the garden apartments and standalone condominium towers that were initially developed in such districts. The preferred model reflects the confluence of available sites, reasonable development and construction costs, efficient and marketable parking solutions, and substantial emerging demand for a more urban-type product in a suburban environment.

A handful of development companies built a series of successful prototypes in the last decade of the 20th century. Post Properties and Columbus Realty, which ultimately merged, were among the pioneers. Largely limiting their work to fast-growing markets in the Southeast and Texas, Post and Columbus targeted overlooked infill sites for the development of moderate-density rental apartments with structured park-

ing and, often, community-serving ground-floor retail uses. The case studies of Addison Circle, Texas; Courthouse Hill, Virginia; and Paseo Plaza, California, are instructive as all three projects integrate multifamily housing into an existing suburban business district—Addison Circle by way of a mixed-use development and Courthouse Hill and Paseo Plaza by way of the addition of apartment buildings to existing multiuse suburban business districts.

Addison Circle

Addison Circle has brought density—and a sense of community—to a fragmented suburban business district. Located in Addison, Texas, a northern suburb of Dallas, the 80-acre mixed-use project is the result of a public/private partnership between Post Properties, Inc., and the town of Addison. Designed by RTKL Associates in conjunction with Post Properties and a team of consultants, Addison Circle ultimately will total 3,000 dwelling units intermixed with neighborhood retail uses, parks, and civic space as well as up to 4 million square feet of office and com-

Addison Circle in Addison, Texas, outside Dallas, has brought density and a sense of community to a fragmented suburban business district.

RTKL

mercial space. At about 55 dwelling units per acre (net), the largely rental project is more than twice as dense as the typical north Dallas garden apartment project. Yet, Addison Circle offers a sense of place and community not often associated with new development.

Creating a Sense of Place for the District

The idea for a higher-density, mixed-use residential neighborhood was first suggested in the 1991 Comprehensive Plan for Addison and reinforced more recently in a community-based "visioning" program (Vision 2020). The town of Addison has always attracted more than its share of commercial development. But, as competition started to emerge from newer suburbs, Addison's town officials focused on the need to create a physical focal point for the town—as well as a stronger population base—to support and anchor the town's commercial uses.

Although about 80 percent built out, Addison claimed a few undeveloped sites, one of which proved to be ideally suited to the concept of a higher-density mixed-used development. The site is adjacent to Old Town Addison and within walking distance of employment, retail, and entertainment facilities. It is also adjacent to a Dallas Area Rapid Transit station (DART) and close to the Addison conference and theater center and was under the control of a single landowner. Encouraged by town officials, the landowner, Gaylord Properties, teamed with Post Properties, an Atlanta-based REIT, to develop a program and plan for the site.

As designed, the master plan for Addison Circle establishes two subareas: a residential neighborhood of mid-rise housing with supporting retail uses, parks, and other amenities and a higher-density office and commercial district adjacent to the North Dallas Tollway. Linking the two areas is an armature of open space: a traffic circle (Addison Circle) and an axial green. Attention to streets and open space—public space in general—is one of the features that makes Addison Circle so appealing. The circle itself is the symbolic center of the project. In addition to its symbolic role, the circle calms traffic along Quorum Drive, a preexisting major thoroughfare that cuts through the middle of

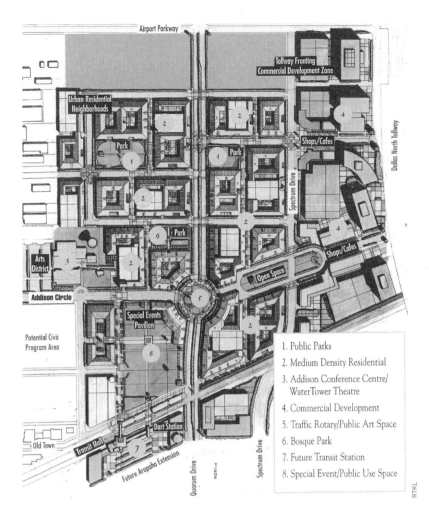

1. Public Parks
2. Medium Density Residential
3. Addison Conference Centre/ WaterTower Theatre
4. Commercial Development
5. Traffic Rotary/Public Art Space
6. Bosque Park
7. Future Transit Station
8. Special Event/Public Use Space

the site. The circle, however, did not come into being without controversy; a special traffic circle consultant convinced skeptical officials to permit construction of what was to be the first public traffic circle in the area in more than 50 years. In addition, Addison sponsored a design competition to create a sculpture for the center of the circle, thereby further establishing the circle as the focal point of both the project and the larger community.

Focusing on the Public Domain

Substantial investment is evident in the treatment of Addison Circle's residential streets and boulevards. In many cases, sidewalks and cross walks are paved in brick, with mature shade trees planted at 25-foot intervals. Larger specimens (in 200-gallon containers) were planted at the outset to vest the streetscape with an instant maturity. Decorative metal guards, similar to those found in English gardens, define the edges

The Addison Circle plan integrates mixed-use retail and residential development into the surrounding suburban business district.

67

RTKL

of tree wells. Bicycle racks, benches, litter containers, and other street furniture add to the usability of the pedestrian-friendly public space.

Both the architecture and site planning contribute to Addison Circle's urban texture. Most residential buildings are four stories in height; in some cases, three residential levels are located above ground-floor shops and small service businesses. The building designs are modern, but they are domesticated by the use of balconies and bay windows, gables, and brick. Typically, the residential buildings have a stone base course topped by a red brick facade. Contrasting brick color bands introduce a variety of detail to the finish. Similarly, window elements and several window types create architectural diversity, including large bay window structures painted to contrast with the brickwork. Facades are further articulated with cast stone sills and lintels, dark-green painted metal balconies, and awnings.

Reversing the typical suburban norm of deep building setbacks and narrow sidewalks, the residential building facades at Addison Circle hug the street while sidewalks are generously wide. Buildings are set just six feet back of the sidewalk (18 feet from the curb), and sidewalks are 12 feet deep on residential streets. The six-foot setback allows for a landscape buffer between sidewalk and building. Along boulevards, buildings are set back 24 feet from the curb, and sidewalks are 14 feet wide, accommodating a ten-

foot zone for landscaping or outdoor dining. In form, most residential structures are doughnut-shaped courtyard buildings. The units are located along both sides of interior corridors, with major entries and windows looking out over the street as well as to the interior pool and courtyard areas. The intent of the "full-block closure" building prototype is to avoid functionally ambiguous space—one is either in the public realm, which is policed by the many windows overlooking the street, or one is within the security of the building.

Parking is provided in above-grade structures located behind each residential block, allowing residences and shops to open directly onto the street. The structured parking provides for one parking space per bedroom, a ratio that amounts to about 1.4 spaces per dwelling unit. Secondary automobile and pedestrian circulation is provided by "mews"—fire and access lanes located between buildings. The 45-foot right-of-way, paved from building face to building face, consists of two 12-foot vehicular lanes flanked by 10.5-foot-wide sidewalks defined with street trees but no curbs. Building entries and apartments face onto the mews, bringing activity to these areas, which also serve as pick-up and drop-off points for building residents.

Some apartments open directly onto several small parks that dot the neighborhood. Low stone walls edge the parks in places, defining pedestrian walkways between park and building. Hiking and cycling paths are under development, and a large open space has been dedicated to Addison for town-sponsored special events.

Meeting New Demographic Needs and Aspirations

Addison Circle features a wide range of dwelling types—from 570-square-foot efficiencies that rent for as little as $645 per month to 3,200-square-foot lofts that rent for more than $4,000 per month (all rental figures as of 1999 completion). While the large share of units (45 percent) are one-bedroom models, the planned mix also includes two- and three-bedroom units, townhouses, and live/work units. To a great extent, the market for Addison Circle is an emerging market segment: those who rent by choice, not out of necessity. As Paris Rutherford, vice president and director of urban design for RTKL/Dallas notes, "They are largely double-income couples ranging in age from 30 to 55: a mix of young childless professionals and empty nesters. They rent by choice, preferring the urban lifestyle Addison Circle affords."

For this market segment, quality of life is a central issue. Developers such as Post Properties are finding that amenities in the form of pools and health clubs are a starting point but that, for many renters, the idea of a community —everything from a dry cleaner downstairs, to a coffee bar, to a secure and attractive place in which to stroll or sit—is an increasingly sought-after amenity. "The success of Addison Circle," notes Art Lomenick, former senior executive vice president of the western division at Post Properties, Inc., "is directly tied to an informal sociability created by the mixed-use development pattern."

Addison Circle is being developed in phases. The first phase, which includes 460 dwelling units, 20,000 square feet of retail space, and a half-acre park, was completed in 1997. A second phase, with 610 units, 90,000 square feet of retail space, 41,000 square feet of office space, and a 1.5-acre park, was completed in 1999. Eight phases are planned, with an expected buildout around 2003 to 2005. Although Post Properties focuses on developing rental projects, it included a small number of for-sale units in the total development program. Within the large-scale commercial portion of Addison Circle, one high-rise office building and a mixed-use mid-rise building have been completed. The remaining phases of this sector of Addison Circle are expected to include corporate housing and other residential uses and office and retail space, ultimately accommodating 10,000 permanent jobs.

Managing the Entitlement Process

To develop a project like Addison Circle—radically different and of higher density than typical suburban rental projects—the developer had to undertake a series of steps both to educate the city and the public about the benefits of the design and to establish the terms of the public/private partnership. In addition to the typical public workshops, the educational process went so far as to arrange for city staff to travel to Chicago and Boston to observe and measure streets and setbacks in several universally admired older urban neighborhoods. Eventually, the developer and the town hammered out a set of design and development standards that formed part of the development approval and covered items such as density, lot coverage, exterior building materials, setbacks, and street landscape standards. Working with town staff, the developer evaluated phasing and development options and their likely impacts on municipal operating and capital budgets. The developer also identified funding gaps that needed to be resolved in order to provide the infrastructure and level of quality mutually desired by town and developer.

The final agreement with the town of Addison committed the town to spending $9.5 million out of its general funds over the life of the project: $5.5 million on upfront infrastructure,

Attractive buildings and public domain treatments create a pedestrian-friendly environment throughout the urban village at Addison Circle.

street, and open-space improvements and the remaining $4 million in the second phase of development. As Lomenick concludes, "It cost an awful lot of money to build Addison, but unlike some other developments, Addison Circle will be there 100 years from now."

Lessons Learned

The lessons learned at Addison Circle point to unsatisfied demand for a choice in housing as America's demographic profile changes. The development of housing options in suburban business districts enhances the attraction of the product by providing convenient access to a wide range of working and shopping experiences plus direct access to public transit. Notwithstanding that Addison Circle involved a higher residential density than the usual suburban location, an innovative, common-sense approach to the entitlement process, coupled with the project's location within a suburban business district, expedited the approval process. The substantial investment made in the creation of place and the attention to detail in the design of Addison Circle has paid a major place-making dividend to the developer and the community.

Courthouse Hill

Courthouse Hill is a 202-unit infill project of townhouses and mid-rise condominiums located in Arlington, Virginia, just one block from the Courthouse Metro rail station in the Rosslyn-

Ballston corridor of suburban business districts in the Washington, D.C., metropolitan area. Despite the fact that the subject site was surrounded by a mix of high-rise offices and residential buildings and was zoned for similar development, developer Eakin/Youngentob Associates was determined to avoid a tower-in-the-park design solution. Instead, inspired by the 18th- and 19th-century rowhouse neighborhoods in the Washington area, the developer focused on creating a pedestrian-oriented neighborhood, taking advantage of the site's urban context.

Creating a Neighborhood

The result is a project of 69 three-story townhouses and 133 condominiums in a mix of four-, five-, and six-story structures woven together by a network of landscaped parks and pathways. At 29 units per acre for the townhouses and 87 units per acre for the condominiums, the project has achieved densities greater than those usually reached in comparable projects. At the same time, because of the high level of building and site detailing—everything from tree-lined brick walkways to molded cornices—the project sold out rapidly and commanded above-average per-square-foot prices.

Given that the standard of pedestrian connectivity in the surrounding suburban business district was poor, Courthouse Hill posed several challenges. Sloping 35 feet from end to end, the site bordered high rises on one side and single-family residences on the other. Although well located, the cleared site had remained vacant for ten years before the developer purchased it. Eakin/Youngentob Associates concluded that a high-rise solution was at odds with the site's potential and local market demand. What was required, the developer and architect reasoned, was a greater connectedness to the site's context, not the lesser engagement implied by high-rise development. The developer recognized an opportunity to reestablish an urban pattern and pedestrian-friendly scale. Architect Chris Lessard, principal of Lessard Architectural Group, noted, "At over five stories up, people start to feel disconnected from the street level." The low-/mid-rise solution would also provide a much-needed break in the skyline and would

At Courthouse Hill in Arlington, Virginia, the clustering of housing around the courtyards creates an intimate and attractive urban place.

Lessard Architectural Group

permit the entry of light and sun from the surrounding streets.

As a first step in integrating the project within its context, the developer decided to bridge the differences in the massing of the surrounding structures. Lessard notes, "The layout of housing units on the site sought to create a 'layering effect' that tied the project into the neighborhood." The developer stepped down the buildings in height from the high-rise office/retail center and Metro rail station to the north to the low-rise housing to the south. The taller condominium building descends from six to five to four stories while the townhouses complete the layering effect by establishing a three-story profile adjacent to a community park and existing residential neighborhood to the south. A second step in the pedestrian-oriented design strategy was to place the building entrances on the street and relegate parking to the site's interior.

Framing Space to Create a Residential Place

Borrowing from 18th- and 19th-century town models, the Courthouse Hill structures are set close to the street, just 14.5 feet from the curb. Entrances to the individual townhouses are raised both for privacy and to accommodate tucked-under parking. Each townhouse has a lower-level two-car garage accessible by an interior driveway. Parking for the condominium buildings is located in below-grade structures. To deal with the site's 35-foot elevation gradient, the interior of the site was regraded, allowing for relatively level driveways and, in some cases, partially below-grade garages. The configuration of open space is another component of the project's design that helps establish a pedestrian orientation. A one-half-acre public park constructed on the southern edge of the project provides a linkage to the recreation center across the street and the neighborhood beyond.

Landscaped pathways thread their way from the park through Courthouse Hill, connecting to the Metro station and the urban core to the north. The walkways are pledged to public use through a pedestrian access easement. Other open spaces are more private, serving as quiet courtyards or recreation areas for residents of

Lessard Architectural Group

the townhouses and condominiums. Tucked within the U shape of the condominium buildings are a swimming pool and a community center; the latter includes an exercise room, a multipurpose room, and bathhouse facilities. Sidewalks at Courthouse Hill, as well as internal walkways, are paved in brick. Lanterns and period streetlights illuminate both sidewalks and internal walkways, further recalling the project's urban antecedents.

The townhouse facades at Courthouse Hill are designed to look like separate buildings— all varied—echoing the eclectic mix typical of older neighborhoods built one house at a time. The highly detailed brick facades are federalist in style, with pedimented doorways, arched window heads, and strong cornice lines. Dormer windows punctuate the steeply pitched roofs. At the street level, raised entry stoops with metal railings provide the facades with a rhythm and unifying theme. The lowest level of the townhouse units includes a recreation room as well as a laundry room and the garage. The main living quarters are located one floor above, with bedrooms on the third level. An additional loft/bedroom is offered as a buyer option above the primary bedroom level (under the standard roofline).

The condominium buildings are a less literal translation of period architecture but employ the same finishes as the townhouses. As with the townhouses, the elevations are highly artic-

The Courthouse Hill development was designed to provide a transition within the suburban business district from the high-rise residential development to the adjoining detached housing neighborhoods.

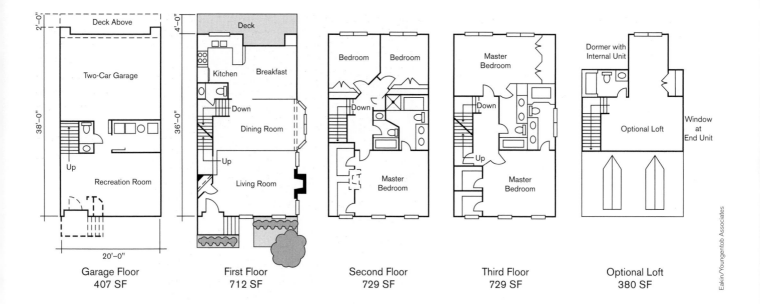

Garage Floor	First Floor	Second Floor	Third Floor	Optional Loft
407 SF	712 SF	729 SF	729 SF	380 SF

Eakin/Youngentob Associates

ulated, with painted wood details contrasting with the brick facades. Recessed balconies further modulate the elevations. Roofs are pitched and accented with dormers and gables of varying sizes.

Meeting the Needs and Aspirations of New Demographic Groups

The market response to Courthouse Hill was extremely positive. Nearly all of the 204 units sold in less than 18 months, a rate of about 11 units per month. At the time of sale in 1997, prices ranged from $115,000 to $280,000 for the condo-

miniums while the townhouse prices ranged from $280,000 to $350,000. Twenty-eight of the 133 condominium units were designated as affordable for-sale housing, fulfilling Arlington County's requirements for the project. At Courthouse Hill, Eakin/Youngentob Associates sought to take advantage of the site's urban location. The proximity to urban amenities was a major selling point for potential residents, who placed a high value on living within walking distance of mass transit, restaurants, movie theaters, shops, and offices. According to architect Lessard, "We were trying to appeal to the young person or the empty nester who is interested in a vibrant street life. So in our design we sought to create a sense of community that related to and enhanced the surrounding urban environment." Adds developer Bob Youngentob, "Our target market was not people who want to live in a gated community, but people who want to feel a part of their neighborhood."

Lessons Learned

The lessons learned at Courthouse Hill demonstrate that buyers often find it easier to move from a detached house to a townhouse or condominium if they can reside in a high-density but low-rise development. One of the project's chief selling points was its access to transit and an extensive range of civic, cultural, community, employment, and retail facilities, most of which are within walking distance. The provision of

Eakin/Youngentob Associates

The sloping site at Courthouse Hill was used to create public spaces for both relaxation and pedestrian connections through the development and to provide an attractive view from the townhouses.

pedestrian-friendly connections to adjoining development played a major role in integrating the project into the surrounding suburban business district. The buildings' enclosure of space created several desirable and special places within the development that were pivotal to marketing the project. The inclusion of 28 for-sale affordable housing units in the project's condominium component provided housing for low- and moderate-income buyers who now have the opportunity to live close to places of employment.

Paseo Plaza

Paseo Plaza represents a hybrid housing form—two-level townhouses at the street level with condominium apartments stacked above. The 210-unit project, located in downtown San Jose (a compact suburban business district in the San Francisco Bay Area), is part of the city's ongoing redevelopment program. Its neighbors are the recently constructed San Jose Repertory Theatre and the San Jose Museum of Art. San Jose State University borders the project to the east. The first two phases of Paseo Plaza were completed in 1997 and 1998, respectively. A third phase of 104 units was completed in April 2000.

Using the Street to Transition from the Public to the Private Domain

From an urban design standpoint, Paseo Plaza's intent is to engage the street rather than turn defensively inward as many new urban projects do. Thus, the mid-rise development has a strong public orientation as well as a more private interior core. The townhouses—each with its own street entrance—line the Third and Fourth Street frontages of the development while retail storefronts edge the Paseo Mall, a pedestrian walkway that forms the project's southern boundary. The townhouses are set back only five feet from the sidewalk along Third Street and 12 feet along Fourth Street. Stacked above the townhouses are single-story condominium units: four stories of flats along Third and Fourth streets and three levels above the townhouses that line the "mews" —an internal pedestrian "street." Along the Paseo, three-story townhouses top the first-floor shops.

Paseo Plaza in San Jose contributes to the streetscape of the suburban business district through its facade design and street tree planting.

Parking is located in a below-grade structure, the top of which forms a podium for the townhouses and for the project's landscaped courtyards. In addition to the multiple street entries to the individual townhouses, a canopy-covered building entry is located on the Third Street

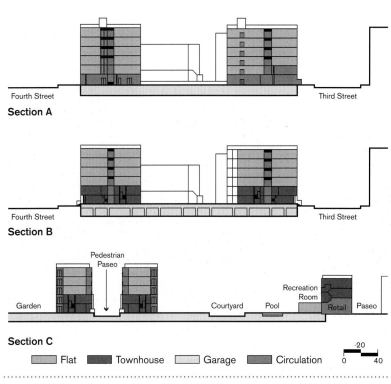

Section A — Fourth Street / Third Street

Section B — Fourth Street / Third Street

Section C — Garden | Pedestrian Paseo | Courtyard | Pool | Recreation Room | Retail | Paseo

Flat | Townhouse | Garage | Circulation

0 20 40

The street building alignment and basement parking are shown on these sections through the Paseo Plaza development.

frontage. A second, less formal building entry is located on the opposite (Fourth Street) frontage. Both entries open onto the main courtyard, a large open space that is differentiated into three smaller areas: a pool terrace, a lawn terrace, and the central paved terrace. A second courtyard, more intimate in scale, conveys the sense of a private garden. Linking the two courtyards is a barrel-vaulted walkway that passes through the residential structures on either side of the mews. A recreation room is also located on the podium level, the roof of which serves as a landscaped forecourt for the townhouses overlooking the Paseo.

Presenting the Public Face of the Project

At street level, the design of Paseo Plaza "draws on the inspiration of Boston's Back Bay townhouses and the Georgian terrace housing in England," notes Bruce Ross, principal of Backen Arrigoni & Ross, Inc. (BAR), the project's architect. The two-story townhouse portion of the facade is sheathed in light-colored stucco scored to recall coursed stone. Projecting stoops and

planter boxes, as well as the deeply inset townhouse entries, add articulation to the facade. The townhouse entries are raised a half-flight to accommodate the partially subterranean garage as well as to increase residents' sense of privacy. Decorative flower planters and closely spaced street trees further enliven the perspective at street level.

Above, the condominium flats are clad in an ocher-colored stucco to contrast with the "stone" of the townhouse facades below. Balconies are recessed five feet from the principal plane of the facade and are grouped together, establishing a rhythm of alternating "in" and "out" planes that break up the bulk of the nearly 400-foot-long project. Through this device, the building begins to recall individual urban structures. The detailing of the building—dark-green painted metal windows and balcony railings as well as cast-concrete sills and trim—ties the upper and lower sections of the facade together into a unified composition.

Along Third and Fourth streets, both the townhouses and flats are double-loaded along hallways, with some units looking out over the street and others looking into the courtyards. Townhouses facing the courtyard have private patios. Along the mews, both townhouses and flats are single-loaded. Typically, the flats are 48 feet wide and sited directly above pairs of townhouses, each 24 feet wide. Gated at both ends, the mews is an intimate space. The pedestrian-only street spans 40 feet from building face to building face. The actual pedestrian walkway is 15 feet wide, lined with ornamental pear trees and decorative street lamps. Private townhouse patios, 12.5 feet deep, flank the walkway on either side.

Paseo Plaza's townhouses have two or three bedrooms and range in size from 1,390 to about 2,200 square feet. Some of the models have large bay windows, and others have double-height living rooms or bedrooms. The townhouse units originally sold in 1998 at prices ranging from the low $200,000s to approximately $500,000.

The condominiums were targeted to a lower price range. The one- and two-bedroom units, from 847 to 1,450 square feet, were priced from $165,000 to about $300,000. With an eye toward

Buildings were used to frame the vista down the paseos to create a sense of place and provide for future ground-floor retail opportunities within Paseo Plaza.

affordability, the two-bedroom units were designed as "double masters," with two equally sized, mirror-image bedroom/bathroom suites that could be marketed to two unrelated singles. The flats have nine-foot ceilings.

Meeting the Market for
New Demographic Groups

The sales program for Paseo Plaza lasted approximately 30 months and averaged seven sales per month. The townhouses, with their entries on the street and higher prices, were more of a pioneering effort for downtown San Jose; they sold at a slower pace than the more affordable condominiums. Sales for all units increased considerably in the final 12 months, and, as the project established itself, resales realized 25 percent capital gains within the first year. Paseo Plaza's retail space has been less successful; it was completed ahead of market demand and failed to achieve the retail mix suited to the locality.

Bruce Ross of BAR credits the Redevelopment Agency of the City of San Jose for the overall success of Paseo Plaza. He notes, "They were like a partner in the deal," programming the site, setting the objectives of a pedestrian-friendly urban environment, and contributing resources, including infrastructure and decorative street lighting. In return, the city has gained an active residential anchor contributing to the rebirth of downtown San Jose.

Lessons Learned

Paseo Plaza shows that housing located proximate to educational facilities and civic and cultural centers meets an important need for several demographic groups in the community and therefore taps an as yet unsatisfied market. Critical to the success of the project was the role of the Redevelopment Agency of the City of San Jose, which transferred the site to the developer at no cost. The dramatic growth in capital value of the housing units within one year of their completion has triggered further housing development within the suburban business district and evidences the desirability of holding such investments in the medium term to maximize financial returns. The poor performance of the

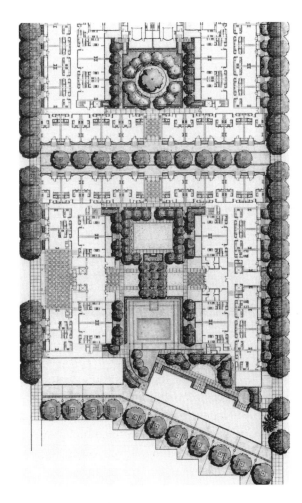

In building to the street alignment, Paseo Plaza created internal courtyards and a landscaped pool and recreation area.

project's retail component demonstrates the importance of properly configuring, mixing, and actively leasing such space so that it becomes an essential place-making component of a project.

Seizing the Market Opportunity

Addison Circle is one of the strongest examples of how housing can help diversify and intensify a suburban business district. Ultimately containing about 3,000 housing units on an 80-acre site, along with 110,000 square feet of retail space and several office buildings, it has integrated a fragmented suburban business district by drawing together an appropriate mix of interdependent uses that reinforce one another to create a critical mass of place-making activity. Despite the nearby presence of several million square feet of retail space in conventional shopping centers of all sizes, the street-level retail uses and restaurants in Addison Circle are a destination for many of the several thousand

The development of multifamily housing in suburban business districts opens up a new world of choice in housing type and location.

nearby office workers. It is a model live-work-shop place that meets the needs and aspirations of America's new demographic profile. To introduce such developments into other suburban business districts will require a high level of public commitment to innovative housing that is fully integrated into the suburban business district. Such was the case with Paseo Plaza. And, as demonstrated by Courthouse Hill, affordable housing units can provide hous-

ing for moderate-income suburban business district employees.

In many suburban business districts such as Tysons Corner, new residential development remains true to conventional types, principally high-end garden apartments that are isolated and self-contained and require their occupants to drive to adjoining retail and office development. They have not been integrated into the surrounding development by way of pedestrian-friendly design and active place making and, as a consequence, add little to the vitality and life of the surrounding suburban business district. They are an opportunity lost.

America's new demographic profile is demanding new living environments rich with transit options as well as with community, cultural, civic, employment, entertainment, and retail opportunities. Multifamily residential development allows residents to live-work-shop—without the hassles of traffic congestion—in a place that they find unique and inviting. The presence of other residents creates life, interest, and a range of opportunities simply not feasible in lower-density development. And a vibrant environment is a prerequisite to increasing real estate values and delivering a place-making dividend to both the developer and the commu-

The Attraction of Suburban Business District Living

While people may not agree with John Sherry's thesis that Americans are guided in their choices by what they read in the newspaper, see on television, or watch at the movies, a series of articles published in the *Washington Post* in July 2001 informed readers of the housing choices now becoming available in suburban business districts. Residents of various multifamily developments in the Washington-area suburban business districts of Pentagon City, Ballston, and Reston were asked why they had chosen to live in a suburban business district. Interestingly, the residents, drawn from various demographic groups, gave the following reasons:

- "To beat the traffic";
- "I love walking to my office";
- "I have the Metro [rail station] within 100 yards";
- "The mall's [Simon Properties's regional shopping mall, Fashion Center at Pentagon City] right next door and the grocery store is downstairs";
- "There is a shopping mall, movie theaters, restaurants, and a Metro station";
- "I can walk up there [Reston Town Center] for coffee or breakfast. It definitely has a European flair"; and
- "We're close to the town center, where things happen, and close to the Reston Hospital."

While these reports are anecdotal, it is significant that the option to live, work, and shop in suburban business districts is being put forward by the popular press as an attractive residential option for America's new demographic profile. It is an option that, until recently, most people would not have known existed. ●

Source: *Washington Post*, July 7 and 21, 2001.

nity. With their underused land and metropolitan locations, suburban business districts are well placed to respond to changing market preferences—they constitute a residential market opportunity that is deep, growing with demographic changes, and as yet largely unsatisfied.

Notes

1. Martha Farnsworth Riche, *The Implications of Changing U.S. Demographics for Housing Choice and Location in Cities* (Washington, D.C.: The Brookings Institution, 2001), p. 2.

2. Edward L. Glaeser, "Demand for Density? The Functions of the City in the 21st Century," *Brookings Review,* Summer 2000, p. 10.

3. John F. Sherry, ed., *Servicescapes: The Concept of Place in Contemporary Markets* (Chicago: NTC Business Books, 1998), p. 51.

4. Christopher J. McIntosh, "Finding Good Dirt—As building sites get harder to find and more expensive to develop, developers are becoming more creative and taking greater risks," *Multifamily Trends,* Spring 2001, p. 22.

5. Suzanne M. Bianchi et al., *American Families* (Washington, D.C.: Population Reference Bureau, 2001), p. 3.

6. Jack McNeil, *Changes in Median Household Income* (Washington, D.C.: Bureau of the Census, 2001), p. 1.

7. Joint Center for Housing Studies, *State of the Nation's Housing 2001* (Cambridge: Harvard University, 2001), p. 12.

8. Edward L. Glaeser et al., *City Growth and the 2000 Census: Which Places Grew, and Why* (Washington, D.C.: The Brookings Institution, 2001), p. 12.

9. Bureau of the Census et al., *American Families and Their Housing in 1997* (Washington, D.C.: Bureau of the Census and U.S. Department of Housing and Urban Development, 1999), p. 4.

10. McIntosh, "Finding Good Dirt," p. 23, and Joint Center for Housing Studies, *State of the Nation's Housing 2001,* p. 21.

chapter 5

Aligning Office Development with Changing Tenant Demand

In many respects, office development is the least complicated type of real estate development—tenants usually lease large floor areas and require long-term leases. Developers who build to tenant demands are likely to enter into long-term leases that represent a lower-risk investment with high capital value. It is significant, however, that office tenant requirements, which have remained relatively constant for the past two decades, are beginning to change.

Frank Mann, Jones Lang LaSalle's executive vice president for client representation, describes the shift. "Our clients are looking for the most flexibility we can give them, to both expand and contract. . . . Access to mass transportation and rich cultural activities are the two pluses of in-town property that aren't now found in outlying counties. Culture and transportation add value because they attract a young work force which my clients seek. . . . These young professionals want the kind of live-work-play environment found in Midtown and Buckhead—not Cobb or Cherokee counties."[1]

Changed Tenant Demands and Needs

In the *2000 Landauer Real Estate Market Forecast,* Chief Economist Hugh F. Kelly forecast imminent market changes. "Demographers have been watching the baby boomer cohort for decades. At the beginning of the 21st century, the leading edge of the boomer generation enters the pre-retirement years. Meanwhile, there will be slow growth in the number of labor entrants, coming out of colleges and graduate schools. After decades of labor surplus, low unemployment is the norm rather than the exception. These demographic patterns will exert a powerful influence on economic and real estate decisions."[2]

Indeed, dramatic market changes are already evident. Citing examples of hot emerging markets, *Emerging Trends in Real Estate 2001*[3] predicts a major shift in real estate investment to compact suburban business districts that provide a live-work-shop environment complete with mass transit. Specifically, the report points to the following markets:

- Buckhead, Georgia, near Atlanta;
- Reston, Virginia, in the Washington, D.C., metropolitan area;
- Bethesda, Maryland, in the Washington, D.C., metropolitan area;
- Walnut Creek in the East Bay area of San Francisco;
- Bellevue, Washington, near Seattle; and
- Birmingham, Michigan, near Detroit.

Compact suburban business districts are ". . . locations which offer a mix of residential, office, retail, hotel and entertainment in an exciting, aesthetically pleasing and pedestrian-friendly environment. Such markets provide a vibrant atmosphere during the work day, evening, and weekend which in turn drives synergistic tenant demand amongst all asset types resulting in above average rental growth and strong investment performance."[4] People are making different choices. As the market changes direction, it is witnessing outstanding financial success for projects such as

- Federal Realty's Bethesda Row in Bethesda, Maryland;
- Post Properties's Addison Circle in Addison, Texas; and
- Terrabrook's Reston Town Center in Virginia.[5]

The success of these 24-hour live-work-shop environments stands in stark contrast to recent somber projections for the suburban office and retail segments of the real estate market. Office vacancies induced by failing dot.com companies and department store closures in shopping malls do not bode well for the future of office and retail development.

Chris Kurz of Linden Associates, Inc., in Baltimore has summarized the sea change taking hold in the market. "The echo boomers are about to flex their muscles! They are becoming the key part of the labor force and the housing

and retail markets. Meet needs as they perceive them and win big! In are 'urban,' 'green,' 'warm,' 'experience,' 'substance.' Out are 'suburban,' 'uniform,' 'appearance,' 'one size fits all,' 'cheap,' 'quantity over quality.'"[6] The market will see finance and investment favoring the 24-hour

Five Principles in Planning Reston Town Center

The formula used by Reston Town Center to deliver a strong place-making dividend is summarized in the following five principles:

1. The town center had to be walkable; its core had to total 100 acres or less.
2. The town center had to contain a mix of uses—office, retail, restaurants, entertainment, and residential.
3. The mix of uses had to be dense enough to bring a critical mass of people (residents, workers, shoppers—live-work-shop) into the town center.
4. The spaces had to be attractive enough that people would choose to go to the town center.
5. The town center had to be easily accessible by car and by transit.

These planning principles have guided the development of Reston Town Center and have differentiated it from its competitors by creating a sense of place. •

Source: David J. O'Neill, *The Smart Growth Tool Kit* (Washington, D.C.: ULI–the Urban Land Institute, 2001), p. 126.

downtown and compact suburban business districts while penalizing their fragmented and disjointed cousins. In fact, Census 2000 found that, after decades of decline, downtowns, inner-ring suburbs, and more urban locations are again gaining population.[7] Real estate finance and investment are already reflecting the demographic shift as new standalone suburban office developments have become more and more difficult to finance and capitalization rates in the sale of such properties have been escalating to account for increased leasing risk.[8]

Metropolitan Office Space Distribution

These emerging trends in labor force and, as a consequence, tenant location requirements are at odds with today's overall picture of a highly dispersed suburban office market that, at least until recently, continued to draw strength away from the traditional downtown office core. In a 1999 study for the Brookings Institution,[9] Robert Lang used data from *Black's Guide to Office Leasing* for 12 of 13 selected U.S. metropolitan areas and data from Cushman and Wakefield for New York City. He found that in 13 of the largest U.S.

metropolitan real estate markets, on average, 37.7 percent of the total office space was located in "primary downtowns" (central business districts), 6 percent in "secondary downtowns" (compact suburban business districts as defined by the Urban Land Institute), 19.8 percent in "edge cities" (fragmented suburban business districts as defined by ULI), and 36.5 percent in "edgeless locations" (dispersed suburban business districts as defined by ULI, or isolated, standalone office developments with less than 5 million square feet of office space). Figure 5.1 details the distribution of office space in the 13 metropolitan areas.

The study also found that total office space in the suburbs of the same 13 metropolitan areas had grown from 2.34 billion square feet in 1979 to 1.123 trillion square feet in 1999, for an increase of 305 percent. By comparison, central city office space over the same period grew from 67.6 million square feet to 1.57 trillion square feet, for an increase of 112 percent. The report noted, "The building stock in cities is signifi-

cantly older than the suburbs, which puts the cities at greater risk of losing total inventory."[10] Of particular interest was the finding that ". . . 38 percent of all metropolitan office space in 1999 was located in the traditional downtowns, while nearly the same amount, 37 percent, was found in highly dispersed, 'edgeless' locations lacking well-defined boundaries and extending over tens if not hundreds of square miles of urban space."[11] These "edgeless locations" represent fragmented and dispersed suburban business districts and isolated, standalone real estate developments with less than 5 million square feet of office space.

The Brookings study concludes with a warning to those who hope that at least some suburban business districts will mature into mixed-use, nearly urban, live-work-shop environments. Many suburban business districts ". . . face the same land cost and congestion pressures as old downtowns, for they too are now central places. Perhaps edge cities are losing their edge. The new metropolitan form shows up less often in

figure 5.1 Distribution of Metropolitan Office Space in 13 Major Metropolitan Areas, 1999

Metropolitan Area	Percent Office Space within Primary Downtown	Percent Office Space within Secondary Downtowns	Percent Office Space within Edge Cities	Percent Office Space within Edgeless Locations
Chicago	53.9	N/A	19.5	26.6
New York	56.7	7.2	6.3	29.9
Boston	37.4	4.6	18.8	39.2
Washington, D.C.	28.6	12.5	27.1	31.8
Denver	30.4	4.2	29.4	35.9
Los Angeles	29.8	7.8	25.4	37.0
San Francisco	33.9	8.8	13.9	43.4
Dallas	20.5	4.5	40.3	34.6
Houston	23.0	N/A	37.9	39.1
Atlanta	23.6	9.9	25.3	41.2
Detroit	21.3	N/A	39.5	39.2
Philadelphia	34.2	3.2	8.9	53.6
Miami	13.1	4.5	16.6	65.8
Average	37.7	6.0	19.8	36.5

Source: Robert E. Lang, *Office Sprawl: The Evolving Geography of Business* (Washington, D.C.: The Brookings Institution, 2000), p. 6.

The Office Market Outlook

The *ULI 2001 Real Estate Forecast* reported that the office sector is likely to experience a considerable slowdown through mid-2002. It projected that corporations would reduce space requirements, thereby adding to the sublease inventory. In 2000, office construction starts increased by 3.2 percent to 286 million square feet following a modest decline in 1999. However, starts are likely to drop to 167 million square feet in 2001—a 42 percent decline—with an additional 2.2 percent decrease expected in 2002. The forecast projected that suburban office markets would likely see major increases in vacancies and downward pressure on rents. The nine-to-five markets are at greatest risk as corporations consolidate their offices in locations that appeal to their labor force and abandon poor-quality office space that dates from the 1970s and 1980s and lacks the floor loading capacity and plate size required for today's office equipment.

Other analysts have concluded that tenants are now demanding office buildings that combine fail-safe voice-data and high-speed Internet access with a reliable source of power. Rooftop antennas and secure ducting with two separate fiberoptic pathways are necessary to ensure that telecommunications and data capabilities "don't go down." Many suburban and some central business district buildings with only single lines are now at risk of obsolescence.

With increasing public awareness of the cost of traffic congestion, office locations that offer a choice of transportation

With increasing public awareness of the cost of traffic congestion, office locations that offer a choice of transportation options and more than a nine-to-five range of activities— and thus promote travel at other than peak hours—will enjoy a competitive advantage.

options and more than a nine-to-five range of activities—and thus promote travel at other than peak hours—will enjoy a competitive advantage. Class B suburban office developments in fringe locations that have already seen an increase in their capitalization rates of 50 to 65 basis points are likely to find themselves at a significant disadvantage. Rising cap rates, declining rents, and increased vacancies add up to a scenario that fragmented and dispersed suburban business districts in particular will wish to avoid. The recommendation in the *Real Estate Report—First*

Quarter 2001 by the Chicago-based Real Estate Research Corporation is blunt. "Buy: CBD office properties located in a 24-hour city that have solid supply and depth of demand . . . Sell: suburban office properties." The best strategy for suburban business districts is to align their product offering with these new and changing tenant demands. ●

Source: Adapted in part from Dean Schwanke, *ULI 2001 Real Estate Forecast* (Washington, D.C.: ULI– the Urban Land Institute, 2001) and Jules A. Marling, ed., *Real Estate Report—First Quarter 2001* (Chicago: Real Estate Research Corporation, 2001).

the Post Oaks (Houston) and Tysons Corner (Virginia) than in the nameless office parks at nearly every exit off the beltway. That is where most of the office space built outside downtowns is now found. Those looking to build better suburbs should not ignore this fact."[12]

In companion research released in May 2001, the Brookings Institution's Edward L. Glaeser found that across the 100 largest metropolitan areas in the United States, only 22 percent of people work within three miles of the city center.[13] Clearly, the suburban office market

The Office Building Formula

The development of a standard office building formula (consisting of a stand-alone building surrounded by acres of surface parking) and its acceptance by both the leasing and capital markets have played a major role in the creation of fragmented and dispersed suburban business districts. The formula's success is rooted in its historical development and the lack of choice available to suburban tenants. This success has led to its unquestioned application across the nation. During the second half of the 20th century, the nature of office work underwent major changes. New communication systems and the computerization of many routine accounting and typing functions changed the work environment. More women entered the labor force. On the roads, traffic congestion was increasing, and the long commutes to and from downtown equated to time away from the family. In addition, the supply of downtown parking could not keep pace with demand.

At the same time, the style of corporate management was undergoing modernization as college graduates were appointed to senior management positions. The new managers found the office building stock in downtowns obsolete and expensive compared with the newer product available in suburban business districts. Fluorescent lighting and air conditioning had recently liberated the configuration of office buildings, allowing for larger floor plates.

Within the nation's downtowns, it was difficult and expensive to assemble fragmented landholdings to construct buildings with 20,000- to 25,000-square-foot floor plates. However, in the spacious suburban business district, the large floor plate could easily accommodate tenant requirements, permitting developers to maximize rentable square footage. The space could be leased to one tenant or divided efficiently into smaller areas to allow the subleasing of space when a business did not require surplus office space. One consequence of larger floor plates was the physical separation of the building from adjoining sites by generously sized employee parking lots, which were made possible by low land and construction costs. For senior managers looking to model their corporate headquarters after the campus environments in which they had earned their academic degrees, the suburban business district offered an attractive and cost-effective alternative.

Some developments followed the pattern established by Corporate Woods Office Park, a project initiated in the late 1960s in Kansas City that carefully sited high-density office development in a woodland setting. Others, however, had more of a visual affinity with the functional but sterile Pentagon parking lots in Arlington, Virginia. In his November 17, 2000, article in the *Philadelphia Business Journal,* Paul Eisenberg quoted Jeanne Leonard, director of investor relations with Liberty Property Trust. "There are differences in what we build and what others build, and there are basic similarities that are dictated by the marketplace. Yes, they all have large parking lots, but that's because you cannot fill a building with tenants unless you have enough parking. That's a truism. That's the way it is. Would we love to build buildings that were not surrounded by parking? Absolutely. Would we go broke in ten minutes? Absolutely. So there are basic marketplace rules that one must adhere to." Until the market changes these rules, fragmented and dispersed suburban business districts will continue to be created, thereby perpetuating the problem. ●

is very deep and with changing tenant requirements, the evidence points to a significant incentive to transform suburban business district office space to meet emerging employment needs.

Why Office Location Decentralized

With the advent of the telephone, telex, facsimile machine, and e-mail, face-to-face communication in commerce is less essential than in earlier decades; thus, the need to locate all corporations, or parts of the corporation, in one central place is now likewise less essential. Moreover, air conditioning and fluorescent lighting have revolutionized the work environment such that desks no longer have to be positioned near windows or internal light wells. The nature of office work has also been transformed from manual accounting and typing activities to a range of knowledge-based skills reliant on automation.

In the second half of the 20th century, corporate management styles also underwent a major upheaval that translated into new office layouts and larger floor plates not readily accommodated by obsolete downtown buildings. At the same time, downtown land values and office rents escalated, and downtown traffic congestion became a problem. As suburban business districts began to offer lower rents, new buildings that bespoke the new corporate style, and an abundance of cost-free employee parking, many U.S. corporations could not resist the lure of more suitable surroundings.

Initially, "the most important variable in determining the direction of a corporate shift was the location of the home and country club of the chief executive officer of the particular company." That location, of course, determined the length of the chief executive's commute to work.[14] At the same time, a different but nonetheless powerful incentive for executives to relocate away from downtown was the opportunity to lease modern suburban offices and thus liquidate their downtown property assets. The proceeds from liquidation permitted companies to expand operations. In particular, for those firms that had leased their downtown premises, the lower cost of suburban land was reflected in lower total occupancy costs and increased profit margins. Lease terms allowed tenants to move at the time of lease expiration if a location proved unsatisfactory or their markets contracted, as had been their experience downtown. Consequently, tenants were now far more mobile, and the real estate development industry boomed to meet their needs. Wall Street analysts and management consultants generally considered such moves the mark of an innovative management team taking advantage of the opportunities offered by the new economy.

The purpose of corporate moves was as much to improve employee morale and productivity as to reduce costs. Free parking and easy access to the interstate highway made a longer working day possible, and landscaped surroundings and a corporate gymnasium made for a more relaxed work environment. Company cafeterias replaced downtown sandwich shops and restaurants, shopping areas, and daytime entertainment in the city center. Some employees found the new environment to their liking while others claimed it was sterile and boring. Today, suburban business districts' lack of choice in transportation options is increasingly a source of frustration as more employees suffer the effects of worsening traffic congestion on their daily journey to and from work.

What Office Tenants Now Require

In a 1997 study of employee travel patterns in the Washington, D.C., metropolitan area's business districts, Dr. G. Bruce Douglas found that 63 percent of office workers in dispersed suburban business districts eat lunch at their desks. When they do leave the building, they are usually on assignment and almost always in an automobile.[15] The *1999 BOMA/ULI Office Tenant Survey Report* found that 82 percent of downtown office tenants rated their existing location as very important; however, the number dropped to 50 percent for suburban office park tenants.[16] Figure 5.2 summarizes office tenant preferences

One of the most pressing corporate needs in the 21st century is access to a high-speed Internet connection and reliable energy sources. Buildings wired for today's technologies enjoy a competitive advantage. However, it is a company's ability to attract and retain its labor force that is likely to become a major factor in the future choice of office location. The 18th annual edition of the *Landauer Real Estate Market Forecast (2000)* concluded, "Vigorous suburban growth depends largely on the cohorts in the child-rearing years. The 90's were still good years for suburban demand, as the ranks of the 35 to 44 years age group peaked. But the coming decade represents a trough in the entire range of young adults in the population . . . the renewed strength of center cities . . . [is] merely a staging point for a significant quickening of urban vitality in the U.S. The comparative shortage of workers in the career-building ages from 25 to 44 will require business to rethink some basic labor strategies crafted during the years of plentiful workers, from 1970 to 1995. The demand side for real estate will be ever more tricky to discern. . . . worker retention is going to emerge as the key challenge to employers. . . . the issue is not just access, but how various forms of real estate will respond to new lifestyles and work-styles."[17]

Employee dissatisfaction with suburban traffic congestion is now contributing to a renewed interest in suburban business districts that provide a complete live-work-shop environment.

figure 5.2 **What Is Important to Office Tenants**

Proximity to Clients

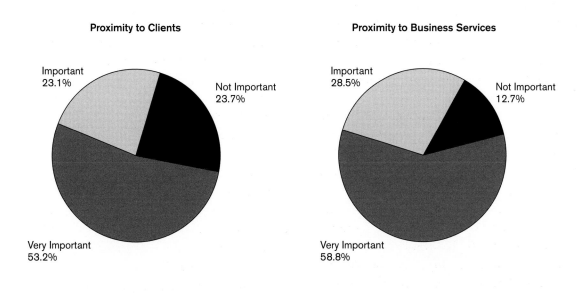

Important
23.1%

Not Important
23.7%

Very Important
53.2%

Proximity to Business Services

Important
28.5%

Not Important
12.7%

Very Important
58.8%

Proximity to Restaurants, Retail Uses, and Personal Services

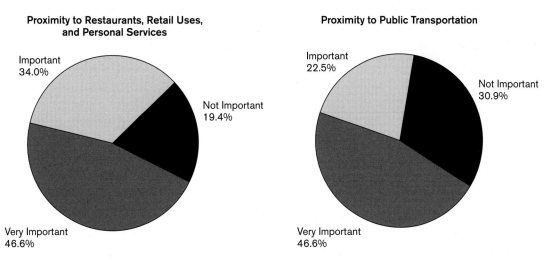

Important
34.0%

Not Important
19.4%

Very Important
46.6%

Proximity to Public Transportation

Important
22.5%

Not Important
30.9%

Very Important
46.6%

Proximity to Home

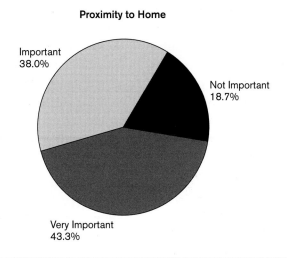

Important
38.0%

Not Important
18.7%

Very Important
43.3%

Source: Jo Allen Gause et al., *What Office Tenants Want: 1999 BOMA/ULI Office Tenant Survey Report* (Washington, D.C.: BOMA International and ULI–the Urban Land Institute, 1999), p. 20.

Elkus/Manfredi, Esto Photographics, Inc.

When office, retail, housing, and entertainment uses are mixed together in healthy portions, the result is 24-hour cities such as the Rosslyn-Ballston corridor in Arlington County, Virginia; Bethesda in Montgomery County, Maryland; and Bellevue near Seattle.

In a recent study of the Washington, D.C., metropolitan area, Terry Holzheimer found that, despite the strength of office development along the Dulles Toll Road and other arterial road locations between 1980 and 1998, transit-served office markets in suburban business districts were surprisingly competitive with nontransit-served office markets in suburban and exurban locations.[18] The transit-served suburban business districts in the study were Alexandria, Rosslyn-Ballston, Crystal City-Pentagon City, Bethesda-Chevy Chase, Silver Spring, and Lanham/Landover. The nontransit suburban markets were Tysons Corner, Reston, Fairfax Center, Merrifield, and Dulles North and South.

Holzheimer's study found that, even given fragmented landownership patterns, tighter zoning controls, and more constrained sites in the transit-served suburban business districts, the districts still delivered 35.3 million square feet of office space over the study period while the comparatively less constrained and less expensive nontransit-served markets delivered only 46 million square feet of office space. The average office rent in 1998 in the transit-served markets was $2 per square foot higher than the average in the nontransit-served markets. Vacancy rates in the transit-served markets were 3 percent lower than in the nontransit-served markets in 1999 and 14 percent lower than in the nontransit-served market at the peak of the office market recession in 1991. The transit markets recovered much sooner from the recession in terms of rental rates and vacancy rates. The evidence suggests that a significant percentage of office tenants will pay a premium for suburban business district transit-linked offices, a factor that will become more crucial as employers are forced to compete for a reduced labor supply demanding greater transportation choice.

Three Aging Suburban Business Districts in America's Heartland

The following three examples discuss aging suburban business districts in Detroit, Kansas City, and St. Louis. While each example differs along several dimensions, all three share several traits. Each location is a major center of employment for the host region, accounting for 3 to 5 percent of total regional employment and, in two instances, approximately the same volume of office employment as in the region's central business district (College Boulevard in Kansas City and Southfield in Detroit).

- Each district comprises a distinct submarket for office space (Southfield and College Boulevard) or for office space together with light industrial, warehouse, and distribution uses (Westport), and each is recognized and marketed by the local and national brokerage community based on that identity.
- Each has been a catalyst for even broader regionally based job and economic growth. Southfield spawned office and diverse industrial growth along the I-496 corridor extending toward Lansing and Ann Arbor. College Boulevard anchors a pattern of office employment growth to the south in Johnson County and continues to have a synergistic effect on the vast inventory of warehouse and distribution space in the same southwest quadrant of the Kansas City region. Westport's growth in the distribution and flex space segments of the market has spread to the environs of Lambert International Airport, to Earth City/ Riverport, and, subsequently, into the I-70 corridor of St. Charles County in St. Louis.
- Finally, each district was established and began to grow dramatically between 1965 and 1975. As the districts age, their ability to support redevelopment to meet changing tenant requirements is governed by local market conditions, varying public policies, and the availability of public financial support.

Southfield—Detroit, Michigan

The Southfield suburban business district is a development corridor located along U.S. Route 10 —alternatively known as the Lodge Freeway— as it extends out from the city of Detroit and the Northwestern Highway to intersect with I-696, which is the northern segment (east/west direction) of the region's circumferential highway. The 1954 development of the Northland Shopping Mall, the nation's first regional mall (designed by Victor Gruen and built by the Hudson-Weber Realty Company), spurred the emergence of Southfield. At its inception, Northland was deemed perfectly located as it was positioned to serve residents of the adjacent city of Detroit as well as residents of the exploding suburbs to the north and west. Northland became and has remained one of the largest shopping malls in America.

Predominant Form of Development

By the late 1960s, Northland had become a catalyst for the development of an array of both build-to-suit and multitenant office buildings. The same pattern quickly repeated itself along the frontage of the Lodge Freeway until a significant cluster coalesced near the freeway's (then future) intersection with I-696, three miles northwest of the mall. Today, the concentration of development around the mall includes 15.5 million square feet of multitenant office space, which is part of a larger total inventory of 27 million square feet of office space in the city of Southfield; single occupants own or lease the balance of the inventory on a long-term basis. In addition to the 2 million square feet at Northland Shopping Mall, an extensive inventory of strip malls and freestanding retail uses has de-

Southfield suburban business district is linear in form, with a length of just over six miles and a width of up to one mile in parts.

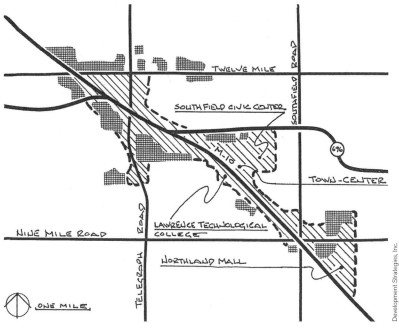

By 1990, South-field Town Center had become the largest concentration of office employment in the Detroit metropolitan area, but it was neither pedestrian- nor transit-friendly.

veloped along the north/south arterials that pass through the district, along with a wide variety of multifamily housing for both rental and condominium occupancy.

In 1958, four years after the opening of Northland Shopping Mall, the city of Southfield was incorporated with 29,000 residents. As a previously rural township, Southfield lacked a traditional main street business district. Today, Southfield has a population of 79,000. At an early point, the city's civic leadership recognized Southfield's strategic location in terms of access to downtown Detroit; the Ford, General Motors, and Chrysler manufacturing facilities; and the Oakland County offices, all of which were driving regional growth. Clearly, Southfield was advantageously positioned not only to capture the residential expansion generated by those departing Detroit for suburbia but also to build a strong tax base by capitalizing on the emerging interest among office employers to locate near the new mall and on the new road to the state capital in Lansing. Traditionally, that route had been the northwest radial arterial, Grand River Avenue, but the construction of the Lodge Freeway/Northwestern Highway and I-496 promised to create new travel patterns and trigger the growth of increasingly affluent suburbs even farther to the north and northwest.

Once completed with its parallel frontage roads, the Northwestern Highway became a magnet for office developers in search of both the visibility and access offered by the highway. From the initial cluster near Northland Shopping Mall, individual owner-occupied and multitenant buildings soon lined the north and south frontage roads for several miles. In the meantime, Southfield purchased a large site for its civic center a half mile north of the freeway. The ambitious young city's commitment to civic infrastructure—a new city hall, library, and community center—provided the catalyst for the Prudential Insurance Company's decision to build a major signature office complex on an adjacent 70-acre tract with extensive frontage on the northern outer road of the Northwestern Highway.

The Town Center

Built between 1979 and 1989, the Prudential Town Center, later named Southfield Town Center, consisted of four major office towers (28 to 32 stories) totaling 2 million square feet, a 377-room hotel (originally a Radisson, now a Westin), and a 300-unit high-rise (30-story) condominium tower, together with a common parking infrastructure of garages and surface lots. The architecture of the town center was striking, its gold mirror glass and skyline visible for miles when approached from any direction, particularly from the Northwestern Highway. With the Northland Shopping Mall on the southeast and the town center on the northwest end of the highway corridor, Southfield became the largest concentration of office employment in the Detroit region, passing downtown Detroit as it struggled with one of the nation's most pervasive patterns of urban disinvestment. The Southfield suburban business district is the headquarters or regional office location for 140 Fortune 500 companies, including BASF, Panasonic, Watson Wyatt Worldwide, Federal Mogal, Lear, Lotus, MSX International, and Progressive Tool and Industries.

Problems Experienced

Despite the many successes associated with the development of Southfield and its regional shopping and office employment base, the story would be incomplete without noting some of the difficulties faced by the city. While Southfield's establishment and growth were initially linked to the departure of families and businesses from Detroit, the influence of race and its associated perceptions and fears have played a major role over the past 30 years. At the outset, the newcomers were all white—the shoppers at the new mall, the buyers of homes in the new subdivisions, and the employees in the new offices. As the population exodus from Detroit accelerated (Detroit's population has declined by over 1 million in the past 40 years), an increasing portion of Southfield's shoppers, residents, and office employees were drawn from several racial groups. Accordingly, Southfield has had to learn to build a multiracial, ethnically diverse residential community and employment base. The effort has required persistence, sensitivity, tolerance, patience, and a belief in the value of diversity on the part of employers, elected officials, and property owners. While the city's relative stability, increasing property values, and continued growth as an employment center may not be the result of a perfect alignment of interests, it should be seen as a success story by anyone who understands the complexity of multiracial community building.

Employment Growth

By the mid-1980s, Southfield's office employment had grown to over 80,000 jobs; today, it stands at over 100,000 jobs. Vacancy rates in its multitenant office inventory is slightly higher than the average for the region (9.9 percent versus 9 percent for the region), and its average lease rate is slightly below the regional average ($19.54 per square foot per year versus $20.16 per square foot per year for the region).[19] The biggest development challenge is how to maintain the quality and scale of Northland given that the shopping center is nearly 50 years old and has a current occupancy of just 70 percent. Despite the efforts of a recent series of investor/owners to maintain the center's condition and position in the marketplace, it seems clear that in time a more radical approach may be needed.

Obsolete Buildings

Meanwhile, the city has initiated the redevelopment of Southfield's older, obsolete office buildings, paying special attention to the structures surrounding Northland Shopping Mall.[20] Two buildings have been demolished, and new construction of freestanding retail and smaller office facilities is underway. The city recently adopted a new economic development plan for the center and its surroundings that is to be implemented under the authority of the Southfield Downtown Development Authority (DDA). In addition to its authority to use the power of condemnation, the DDA commands the financial resources to implement its plans by means of tax-increment financing and a 2-mill tax rate applicable to properties within the district. Further, Southfield uses tax abatement as a business retention tool in selective instances involving the relocation, expansion, or rehabilitation of businesses within the city.[21] In fact, several small, older multitenant office buildings located along the expressway frontage have already been renovated.

Perhaps because of the challenges Southfield faced over the years relative to demographic change and the obsolescence of older retail and office facilities, the community has dedicated considerable resources to answering two interrelated questions: How can Southfield maintain

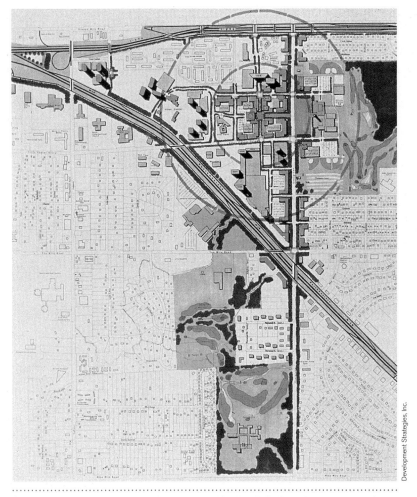

The strategic plan developed for Southfield in the early 1990s provided for the linking of green space to create improved pedestrian linkages within the suburban business district.

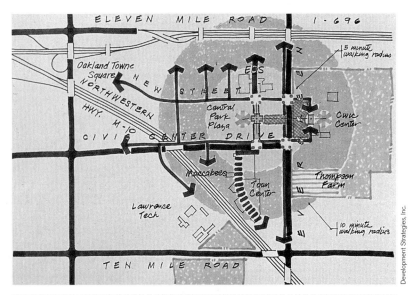

To create a pedestrian-friendly town center in Southfield, the plan calls for breaking up the superblock plat with a series of new roads that provide increased pedestrian access and reduce traffic congestion. The plan also provides for a new central park plaza and released parcels for infill development.

its advantageous position within the region? and How can Southfield foster a process of sustained reinvestment for the improvement or replacement of its older buildings?

Civic Vision

About a decade ago, the city retained a team of national urban design and economics firms to consider these questions.[22] A critique of the city and its built environment yielded a consensus among participants in a public planning process. In short, Southfield lacked a focal point or place that distinguished the community and brought together its residents and those who work there. This conclusion then led to a challenge to the consultant team to develop a strategic plan aimed at creating a needed focal point.

While as yet not fully realized, the plan is progressing toward implementation of the vision developed a decade ago for a pedestrian-friendly "city center" for Southfield. A public plaza has been created as the principal focal point. Construction of a new city library is underway on a site well served to fill some of the excess open space in the city's adjacent Southfield Civic Center and to create an enhanced pedestrian link to the new plaza. In the core area, 140 new townhomes have been built, with more constructed adjacent to the Southfield Town Center.[23]

Lessons Learned

Southfield's experience demonstrates that a fragmented suburban business district can enhance its attractiveness as a retail and office location through the addition of civic and cultural facilities. These facilities provide a focus and identity for the district. Infill housing helps link the district's office and retail components and translates into pedestrian traffic for retail businesses. The standalone Northfield Shopping Mall remains a challenge, particularly as the shopping mall approaches its 50th anniversary. With only a 70 percent occupancy rate, the mall needs to adopt a main street element, reconsider its mix of uses and tenants, and explore the possibility of adding multifamily housing. Such a strategy would realign the property with changing community needs and provide enhanced transit and pedestrian connections to the sur-

The new streets of Southfield town center are limited in width, well streetscaped, and designed to be attractive and safe for pedestrians and automobiles.

rounding suburban business district. The innovative use of public/private financing will play a major role in transforming the Southfield suburban business district.

College Boulevard—Overland Park Kansas City, Kansas

One observer noted that the best thing that happened to establish College Boulevard as the Kansas City region's premier office address was a change of name from 111th Street to College Boulevard. The change occurred in 1970 in response to the establishment of Johnson County Community College at the intersection of 111th Street and Quivira Road in what was then the southwest corner of the city of Overland Park, Kansas.

Overland Park is home to 150,000 residents in a bistate region of 1.7 million people. After growing steadily in both population and resident jobs for over four decades, the city is today the centerpiece of a set of communities that includes Lenexa, Prairie Village, Leawood, Shawnee, and Olathe in the southwest quadrant of the Kansas City region. These communities in combination and Overland Park alone account for a dominant share of the region's wealth, talent, and resources as measured by household income,

percent of population with college and graduate degrees, taxable real property valuation, and so forth. To most observers, Overland Park also epitomizes good government with its council/manager form of governance and a commitment to planned growth. A close association with and pipeline to the talent pool of the highly acclaimed graduate schools of public adminis-

College Boulevard suburban business district is linear in shape, with a length of just under six miles and a width of up to one mile in parts.

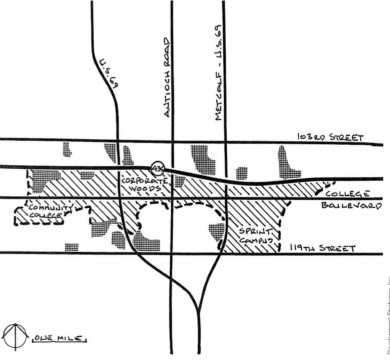

The concept of Corporate Woods in Kansas City was to create office buildings nestled in a forest. Shown in the foreground of the photograph, this project was started in the early 1970s and contrasts with the other dispersed development in the College Boulevard–Overland Park suburban business district.

tration and urban planning at the nearby University of Kansas in Lawrence have contributed greatly to the quality and many achievements of this proud community.

Partnership in Development

The growth and development of Overland Park, incorporated in 1960, has been a case study of cooperation between local government and the chamber of commerce. In fact, legend has it that Overland Park's city fathers, comprising city officials and chamber executives, came together regularly over coffee at a favorite restaurant to formulate an eventual vision for the young city. The initial "wish list" for the city that evolved in 1967 concluded that the new city should exhibit the following characteristics:

- fine residential neighborhoods;
- the best public schools in the nation;
- the best city services available anywhere;
- appealing shopping districts and centers;
- no ugly "smokestacks" and associated industrial employment; and
- no public incentives such as tax abatements to spur private investment.

Citizens and officials soon recognized, however, that the trouble with Overland Park's lofty goals was that there was no means to pay for them. This realization led to a final goal of developing a number of office buildings that would create a commercial tax base to help fund the quality of life and infrastructure envisioned for the emerging city of Overland Park.[24]

Office Park Development

The concept of the planned suburban office park was just beginning to be tested and refined across the country in the mid- to late 1960s. In fact, the development of several small office parks was already underway in the Kansas City region when, in the early 1970s, a local developer named Thomas Congleton joined forces with Metropolitan Life Insurance Company as his financial partner to propose the creation of Corporate Woods. Located on a densely wooded tract between College Boulevard and the recently completed I-435 regional beltway as it passed through Overland Park and Johnson County, the park called for a series of distinctive contemporary office buildings individually nestled in the forest. Much of the land, including a creek and its associated flood plain (Indian Creek), would be preserved as a natural amenity.

Recognized today as a national model and a winner of numerous awards, Corporate Woods became the third catalyst for the emergence of an office corridor focused on College Boulevard.[25] The first two catalysts were the nearby community college campus and superb access and visibility provided by the parallel I-435 circumferential highway. Soon to follow Corporate Woods were the more modest Fox Hill and Executive Hills office parks and a series of small clusters and individual office and retail projects—all of which firmly established the corridor as a regional node and multiuse concentration of employment, shopping, and multifamily housing.

Corporate Woods remains the flagship of the College Boulevard corridor, with almost 2.4 million square feet of office space already completed and the capacity to build another 1 million. The entire College Boulevard corridor contains 13 million square feet of office space (both multitenant and owner-occupied, completed or under construction) and is zoned for an additional 4.7 million square feet. In addition to the office space that currently accommodates an estimated 50,000 employees, the corridor contains 1.5 million square feet of diverse retail space, over 3,000 hotel rooms, 8,200 multifamily units, a 600,000-square-foot trade center, a children's hospital, and a rehabilitation center.

Included in the inventory of existing office space in the College Boulevard corridor is the new 3.6 million-square-foot corporate headquarters and training complex of the Sprint telecommunications firm. Under construction and approximately half occupied, the complex is designed to accommodate up to 15,000 employees and is one of the largest corporate headquarters campuses under development in the world today.[26]

Access and Regional Impact

Seen within a larger context, the College Boulevard corridor anchors an even larger sector of the Kansas City region. Extending south from College Boulevard is the Metcalf Avenue corridor, which merges into the U.S. 69 highway corridor. The U.S. 69 corridor in turn intersects with 135th Street, which is emerging as a next-generation commercial corridor paralleling College Boulevard. Overall, the extension of the College Boulevard development pattern includes another 5.4 million square feet of nonresidential development. However, its character differs markedly from that of the early developments along College Boulevard in that about

The 3.6 million-square-foot Sprint telecommunications headquarters and training complex in the College Boulevard corridor almost constitutes a suburban business district in its own right.

half the space is retail and less than 1.5 million square feet is set aside for office use. Also included in the mix are two community hospitals totaling about 1 million square feet.

In addition to the office-focused development pattern of College Boulevard, it should be noted that extensive high-quality industrial space, primarily distribution and warehousing uses and flex space, is located just to the west of Overland Park and north of College Boulevard. Given that Overland Park's land use plan and regulations shunned industrial uses, the distribution and warehousing facilities are concentrated in the abutting communities of Lenexa and Olathe. Yet, when the combined office and industrial base in this southwest corner of the region is seen as a whole, it presents a picture of a dynamic economic engine comprising both office and industrial uses that contribute to the well-being of the greater region and the individual host communities.

Future Development Form

In view of the scale and mix of land uses and the quality of the labor force attracted to the College Boulevard corridor, the question arises, What is the future of the corridor over the next decades? Apparently, city and business leaders have yet to give this question much thought. With their attention focused almost exclusively on achieving the vision for today's College Boulevard corridor, the area's leaders have not considered the corridor's longer-range future, especially its capacity to add another 4.7 million square feet of office space, 235,000 square feet of retail uses, and 850 hotel rooms. On the near-term horizon is the completion of the massive Sprint complex and the development of a 550,000-square-foot subregional convention center and associated 400-room Sheraton Hotel. Further, the Metcalf/U.S 69 and 135th Street corridors are zoned for almost 9 million square feet of additional office and retail space.[27]

Another factor bearing on any planning for next steps is the growing community concern that the area's roadway system may be unable to handle the traffic associated with current development, much less the potential traffic associated with future development. Of particular concern is the imminent completion of the Sprint campus. The current climate of community concern over traffic congestion will prove pivotal not only in increasing overall development densities but also in responding to changing tenant demand. Through aggressive civic leadership and early commitment to strategic planning and place making, the community may provide strong support for the possible construction of a mass transit system to serve the suburban business district and the development of a mix of intensive land uses, including multifamily housing and the creation of a pedestrian-friendly "town center."

Lessons Learned

The College Boulevard-Overland Park suburban business district demonstrates, first, how to accommodate future growth through increased density and, second, how to translate a high standard of design excellence into the creation of place and a districtwide identity. Clearly, the district's strong form of government, relative affluence, and access to intellectual capital provide a solid foundation for formulating a strategic plan to tackle the problems of increasing congestion, particularly as College Boulevard-Overland Park lacks well-developed transit service.

Hence, the greatest challenge before the Kansas City region is to ensure a steady flow of investment capital to maintain and upgrade the quality of the district's office buildings and site infrastructure, along with its roads, lighting, pedestrian circulation, street trees, and parks and open spaces. In the interim, the region will have to adapt to higher levels of congestion and accommodate greater volumes of traffic even before it forges the political consensus necessary to address issues of transit provision and increased development density. The time-tested civic vision that has guided development for the past 30 years needs to be cast into a strategic plan for the transformation of this suburban business district.

Westport District—St. Louis, Missouri

The Westport District is located in the city of Maryland Heights in the heart of St. Louis

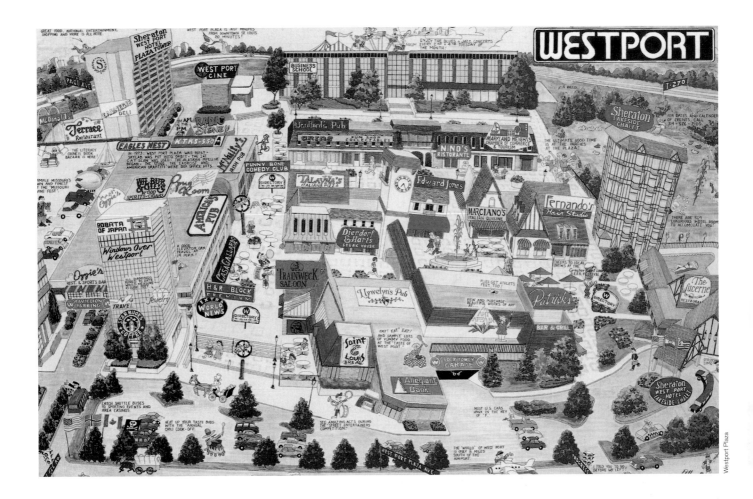

County (population 1 million) within the bistate St. Louis region, which is home to 2.6 million people.[28] Dating from the mid-1960s, the district has earned acclaim for its modern industrial park that is the product of several developers' efforts. The centerpiece of Westport is Westport Plaza, the St. Louis region's first suburban mixed-use development, with offices, a specialty retail "village," both a cinema and live theater, and two hotels, all sharing a common parking infrastructure. As the last phase in Westport's development, Westport Plaza made a major contribution to the creation of place and community life in this suburban business district.

Employment Growth and Development

The district grew dramatically through the 1970s and 1980s, stimulated primarily by the intersection of the I-270 circumferential highway in St. Louis County with Page Boulevard, a radial highway extending from the Mississippi River in downtown St. Louis 18 miles to the east and terminating at Westport. In aggregate, the district includes 2.8 million square feet of office space and 16 million square feet of industrial space, almost all in one-story structures and two-thirds of which would be classified as office, warehouse, or flex space.[29] Over half of the industrial space entered the market between 1965 and 1975 when the inventory reached 10 million square feet in 270 buildings. Since 1975, the inventory has increased steadily to a total of 450 industrial buildings encompassing 16 million square feet of industrial space. The development of office space lagged behind industrial growth for almost 15 years, with the 1980s accounting for construction of about 40 percent of the office inventory.

The primary developer and visionary of the Westport area was Thomas White, Sr., founder of the White Company. White, along with several partners, foresaw the development opportunities that would be created by the completion of the intersection of Page Boulevard and the circumferential interstate highway. In the first stage of development, White and partners literally

Westport Plaza in the Westport suburban business district in St. Louis functions as a mixed-use town center combining retail, entertainment, education, and residential uses that create a place for community life.

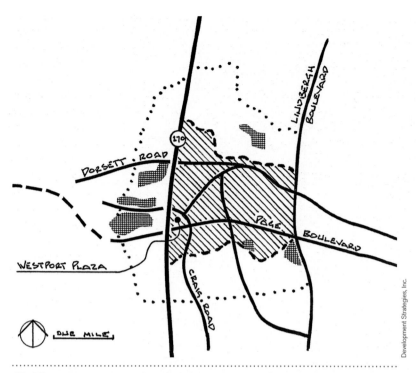

The Westport suburban business district covers approximately five square miles in and around its core that is bounded by I-270 on the west, Dorsett Road on the north, Lindbergh Boulevard on the east, and Page Boulevard on the south.

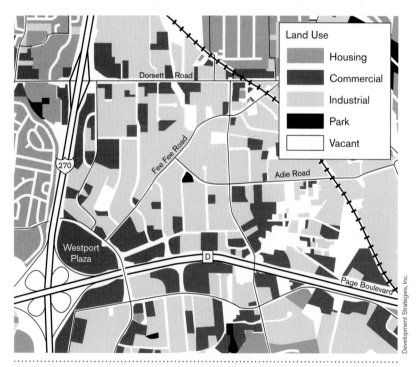

Land Use

Housing
Commercial
Industrial
Park
Vacant

The commercial uses within the Westport suburban business district are scattered, making it difficult to provide public transit service cost effectively. The town center of the suburban business district, Westport Plaza, is located at the interchange of I-270 and Page Boulevard.

"bought the farm" (actually three farms) through which the highway would pass and planned a multistage commercial/industrial development. Their strategy called for rapidly building up the area's employment base primarily by satisfying the needs of small to medium-sized distributors, wholesalers, and light manufacturers previously located in century-old multistory loft buildings in the urban core. The demand for primarily one-story, build-to-suit facilities tailored to the needs of each business was so strong that White sold a portion of his land inventory to another developer (the Linclay Corporation) to accelerate the pace of delivery.

The second stage of the Westport land development strategy was to build larger multistory, multitenant office buildings on prominent sites reserved along the Page/I-270 frontage. The result was the development of several Class A and near–Class A office buildings that provided a strong catalyst for a wide array of smaller build-to-suit and multitenant facilities, adding to an eventual inventory of almost 50 office buildings with 2.8 million square feet of space.

The Town Center and Multifamily Housing

The third phase was the fulfillment of the White Company's dream of a unique mixed-use complex to occupy Westport's most prominent site— 42 acres reserved at the northeast quadrant of the Page/I-270 interchange. It is Westport Plaza that gives the district its identity today. It concentrates 1 million square feet of space in five office buildings (the district's highest-value office space), two separate but commonly managed Sheraton Hotels with a total of 510 rooms (one a high-rise tower, the other a three-story, half-timbered lodge), a specialty shopping and entertainment center with 175,000 square feet of retail shops and 18 restaurants, a 1,000-seat multiscreen theater, and a 990-seat live theater.

The last part of the equation, which completes Westport (though not part of the White Company's original corporate strategy), is the array of multifamily developments at the periphery of the district. More than 4,700 multifamily units are located in 12 separate multifamily rental projects.

Development Strategies, Inc.

The detached housing shown on the west side of I-270 provides a useful comparison to the size of the superblock plat on which the commercial and industrial buildings have been constructed in the Westport suburban business district. The commercial buildings all exhibit large surface parking areas that increase the separation of buildings and make the environment pedestrian-unfriendly.

Light Industrial and Flex Space

A particularly interesting aspect of Westport is the extensive inventory of light industrial space, especially the large flex space component, which is widely regarded as the best place to incubate a business in the St. Louis region. The space is relatively inexpensive and flexible in the sense that many small buildings offer different sizes and configurations of space, along with various loading, parking, and visibility options. At the same time, though, some industrial users say that Westport is inadequate for their needs. In particular, bulk warehouse users find the Westport industrial buildings functionally obsolete. The structures are generally too small and lack needed ceiling heights; they are under 100,000 square feet with 18- to 24-foot-high ceilings versus the 26-foot minimum for contemporary buildings. Further limitations for some users

are the inability of the street system to meet the size and capacity requirements of today's trucks and the restricted amount and tight layout of on-site parking and loading space.[30]

Office Development

While Westport boasts several first-class office buildings that are well maintained and marketed by both national and local real estate firms, it has never emerged as a premier office address. Westport is a little too removed from the primary corridor of neighborhoods preferred by executives and managers. In addition, the industrial character of the larger Westport area detracts from the prestige expected by those willing to pay Class A office rents. The area's office buildings average less than 50,000 square feet of floor area versus the 100,000-square-foot minimum in the newer buildings along the I-64/U.S. 40 corridor to the southwest. Even so, Westport derives a significant market advantage with its proximity to Lambert International Airport.

Interstate Access

A major factor in considering the future of Westport is the potential impact of the opening of the Page Avenue Expressway. At present, this east/west arterial highway stops just beyond the interchange with I-270, although plans for its extension have been on the books for 30 years or more. Now, however, those plans are about to become a reality; construction has commenced on the link that will carry Page Avenue west as an expressway across the Missouri River to a connection with Route 94 in St. Charles County. Within a few years of completion of the connection to Route 94, the expressway will be extended farther west to tie directly into I-64 and, by extension, into I-70, the primary east/west highway in the central Midwest (connecting St. Louis to Kansas City and running from Philadelphia to Denver and beyond to San Francisco and Los Angeles).

Lessons Learned

The Westport suburban business district offers important lessons related to the quality of Westport Plaza and the anchor it provides for multi-family development. Without question, the district is a live-work-shop place that is affordable and complements Westport's employment incubation role. However, the challenges facing Westport relate to how the district will reconfigure its obsolete industrial space and evolve to take advantage of significant improvements in regional and national road access. Westport's evolution could follow any one of several potential scenarios.

- Westport could assume an even stronger role in regional business incubation and entrepreneurial activity given its outstanding access to nearby neighborhoods and the affordable housing stock of St. Charles County. Such housing is particularly well suited to the needs of young entrepreneurs and their families.
- Westport could expand its office inventory by redeveloping portions of the older low-density industrial products, thereby increasing the district's overall density of jobs.
- Westport could redevelop portions of the industrial inventory to accommodate expansion of the retail offerings, especially given the relative paucity of big-box operations on either Page Avenue or along the Olive Boulevard corridor to the south, although such retail expansion would likely result in a net reduction in the number of jobs in the district.
- Page Avenue could be reconfigured to accommodate a light-rail corridor, thereby suggesting the possibility of an overall increase in density to create a far more urban center, expanding on the mixed-use theme of Westport Plaza.

The preferred scenario is to transform the suburban business district's configuration, access, and mix of space to match the changing needs of business and the community.

Transforming to Meet Changing Tenant Needs

It is clear from the suburban business district examples that many aging suburban business districts occupy important positions in their respective metropolitan economies. Figure 5.3 summarizes the major role played by each suburban business district in its metropolitan region.

Reports issued by the Brookings Institution, as well as the above examples, clearly demonstrate the historic decentralization of metropolitan employment into fragmented and dispersed suburban business districts that cover extensive land areas of up to five square miles. Such business districts are by their nature neither compact nor walkable. They were built to meet the needs of an economy based on manufacturing and services rather than on information. That suburban business districts need to evolve in response to changing economic, tenant, and community needs is beyond question, but it is clear that not all parts of suburban business districts can or will need to develop into mixed-use town centers like Reston, Virginia.

figure 5.3 Comparative Data—Examples of Suburban Business Districts (SBD)

	Southfield, Detroit, Michigan	College Boulevard, Kansas City, Kansas/Missouri	Westport, St. Louis, Missouri
Metropolitan population	4.4 million	1.7 million	2.6 million
Host city population	79,000	150,000	24,000
Metropolitan employment (jobs)	2.24 million	1.00 million	1.32 million
SBD employment (jobs)	100,000	50,000	35,000
SBD as percent of metropolitan employment	4.5%	5%	3%
Area of suburban business district (square miles/acres)	4.5/2,900	5/3,200	4/2,500

	Commercial/Industrial Land Use (million square feet)		
	Southfield, Detroit, Michigan	College Boulevard, Kansas City, Kansas/Missouri	Westport, St. Louis, Missouri
Office	27.0	13.0	4.2
Industrial	NA	NA	16.0
Retail	2.4	1.5	0.3
Total	29.4	14.5	20.5
Hotel rooms	377+	3,000	510+
Multifamily	NA	8,200	6,700

Source: Richard Ward, Development Strategies, Inc., 2001.

Instead, it is most likely that live-work-shop places will be developed within suburban business districts and that such places will be linked by improved transit service. They will provide employees with wider choices than just a detached single-family home in the suburbs, a trip to the shopping mall at lunch hour, and a long commute. They will place greater emphasis on improved pedestrian linkages and the achievement of place-making standards beyond the realm of traditional zoning plans. Public agencies are likely to be called upon to become full financial partners in the transformation of suburban business districts. At the same time, the automobile, far from being abandoned as a mode of transportation, should be put in its proper place and become part of a balanced choice of transportation options. Limited government spending on infrastructure expansion and the proliferation of smart growth programs will severely curtail the practice of abandoning obsolete buildings for new greenfield development on the exurban fringe A more rational approach to growth will support the efforts of suburban business districts that wish to transform themselves to meet the needs of America's new demographics. Indeed, employers faced with a tight labor market will compete for the best employees by touting the quality of life that distinguishes the areas in and around their place of employment.

In the words of Neil Uebelein, general manager of Corporate Woods Office Park, "Most people create an idea and marry themselves to it. What Tom Congleton did was to create a principle and then reshape his ideas to reflect the market. . . ."[31] Herein lies the embodiment of sustainable development as suburban business districts transform themselves to meet changing tenant needs and demands.

Reston Town Center–Reston Suburban Business District

Reston Town Center is considered the heart of one of the most prominent master-planned communities in the United States. Its urban ambience has transformed the town center into a 24-hour central gathering place—a civic center where people go to the movies, dine in a restaurant, or enjoy a community event in the central plaza.

Reston is the product of Robert E. Simon, Jr., and his vision for an alternative to conventional suburban development. Its development began in 1963 on 7,400 acres of land 18 miles southwest of Washington, D.C., in Fairfax County, Virginia. Reston is now home to nearly 100,000 residents, 3,500 businesses, and almost 50,000 employees. The town center is an 85-acre component of a larger 460-acre mixed-use district identified in Reston's original 1962 master plan. The first phase of the town center, Fountain Square, includes 530,000 square feet of office space; 240,000 square feet of retail, restaurant, and entertainment space; and a 514-room Hyatt Regency Hotel. The centerpiece of Fountain Square is an open-air civic plaza featuring a large fountain, outdoor seating, artwork, and—in the winter—an ice-skating rink.

The development of Phases II and III, known as Freedom Square and Explorer Square, respectively, began in 1998 with the construction of One Freedom Square, an 18-story, 400,000-square-foot office and retail building. Completion of the two phases enhanced Reston Town Center's urban character by providing additional street-level retail uses and more office space. Together, Phases II and III consist of 1.6 million square feet of office space, 250,000 square feet of retail space, another premier 500-room hotel, 700 residential units, six acres of open space, and a four-acre park.

The residential components have been codeveloped by Reston-based Terrabrook and Atlanta-based Trammell Crow Residential and include Stratford at Reston Town Center, a 334-unit condominium community that began development in 1998. A second residential neighborhood at Explorer Square will feature 700 luxury rental apartments. At buildout, Reston Town Center will contain 1,034 residential units.

Unlike many other suburban business districts, Reston Town Center has distinguished itself as a vibrant place to live, work, and shop. It is as active in the evening as it is during the business day. Reminiscent of the main streets of a bygone era, Reston Town Center has become a regional destination for people looking to shop, eat, or spend leisure time.

Town Center

In 1981, recognizing that the Reston community soon would be large enough to support its own business district, Reston Land Corporation (RLC)—a subsidiary of Mobil Land Development Corporation and Reston's master developer from 1978 through 1996—initiated detailed planning for an 85-acre mixed-use district that would function as the community's urban core. The first section of Reston Town Center,

Fountain Square, an open-air civic plaza featuring a large fountain, outdoor seating, and–in winter–an ice-skating rink, is the centerpiece of Reston Town Center in Virginia.

Terrabrook

occupying 20 acres on the eastern end of the 85-acre urban core, opened in 1990. The mixed-use project includes twin 11-story office buildings; a 514-room Hyatt Regency Hotel with extensive conference facilities and an executive fitness center; street-level retail, restaurant, and entertainment uses with professional offices above; and surface and structured parking for more than 3,000 cars.

Terrabrook bought the future sections of Reston Town Center from RLC in 1996 and has been the master developer since that time. One Freedom Square, the first of six office towers in Phase II, was completed in fall 1999 and is home to Andersen Consulting (Accenture, as of January 1, 2001) and the prestigious law firms of Cooley Godward and Hale & Dorr. The 400,000-square-foot building is one of Reston's most visible landmarks.

As part of the approval process for Reston Town Center, RLC negotiated a shared-parking agreement with the local government in recognition of the mixed-use project's efficiencies, thereby reducing the parking requirement for the first section from 4,100 to 3,100 spaces. A transportation management association known as LINK also was formed to educate the public about transportation alternatives, refine regional transit systems' routing to the development, and advocate various demand-reduction strategies.

Traditional Neighborhood Design

The plan for Reston Town Center intentionally incorporated the characteristics of both urban and suburban development—pedestrian-scaled streets, a variety of land uses and services, open spaces, easy vehicular access, and ample parking. Custom-designed paving and benches complement the architecture and reinforce human-scale comfort and overall access. Large trees and seasonal planting beds vest the streets

The mixed-use buildings that comprise the Reston Town Center have retail and entertainment uses at street level with office, hotel, and residential uses above, which keeps the center active and busy outside office hours.

and plazas with a sense of liveliness and maturity. Streets and sidewalks are proportioned to balance spaciousness and ease of movement with an intimate, human scale. The sidewalks are wider on the sunny side of the street, and the roadway is narrow so that the pedestrians are encouraged to cross from one side of the street to another.

Reston Town Center's developers realized that a variety of retail storefronts would help create a vibrant pedestrian experience. Buildings were designed to accommodate a continuum of storefronts at the ground level of every building, with variations in setbacks, entrances, awnings, bay windows, and signage producing a recurring sense of surprise and the impression that the town has evolved over time. Reston Town Center has become a central gathering place for residents of Reston and surrounding communities. Innovative and attractive community amenities foster a sense of place. As the first of the amenities, the 5,400-

square-foot pavilion in Fountain Square is the setting for community concerts during the summer and ice skating in the winter. The second of the amenities, to be built by Terrabrook in a future phase, will be a 4,000-square-foot enclosed art gallery.

Regulatory Barriers

Reston Town Center could not move ahead without Fairfax County's approval for a rezoning. The process began in 1984, took approximately three years, and involved several revised submissions. RLC's initial rezoning request for the 460-acre town center district was for rights to develop 8.4 million square feet of commercial space and at least 1,400 residential units. The predominant issue was traffic. Negotiations led to the creation of a performance rezoning for a minimum of 6.8 million square feet of commercial space, including 5.5 million square feet of office space and 1,400 residential units. Up to 1.6 million square feet

continued on next page

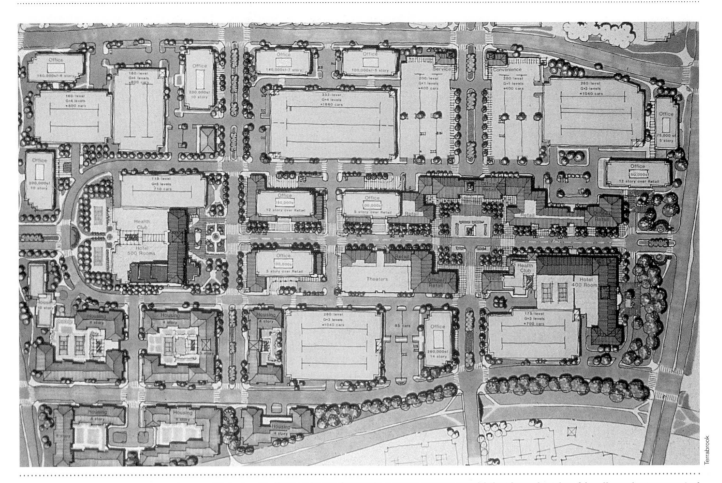

The plan for Reston Town Center is a compact street grid that is pedestrian-friendly and uncongested compared with the automobile-oriented supergrid layouts of other suburban business districts.

of additional office space will be permitted if traffic forecasts prove to be accurate and the project meets the developer's objectives for trip generation. Transportation proffers (developer-funded and -implemented improvements), including pavement and rights-of-way, are valued at $45 million.

Untested Market

The county initially was concerned that Reston Town Center's retail and residential components were too small and that the residential component was not sufficiently integrated with the commercial development. RLC committed to expanding the retail component (thereby reducing the office and/or hotel components) if demand proved sufficient. RLC also argued that

since Reston already had a strong and diverse residential base, the town center did not need to be self-sufficient. The county and RLC agreed to defer residential building in the remaining portions of the town center district until after the amenities necessary to support an urban lifestyle were in place.

A maximum of 3.47 million square feet of development is permitted in the 85-acre town center district, including 2.15 million square feet of office space, 315,000 square feet of retail space, and 1 million square feet of hotel space. The maximum floor/area ratio for the site is therefore 0.94; there is no density limit on specific parcels.

Timing is critical for a major mixed-use center. The density and mix of Reston Town

Center's first phase required the critical mass of population, employment, and income that Reston and the surrounding area had achieved by the late 1980s.

Lessons Learned

The lessons learned at Reston Town center are that it is important to define a project's market niche carefully and prepare a development plan accordingly. The market demand for space in a well-planned mixed-use development was found to be greater than that for space in a comparable single-use development. To keep a town center vibrant and give it a sense of place, entertainment uses as well as programmed cultural and recreational events are essential elements. ●

Notes

1. Judith Potwora, "Mann Says Culture, Transportation Keep In-town Hot," *Atlanta Business Chronicle,* April 9, 2001, p. 8.

2. Hugh F. Kelly, *2000 Landauer Real Estate Market Forecast* (New York: Landauer Realty Group, 1999), p. 6.

3. PricewaterhouseCoopers, *Emerging Trends in Real Estate 2001* (New York: PricewaterhouseCoopers and Lend Lease Real Estate Investments, 2000), p. 12.

4. Robert B. Bellinger, *The Case for Real Estate in an Investment Portfolio* (New York: Lend Lease Real Estate Investments, 2000), p. 8.

5. David J. O'Neill, *The Smart Growth Tool Kit* (Washington, D.C.: ULI—the Urban Land Institute, 2001), p. 124.

6. Dean Schwanke, *ULI 2001 Real Estate Forecast* (Washington, D.C.: ULI—the Urban Land Institute, 2001), p. 9.

7. Rebecca R. Sohmer et al., *Downtown Rebound* (Washington, D.C.: Fannie Mae Foundation and The Brookings Institution), p. 5.

8. Geoffrey Booth's discussions with Stephen Blank, ULI senior resident fellow in finance and author of ULI's *Capital Markets Update,* at ULI offices in Washington, D.C., July 17, 2001.

9. Robert E. Lang, *Office Sprawl: The Evolving Geography of Business* (Washington, D.C.: The Brookings Institution, 2000).

10. Ibid., p. 3.

11. Ibid., p. 5.

12. Ibid., p. 7.

13. Edward L. Glaeser et al., *Job Sprawl: Employment Location in U.S. Metropolitan Areas* (Washington, D.C.: The Brookings Institution, 2001).

14. Kenneth T. Jackson, *Crabgrass Frontier: The Suburbanzation of the United States* (New York: Oxford University Press, 1985), p. 256.

15. G. Bruce Douglas et al., "Urban Design, Urban Form, and Employee Travel Behavior" in *TRB Transportation and Planning Applications Conference Papers* (Washington, D.C.: U.S. Department of Transportation, 1997), p. 306.

16. Jo Allen Gause et al., *What Office Tenants Want: 1999 BOMA/ULI Office Tenant Survey Report* (Washington, D.C.: BOMA International and ULI–the Urban Land Institute, 1999), p. 20.

17. Kelly et al., *2000 Landauer,* p. 6.

18. Terry Holzheimer, *A Comparison of Office Growth in Transit-Served Edge Cities with the Growth of the More Suburban and Ex-urban Non Transit Locations in the Washington Metro Area* (Washington, D.C.: unpublished, 2000).

19. CB Richard Ellis, *Detroit Market Index Brief— 4th Quarter 2000* (Los Angeles: CB Richard Ellis, 2001), p. 2.

20. Douglas Ilka, "Northland Renaissance in the Works," *Detroit News,* April 12, 1996, p. 1.

21. Southfield Business Development Team, (248) 208-8080.

22. Consultant team led by LDR of Columbia, Maryland, together with Development Strategies for economic and real estate development and Harley Ellington Design for local design and planning input.

23. Richard Ward's interview with Donald J. Gross, city administrator (former director of planning), city of Southfield, March 15, 2001.

24. Richard Ward's interview with Mary Burch, president, Overland Park Chamber of Commerce, May 8, 2001.

25. Jim Davis, "Maturing Corporate Woods Still Breaking New Ground," *Kansas City Business Journal,* May 2, 1997, p. 4.

26. Richard Ward's interview with Robert Lindeblad, chief of current planning, Overland Park Department of Planning, May 8, 2001.

27. Compilation and assessment of data provided by the Overland Park Department of Planning.

28. St. Louis County does not include the city of St. Louis, which is a separate county with a population of 350,000.

29. Colliers Turley Martin Tucker, special tabulation from database, March 2001.

30. Richard Ward's interview with Steven J. Tharpe, principal of the Discovery Group, both a broker and investor/owner long active in Westport, May 18, 2001.

31. Davis, "Maturing Corporate Woods," p. 4.

chapter 6

Helping the Mall Meet Main Street

General Growth Properties owns or manages 147 shopping malls, totaling more than 116 million square feet of retail space across 39 states. Chief Executive Officer John Bucksbaum recently provided an insight into the future of mall retailing in America. "I believe the role of the department store will continue to diminish, the specialty store will continue to grow, entertainment will continue to expand, and non-retail uses will continue to populate the mall of the future. Consumers want more community and spirit in their malls. I believe the mall of the future will require different thinking from all of us."[1] The question is not how much retail floor space has grown in America but rather how much has grown obsolete. Suburban business districts grew around the enclosed shopping mall, many of which are now obsolete. Of America's approximately 1,800 shopping malls, PricewaterhouseCoopers found in its May 2001 study that 140 were obsolete and another 200 to 250 were at serious risk of obsolescence.[2]

The transformation of suburban business districts into live-work-shop places can throw a lifeline to America's shopping malls by creating a sense of place targeted at the needs and aspirations of America's new demographic. It requires, however, that both the big-box retailer and the enclosed shopping mall meet main street. At Morgan Stanley's Real Estate Conference in May 2001, the executives of America's three largest regional mall REITs, General Growth CEO John Bucksbaum, Simon CEO David Simon, and Taubman CEO and President Robert Taubman announced their plans to reinvent their property portfolio by focusing on indoor/outdoor malls.[3] Dean Schwanke, ULI's vice president for development trends and analysis, says, "[T]he move to strengthen shopping malls with the addition of a main street is an important trend as retailers like Talbots, Williams-Sonoma, and Restoration Hardware are looking to open new stores in nonmall environments. If your real estate asset includes both a mall and main street component, you can retain your tenants as they respond to the changing demographic needs of their market. In this way the property owner maximizes his rental income stream and diversifies the retail offering at that location."

For Talbots, Inc., an apparel retailer, 20 percent of its 750 stores are in nonmall locations, up from less than 10 percent three years ago, and the company is aiming for 30 to 35 percent in main streets and town centers by 2004. Schwanke, who organizes ULI's annual Place-Making Conference, says, "We can also expect to see the acceleration of the trend toward opening up existing shopping malls to natural light—

the creation of main streets under glass—which retain the all-weather advantages of shopping malls but create that sense of place demanded by America's changed demographic profile and achieve energy savings into the bargain."[4]

The changing nature of America's demographic profile is also evident in changing retail store hours. There are now 237 Home Depots, 1,298 Wal-Marts, and four Staples office supply stores that literally never close—they represent the arrival of the 24/7 retailing environment. Before 1995, no Home Depot store was 24/7. Kramerbooks in the Dupont Circle area of Washington, D.C., is open 24 hours on weekends and posts 10 percent of its sales between midnight and dawn. Shoppers in the 21st century are now more likely to make retail purchases as part of a recreational, entertainment, or dining excursion; thus, to make the sale, the shop must be open at the time the consumer wants to make the purchase. David Scholl, senior vice president of Phoenix-based retail owner/developer Westcor, says, "A lot of this is tied to the baby-boomer segment, people in their mid-40s to late 50s . . . their days of buying toys for their kids are over. Now they're looking for special experiences in life—in vacations, dining, entertainment—and shopping."[5]

The 1990s witnessed a dramatic decline in the number and frequency of shopping trips as well as a reduction in the duration of stay in shopping malls. Few people are likely to take their partners for a romantic evening at the shopping mall food court, but they are likely to seek out main street restaurants that allow them to watch the passing parade and extend the enjoyment of the interlude with some special shopping, a theatrical performance, or some time in the bookshop. With more Americans eating out and more of their lives revolving around their work and leisure activities, Paris Rutherford, vice president of RTKL Associates, believes that the demand for main streets and town centers is being driven by America's social and consumer trends. "Today we are attempting to reproduce those earlier models where the street was the center of activity for a community—a bustling urban environment combining shopping with office, housing, civic, and cultural uses."[6] The successful transformation of suburban business districts will depend on their ability to integrate mixed-use, pedestrian-, and transit-friendly development forms that reestablish the subliminal patterns of repeat visitation that once guaranteed their market preeminence.

The Importance of Retail Development to Suburban Business Districts

The subliminal habit of repeat visitation is a powerful force in the retention and growth of retail market share. Some refer to repeat patronage as brand loyalty. In essence, it works on the premise that once a shopper develops a pattern or habit of shopping with satisfaction in one center, it will take either an unpleasant experience (more likely a series of unpleasant experiences) or a significantly improved experience at another shopping center to supplant that subliminal habit of repeat visitation. In his July 25, 2001, *Wall Street Journal* report, Dean Starkman highlighted behavior now typical of American shoppers. "Wanda Dvorak, a middle-school teacher, needed a pair of shoes. She could have driven to the big air-conditioned Oak Park Mall, about 20 minutes away, but opted instead for the slightly closer Town Center Plaza. There she parked her car about 30 feet from the front door of the Nine West shoe store, walked along a brick path under green awnings, past a spray of orange day lilies

Shoppers in the 21st century are more likely to make their purchases as part of a recreational, entertainment, or dining excursion. Pictured here is 2 Rodeo Drive in Beverly Hills, California.

and big potted shrubs and went inside where she picked up a fashionable pair of mules. It was pleasant and it was fast. 'You can never find a space [at the mall]; you have to park in Timbuktu,' Ms. Dvorak said. 'Then you have to walk all over the mall. . . . It's a pain. . . . The Town Center Plaza has trees, bricks, flowers,' she adds. 'It's got great curb appeal.'"[7]

It is generally easier for an existing shopping center to increase its market share by offering its customers a greater range of goods and experiences than to hold its retail offering constant and seek to poach new customers from its competitors. This explains why shopping center owners are adding main streets to their malls—not to do so invites their tenants and their customers to take their business elsewhere. Access is also an important ingredient in the retail equation. The shopping center that provides easy access and convenience is likely to enjoy a competitive advantage over the more remote, less accessible shopping center. Thus, until the second half of the 20th century, the central business districts of U.S. cities were the nation's major shopping centers. From the 1960s on, the situation changed rapidly as the suburban shopping center evolved through its various forms into the prototypical department-store–anchored, climate-controlled, regional shopping mall surrounded by acres of surface parking and located at the interchange of two interstate highways. This is the seed that germinated into many of today's suburban business districts.

In *City Center to Regional Mall,* Richard Longstreth described how the enclosed shopping mall set the form and character of America's suburban business districts ". . .[R]etail development is a key indicator of urban form and identity. . . [It is clear that] no other single component of the city attracts so many people so frequently and for so many reasons. No other more frankly reveals current attitudes toward public assembly and decorum. No other clearly reflects change in both market conditions and consumer taste. No other embodies more fully the unyielding impact of motor vehicles on the landscape. . . ."[8]

In 1925, Robert E. Wood, Sears's vice president in charge of factories and retail stores, noted

Main streets afford the shopper a greater variety of sensory experiences by using built and natural forms, sculpture, and color in a configuration that invites exploration and enjoyment. In this photograph of Valencia Town Center Drive in California, even the movement of cars up and down the street combines with the configuration of the streetscape and the street's sound system to provide an environment that generates repeat visitation and retail sales.

that motor vehicle registrations were outstripping the parking space available in the central city. At his instigation, Sears built its new "A" stores in low-density areas that commanded lower rents. In addition, the low-density areas provided adequate parking and, because of rising automobile ownership, were well within the reach of potential customers.[9] In the nation's downtowns, the foot traffic generated by department stores had long underwritten the retail sales of specialty retailers. However, once the department stores relocated to the suburbs, specialty retailers had to follow their customers. In the second half of the 20th century, the suburbanization of U.S. cities accelerated as the following conditions converged:

- universal car ownership;
- affordable suburban housing;
- plentiful and low-cost gasoline; and
- rapid construction of urban freeways and the interstate highway system.

Traffic congestion and declining standards of transit service meant that the central city was no

The Shopping Center Formula

The enclosed shopping mall layout followed a standard pattern, with department store anchors built at either end of a pedestrian mall lined with specialty shops. The specialty shops paid higher rents and occupancy costs that subsidized the lower-rent–paying but customer-generating department stores. The center was an enclosed, air-conditioned, all-weather environment. Unlike downtown shoppers, mall shoppers were segregated from vehicular movement and traffic congestion. The surrounding parking lot ensured separation from competing centers and adjoining sites and maximized tenant and customer capture and retention. The entry points from the parking lot into the mall were limited and strategically located to maximize sales and duration of stay. Inside the mall, developers made significant investments to create a stimulating and irresistible environment as reflected in the following marketing jingle: "Pacific Fair, Pacific Fair, there's a whole world of shopping there. A trip away, each shopping day, is waiting there, at Pacific Fair."

Clearly, the nation's new shopping malls conveyed a message of affordability—with

The aerial photograph of Valencia Town Center Mall, California, before the construction of Town Center Drive shows the standard shopping mall layout–a standalone building surrounded by parking lots.

Newhall Land and Farming Company

the price of goods not inflated to cover the cost of an architectural masterpiece. In the postwar era, consumers were interested in "value-for-money" acquisition of goods. It was the merchandise that was important, not the quality of the building where it was sold. Those department stores that had invested their capital in downtown flagship

longer central, or, more important, accessible to a wide range of customers. As downtowns grew progressively congested, pedestrian-vehicle conflicts and declining air quality made the shopping experience far less appealing. In contrast, the suburbs' retail environment offered a pleasant shopping experience. Cheaper land allowed the provision of adequate on-site parking in surface lots and the clustering of shops around a mall free from pedestrian-vehicle conflicts. By anchoring each end of the mall with a department store, specialty retailers could line up on either side of the connecting space and benefit from the tide of shoppers washing up and down the pedestrian route linking the anchors. The

advent of air conditioning allowed the malls to be roofed and designed as all-weather retailing environments. The surrounding surface parking areas, if large enough, prevented leakage of either tenants or customers to adjoining developments. Thus, retail sales could be maximized, and rents increased as the capital value of the real estate asset ballooned. With road capacity to burn and a highway design standard that allowed high-speed automobile travel, the arterial roads providing access to shopping malls dramatically increased the malls' market penetration into the surrounding region. As penetration increased, so too did the new shopping malls' prospects for growth.

buildings eventually watched their market share and capital value erode. They had no choice but to follow their market and relocate to the suburbs in building forms and configurations that were comparatively inexpensive and functional but hardly masterpieces of civic design or rich with a sense of place. From the late 1980s through the 1990s, the big-box retailers, off-price outlets, power centers, and "price club" stores took the no-frills retail format to the extreme. But all these developments lacked aesthetic appeal, community identity, a sense of place, and the integration of public domain and public spaces–the essential elements of community building. The new-breed retail projects such as Valencia Town Center in California and Washingtonian Center in Maryland build on the success of the shopping mall and big-box retailing formulas by adding a sense of place and community-building elements so as to align their offerings with the needs and aspirations of America's new demographic profile. These projects are the new retail formulas that will play a major role in the transformation of suburban business districts. ●

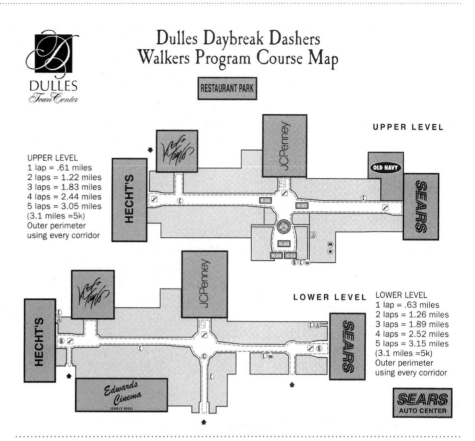

Dulles Daybreak Dashers Walkers Program Course Map

DULLES
Town Center

RESTAURANT PARK

UPPER LEVEL

UPPER LEVEL
1 lap = .61 miles
2 laps = 1.22 miles
3 laps = 1.83 miles
4 laps = 2.44 miles
5 laps = 3.05 miles
(3.1 miles =5k)
Outer perimeter
using every corridor

LOWER LEVEL

LOWER LEVEL
1 lap = .63 miles
2 laps = 1.26 miles
3 laps = 1.89 miles
4 laps = 2.52 miles
5 laps = 3.15 miles
(3.1 miles =5k)
Outer perimeter
using every corridor

SEARS
AUTO CENTER

Dulles Town Center in Loudoun County, Virginia, follows a standard dumbbell form with department stores located at each end of an enclosed pedestrian-only mall lined with specialty shops. Entry and exit points to the mall are carefully placed to ensure that shoppers are exposed to the maximum number of specialty stores as they stroll to and from the department store anchors.

The same regional access that created retail opportunities also offered a competitive advantage for office development, particularly for firms competing for a regionally distributed, often highly educated, and mobile labor force. Although office development in and around shopping malls tended to lag behind retail development by a decade or so, such development transformed mall areas into suburban business districts of which Tysons Corner, Virginia; South Coast Plaza, Orange County, California; and Perimeter Center in Atlanta are prominent examples. Over time, the addition of substantial amounts of office space altered the retail mix. Business services, convenience-oriented retail,

and restaurants emerged as office-serving amenities.

Strong office concentrations also generated hotel demand. For their part, business visitors drove an additional increment of demand for certain types of retail uses, notably eating and drinking establishments. The strongest of these concentrations, by virtue of both their overall retail mass and their breadth, emerged as the dominant retail hubs in their respective regions, and many became proving grounds for further innovation in retail format and concepts.

Today, worsening traffic congestion, favorable demographics, and an increasing preference for urban living have combined to make moderate-

The internal environment of the shopping mall is controlled and predictable. However, the level of natural light is on the increase in enclosed shopping malls with the use of glass roofs that bring the outside indoors to make the mall environment feel more natural. Pictured is Tysons Galleria in Fairfax County, Virginia.

to high-density housing resurgent in many of today's suburban business districts. Increasingly, office location decisions favor those locations with appropriate nearby housing. This trend will also play a major role in the transformation of retail development within suburban business districts.

The Impact of the Standalone Big-Box Suburban Retailer

In the 1980s and 1990s, a range of standalone, big-box, value-oriented mass merchants moved into large, low-rent, nonshopping mall locations in the suburbs. In large part, substantial investments in information technology precipitated the moves. For example, Wal-Mart, the first retailer to employ automated distribution systems and electronic data interchange with suppliers, innovated continuously through the 1970s and 1980s. By the mid-1990s, the chain was one of the nation's largest purchasers of information technology. Technology innovation, which ultimately found widespread use among the big boxes, was a response to a perceived shift in consumer orientation toward value. The pursuit of

ever-lower prices required the most efficient operation possible and, in turn, led to larger and larger stores in low-cost locations. The debut of the big boxes was primarily a suburban phenomenon driven by value and low suburban land costs.

This trend had two important implications for suburban business districts. First, it meant that the suburbs experienced an invasion of big boxes and power-center formats that dramatically altered the perceptions of land use and density and exacerbated the challenges of traffic congestion and circulation within suburban business districts. Second, the big boxes and power centers posed formidable competition to the dominant regional mall format. Many of the new merchants generated sales per square foot as high as $1,500 per year, significantly outclassing the $250 to $300 sales per square foot per year generated in traditional mall stores. Because the inventory of retail space in most markets was growing substantially faster than demand, the upshot was a decline in rents, increases in vacancy, and the functional obsolescence of existing retail space, much of which was less than a decade old.

Standalone big-box retailers like this Lowe's home improvement store in White Marsh, Maryland, consume extensive areas of land for single-level stores and surrounding surface parking lots. The latter impede pedestrian movement and work against shared parking.

The Golden Ring Mall in Baltimore, one of several hundred obsolete malls in the United States. An alternative strategy to demolition is to create a main street connecting to the mall while introducing multi-family housing and mixed uses to reinvigorate the development.

Indeed, the relatively short shelf life of retail concepts and formats has been a hallmark of the retail landscape for the past 15 years. In a race for market share, the big boxes continually refine the model, often leading to closures of relatively new stores. From the perspective of those planning and managing suburban business districts, this dynamism comes at great cost. The land use implications are disproportionate. The loss of a single business may leave a dramatic impact on individual retail property investments. The long-term vacancy of retail premises can undermine the interconnectivity of the aggregate retail offering within the suburban business district.

So what becomes of the traditional formats? Regional and super regional malls are very much alive; most did not stand by idly as the big boxes emerged. They have, however, sought to differentiate themselves by introducing new merchandising strategies; by adding innovative uses, particularly entertainment-oriented uses; and by responding to the demands of the changing demographics of their market areas. Where the formula was once driven mainly by household purchasing patterns of nonworking suburban women, malls today must respond to a completely different customer mix, including nearby office workers, time-scarce families, burgeoning suburban minority populations, and visitors craving diversion and new entertainment experiences.

The Transformation of Retail Development in Suburban Business Districts

Traffic congestion poses the greatest threat to the future prosperity of suburban business districts. Traditional Euclidean zoning—with its separate districts for each land use and relatively low density of overall development—and the suburbs' lack of transit options have combined to increase dependence on the automobile while choking local streets and highways. In addition, the nature of contemporary development finance and leasing, which depends heavily on past performance of comparable projects, has resulted in a relatively homogeneous and predictable retail pattern. Despite the emergence of new formats and ongoing efforts to diversify the re-

tail mix in shopping malls, the public perceives retail projects as largely similar regardless of the distinguishing characteristics of a given region. The transformation of the shopping mall assets through new entertainment uses and the use of "street retail" formats such as main streets and mixed-use town centers allows these retail assets to keep pace with the needs and aspirations of America's new demographic profile.

Street Retail

The reemergence of street retail as an innovative development strategy dates to the mid-1990s. It was a competitive strategy—a niche play— in an era when large amounts of real estate investment capital had bid up the price of conventional shopping center product and creative retail developers sensed that the interests of both markets and tenants might align. This period also coincided with a more entertainment-rich

The Retail Market Outlook

As it enters the current slowdown, the retail real estate sector may not be overbuilt, but it is burdened by an oversupply of obsolete space. The department stores anchoring the suburban shopping malls have experienced a significant decline not only in retail sales but also in market share. Montgomery Ward, Bradlees, Heilig-Meyers (furniture), and Pathway are just some of the chains that went into Chapter 11 in 2000. It was reported that Neiman Marcus Group, Inc., failed to meet its most recent quarterly earnings estimate. Federated Department Stores, Inc., lowered its sales numbers for May and then said that, because of even lower sales, the company may not even meet its revised expectations. Sears announced that it would close selected stores across the country.

Traditional mall-based specialty shops such as Talbots, Williams-Sonoma, Crate and Barrel, Banana Republic, Urban Outfitters, and Old Navy have joined Restoration Hardware, Starbucks, and the big

booksellers such as Borders and Barnes & Noble in the pursuit of streetfront or main street locations in suburban business districts offering a full live-work-shop experience in pedestrian-oriented concentrations. Target, Kohl's, and Galyan's Sporting Goods have pioneered big-box retailing on main street in the Peterson Group's Washingtonian Center in Gaithersburg, Maryland, and, in the current weak economic climate, have increased their sales.

The *ULI 2001 Real Estate Forecast* reported, "Many retailers are looking to expand, but in a selective way and combined with closings of less profitable stores. They are giving serious consideration to location choices because of cannibalization of their other stores. Thus, many retailers will likely use a strategy of taking two steps forward and one step back, opening new stores while closing unprofitable ones." Grocery stores locating in compact suburban business districts are, in view of strong demographics, considered good

investments. The most promising sectors for retail development, according to the ULI survey, are urban mixed-use properties and mixed-use town centers.

In light of current trends, a strong hedging strategy for major shopping malls that anchor suburban business districts is to develop a main street entry that provides tenants and shoppers with a mix of retail locations and experiences as well as with infill housing and a transit facility. The Valencia Town Center in California and The Mall of Georgia in Atlanta have used the main street approach with considerable financial success. The smart money is being drawn to the market created by America's changing demographic profile. ●

Source: Adapted in part from Dean Schwanke, *ULI 2001 Real Estate Forecast* (Washington, D.C.: ULI–the Urban Land Institute, 2001) and Jules A. Marling, ed., *Real Estate Report–First Quarter 2001* (Chicago: Real Estate Research Corporation, 2001).

brand of retail development that attracted significant attention nationwide.

Street retail attempts to marry the diversity and richness of a traditional shopping street with the proven virtues of centralized leasing and management. Two distinct approaches have emerged. The first targets existing urban and older suburban neighborhood retail districts, assembles a combination of sites and buildings, and crafts a retail mix that usually brings together proven national tenants with local restaurants, business and personal services, and other uses. The second approach is greenfield development, or wholesale redevelopment of existing low-density suburban development.

Through its subsidiary Street Retail, Inc., Federal Realty Investment Trust has been involved with both types of street retail. Howard Biel, who for many years led Federal Realty's street-level business, notes that while the initiative had many seeds, an important early driver was key tenants who saw streetfront retail as a way to tap strong underserved markets by offering an innovative product. These tenants recognized that, with the addition of the right tenants, the strategy was feasible. The economics were also favorable, particularly the prospect of lower total occupancy costs as tenants escaped the high common-area management charges of malls and the control exerted by mall manage-

ment over store trading hours. Federal's first efforts focused on individual buildings and relatively large-scale tenants, including the redevelopment of the old Woolworth store on the main street in affluent Greenwich, Connecticut, as a Saks Fifth Avenue. After its initial success, the company moved to larger-scale efforts involving multiple properties or multiple blocks as a means of capturing an additional increment of value added. Federal's projects tend to be located in fairly densely settled, close-in suburban districts, such as Manayunk, a historic neighborhood outside Philadelphia, or Bethesda Row in Bethesda, Maryland, just outside Washington, D.C.

Federal Realty's latest project, Pentagon Row, is a mixed-use retail and residential infill project in Pentagon City, a suburban business district in Arlington, Virginia, that includes a Metro rail station, multifamily residential apartments, and one of the Simon Group's most successful regional malls, Fashion Center at Pentagon City. Federal's intention is to use the residential population to give the project extended retailing hours, moving it beyond the typical suburban business district's weekday 9:00-to-5:00 operation. Federal Realty plans to push the mixed-use envelope by undertaking an even larger project—the transit-oriented Lindberg Center in Atlanta that will include the 900,000-

113

The incorporation of urban entertainment destinations into suburban business districts has been prompted by a desire to protect and enhance the districts' real estate value. By extending operating hours to a more urban 24/7 operation, owners can work real estate assets harder and increase sales. Pictured is the Edwards Entertainment Center on Town Center Drive, Valencia, California.

square-foot Bell South Towers. Howard Biel makes the important point that street retail is inherently more complex than conventional retail approaches and suggests that future successes will occur only in those environments that "demonstrate an unambiguous political will to understand and underwrite main street repositioning, re-merchandising, redevelopment, and ongoing marketing."[10]

Urban Entertainment Destinations

Such was the level of interest in urban entertainment at the end of the 1990s that one of the most significant real estate growth sectors was seminars and conferences devoted to the topic. The field was so fast-paced that the Urban Land Institute published a second, updated edition of its *Developing Urban Entertainment Centers* a mere two years after the book's initial publication.[11] Each new trend, it seemed, was quickly supplanted by the next. The "black box" (the movie theater) was replaced by theme restaurants, then megaplex cinemas, then live entertainment venues. By 2000, the shakeout in the cinema business and the theme restaurant business suggested that the silver bullet approach

would never succeed. Reliance on a formulaic approach is not a recipe for success. Most successes in the urban entertainment field involve a complex mix of activities—a blend of commercial and civic activities, a rich sense of place, a regionally appropriate and resonant design, and activities demanded by the market.

The incorporation of urban entertainment destinations into suburban business districts has been prompted by a desire to protect and enhance the districts' real estate value. By extending hours from the weekday nine-to-five business cycle to a more urban 24-hour/seven-day operation, owners and operators can work real estate assets harder and increase sales. Similarly, extending the range of services and experiences offered by suburban business districts makes the districts attractive live-work-shop environments, creating a memorable place, a critical mass of human activity, and a subliminal habit of repeat visitation.

New Approaches in Suburban Business Districts

Suburban business districts once stood at the pinnacle of the free market. Their success was at least in part predicated on their ability to grow and develop in a relatively unencumbered regulatory environment. As a consequence of zoning ordinances' provisions and intent, the shopping centers in these districts tended to relate less to their surroundings and instead functioned as large, freestanding, relatively independent projects that competed for shoppers' attention. Office buildings were developed in a similar freestanding fashion. The result is familiar: the lack of any cohesion or continuity, a terribly inefficient infrastructure pattern, unremitting traffic woes, and frustrated consumers.

Increasingly, suburban districts are availing themselves of the tools long familiar in American downtowns, where fragmented property ownership and the lack of unified management often created a competitive disadvantage vis-à-vis the suburbs. Now, ironically, some suburbs are turning to special-assessment districts, business improvement districts, tax-increment financing, and other tools associated with downtown management. The motivation, of course,

is the threat of declining market share. In effect, suburban business districts are fighting the same outward migration of retail sales that they themselves hastened in earlier decades. The examples of Country Club Plaza, Uptown Houston, Valencia Town Center, and the Washingtonian Center show how four different suburban business districts are leveraging their existing assets to expand their market share and reinforce their customers' subliminal habit of repeat visitation.

Country Club Plaza—Embracing a Public/Private Partnership

In 1997, the city council of Kansas City ratified the creation of a tax-increment financing district to support a $240 million redevelopment program for Country Club Plaza. The plaza began development in the 1920s and has remained under the ownership of the J.C. Nichols Company since then. The name Country Club Plaza refers to both the centrally managed retail component as well as to a surrounding suburban

The use of a $240 million tax-increment financing package has allowed Country Club Plaza in Kansas City to provide structured parking, public amenities, and streetscape improvements to ensure that this model suburban business district continues to meet customer needs and protects the city's tax base.

business district. The shopping center and district currently encompass about 1 million square feet of diverse retail space, 2.4 million square feet of office space, 700 hotel rooms, and just over 7,000 housing units. The plaza, which has received the Urban Land Institute's Heritage Award, has influenced several generations of developers and planners and remains a national model of suburban business district development. Well before the mid-20th century, the plaza supplanted downtown Kansas City as the region's premier shopping district. Since then, it has reinforced its position at the top of the market by drawing and retaining nationally and regionally exclusive retailers such as Saks Fifth Avenue, Mark Shale, Polo/Ralph Lauren, Armani A/X, and others. Office, hotel, and residential projects also perform at or near the top of the market.

Adapting to a Changing Market

In the past several years, however, the plaza started to face serious competitive pressure on many fronts. In a pattern experienced by most of the nation's downtown areas, much of the market erosion stemmed from the ongoing dispersion of population and income—in this case, to the southern and western portions of metropolitan Kansas City. In 1996, Leawood Town Center, a 750,000-square-foot open-air center, opened in Johnson County, Kansas, ten miles from Country Club Plaza. Leawood, anchored by Jacobsen's and specialty stores Pottery Barn and Galyan's Sporting Goods as well as by a 20-screen AMC cinema, drew several upscale tenants that previously had only one location—the plaza. In late 1996, Nordstrom, which had been eyeing the Kansas City market for several years, announced plans to open the region's first store. While the J.C. Nichols Company had been in discussions with Nordstrom over the years, the Seattle retailer decided to locate in Oak Park Mall, a middle-market mall in suburban Johnson County. In addition to the 200,000-square-foot Nordstrom anchor, the mall was expanding to accommodate an additional 50,000

The inherent strength of Country Club Plaza in Kansas City lies in its mix of retail, entertainment, residential, and office uses, all of which are provided within a compact and aesthetically pleasing pedestrian- and transit-friendly environment.

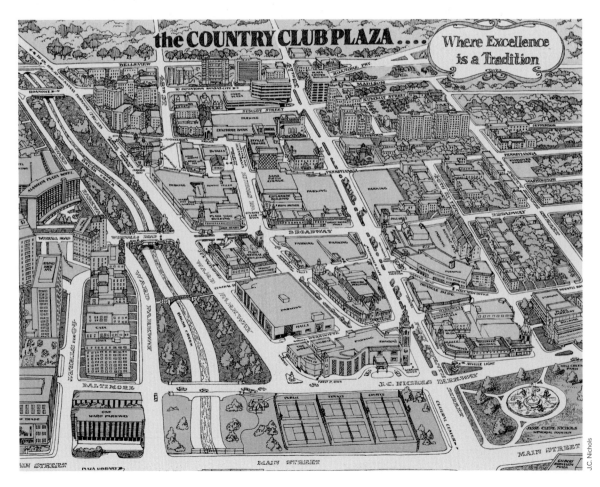

square feet of new specialty retailers. Reportedly, to secure the project, the county offered Nordstrom and Oak Park significant financial incentives in the form of tax abatements and infrastructure improvements.

Office vacancy increased sharply in Country Club Plaza from 1994 to 1995, moving from 9.8 to just over 16 percent. A number of new suburban buildings had opened with larger floor plates and significantly lower rental rates. Apartment occupancies also fell—from 96 to 93 percent even while the rest of the market saw gains of one to two percentage points. Like prospective office tenants, apartment renters shopping the plaza generally were deterred by older product and higher rental rates.

Retail sales at the plaza, after growing at rates of 3.9 and 5.3 percent in the previous two years, fell by 2.4 percent in 1996 as the regional economy surged. In late 1996, the J.C. Nichols Company, with new leadership and a new sense of urgency, set out to restore the plaza to its once-dominant position. The company's resulting strategy involved five key components as follows:

- expand the competitive offerings of the plaza's retail core by expanding and renovating the anchor stores;
- reposition the weaker components and re-tenant with an eye toward the ever-stronger visitor market;
- drive additional demand by providing new office, residential, and hotel product in the surrounding district;
- embark on a program of public amenities and streetscape improvements to enhance the publicly owned streets and sidewalks in the plaza district; and
- dramatically expand the supply of parking.

The Need for a Public/Private Partnership

The estimated cost of the redevelopment project totaled $240 million, about $58 million of which was for parking structures and public amenities. The only hitch in the plans was the cost associated with expansion of the structured parking. Both the lack of land needed for surface parking and the plaza's overall design theme made structured parking a necessity. Further,

the plaza had long acceded to retailers' demands for free parking. In view of these conditions, the capital and operating cost burden reduced the expected return on equity in the redevelopment plan to levels below that demanded by investors. But all was not lost. Missouri's aggressive tax-increment financing (TIF) statute allows projects that meet certain community development criteria to finance selected capital costs through future tax revenue streams. Kansas City had several TIF districts already in place. In the case of the plaza, though, the initial public reaction to the TIF proposal was one of incredulity —first, that the plaza was in any type of financial trouble and, second, that a public redevelopment tool usually associated with blighted neighborhoods would play a major role in the development's recovery.

Despite initial public resistance, the TIF commission, its staff, and the city council, along with the school district and other interested parties, eventually came to support the creation of a TIF district for the plaza. Simply put, the compelling argument was the documented market erosion and the clear demonstration that, without tax-increment financing, the strategic plan for redevelopment would not be implemented, the plaza's competitive position would continue to erode, and the city would lose tax revenue not only to a neighboring county but also to a neighboring state. The TIF district gained approval in May 1997, and construction on a new office and retail building, the first of several redevelopment projects, began in early 1998. With the new building, the Nichols Company won the bidding for a significant regional insurance company headquarters that likely would have otherwise relocated to Johnson County. In addition, encouraged by the strategic plan, several new retail establishments and restaurants have signed leases.

Lessons Learned

Despite the fact that Country Club Plaza is a pedestrian-friendly suburban business district that benefits from a predominantly single-ownership management structure, it is clear that to maintain its market position it had to keep its retail, office, and multifamily offerings fresh and its rental rates competitive. To stay in tune with the shifting demographic structure of its trade area, it had to provide greater convenience in the form of additional parking facilities. Financial inducements and support offered to competing centers by a neighboring county meant that a public/private partnership complete with TIF financing was essential to the transformation of Country Club Plaza. The plaza has maintained its patrons' subliminal habit of repeat visitation and thereby its market dominance into the 21st century.

Uptown Houston—Breaking Up the Superblock to Maintain Regional Competitiveness

The rapidly expanding Houston regional market provides ample opportunities for growth in the retail sector. However, much of the new demand is generated in Houston's expanding suburban ring. One suburban area of note is Uptown Houston, Houston's hub for high-end and luxury retail merchandise. The 2 million-square-foot Galleria Shopping Center, located in Uptown Houston, not only boasts a loyal local following but also enjoys an international reputation developed over the past 30 years. Despite the proliferation of new retail projects farther outside the city, Uptown Houston has so far retained its market position as a retail destination. However, by 1998, limited access, traffic congestion, and other issues were beginning to undermine the appeal of Uptown Houston as a convenient place to shop. The perception of *inconvenience* was threatening to erode Uptown's market share.

Starting with a freestanding Dillard's store in 1963, retail space in Uptown had grown by the late 1990s to include more than 3.4 million square feet in shopping centers, plus an estimated 600,000 square feet in freestanding space. Much of the space is concentrated in the 2.1 million-square-foot Galleria, with five major high-end department stores and 300 smaller shops. Other notable projects include Pavilion on Post Oak (286,000 square feet), Post Oak Shopping Center (201,000 square feet), and Center on Post Oak (182,000 square feet). Uptown

added almost 500,000 square feet of shopping center space between 1990 and 1998.

Reducing the Vacancy Rate and Increasing Market Share

While retail vacancy rates in Uptown Houston fell from 7 percent in 1990 to 5.5 percent by 1993, the addition of new retail space drove the vacancy rate up to almost 10 percent by 1998. Retailers and property owners saw increasing competition from projects with better market access as a probable factor in forcing up Uptown's vacancy levels. In 1997, Uptown captured about $1.8 billion of the $51.5 billion in *total* retail sales generated in the Houston Consolidated Metropolitan Statistical Area (CMSA). Uptown's market share had peaked at about 4.4 percent of metropolitan sales during the 1980s as consumers with rapidly rising incomes sought the upscale merchandise offered by Uptown's stores. Uptown's share then declined to 2.7 percent during the 1991–1992 recession. By the mid-1990s, Uptown had regained some of its lost market share, which had stabilized at around 3.5 percent.

In 1998, the Harris County Improvement District No. 1, also known as Uptown Houston, began planning a dramatic series of access and mobility improvements for the district. Analyses completed at the time clearly showed how the outward progression of retail uses in metropolitan Houston led inexorably to a decline in sales in closer-in centers. Faced with significant retail expansion on the west side of the city, Uptown Houston sought to avert the erosion of Uptown's comparative retail offering. As at Country Club Plaza, the vehicle was tax-increment financing—in this case, a tax-increment reinvestment zone, or TIRZ.

Part of the process of petitioning the city to create a TIRZ involved documentation of Uptown's expected retail sales both with and without the proposed improvements. The improvements were designed to alleviate traffic congestion and to increase the "navigability" of the suburban business district's retail core. Uptown's shopping centers would benefit from an improved image associated with ease of movement and convenience and stave off a rapidly eroding capture rate for everyday goods. The long-term projections computed for Uptown Houston as part of the TIRZ approval process estimated that stabilizing Uptown and maintaining its competitive position within the region would mean substantial additional support for retail uses. Projections called for incremental sales of $714 million over the expected baseline scenario—a level sufficient to support about 1.8 million square feet of additional retail space in Uptown.

Creating a New Pedestrian-Friendly Suburban Business District

Since the approval of the TIRZ in 2000, Uptown Houston has embarked on an improvement program that includes mobility upgrades—breaking superblocks into street grids, an ambitious set of streetscape betterments, and a detailed approach for coordinating with regional highway reconstruction projects. An initial bond offering of $30 million is targeted to fund these initiatives as well as to assist with housing development. Without question, the most significant post–TIRZ development initiative is the upcoming expansion of the Galleria, Uptown's signature shopping center. Urban Retail Properties plans to add another 750,000 square feet of retail space, including Nordstrom, Foley's, and Neiman Marcus. In the view of Uptown Houston executives, the mobility improvements and urban design initiatives were a significant factor in Urban Retail Properties's decision to expand the Galleria. The resulting incremental tax revenues will be earmarked to support ongoing public investment in Uptown. David Staaf, director of planning and development for Uptown Houston, noted that the ultimate objective is to create a "great, *urban,* place." He commented, however, that individual property owners continue to consider their own projects as "domains unto themselves," which poses a great challenge to creating the type of effortless connections and diversity that exemplify strong urban places. Still, he is convinced that the long-term competitiveness of places such as Uptown Houston, Tysons Corner, and others depends in part on responding to the need to be not just accessible, but also memorable.

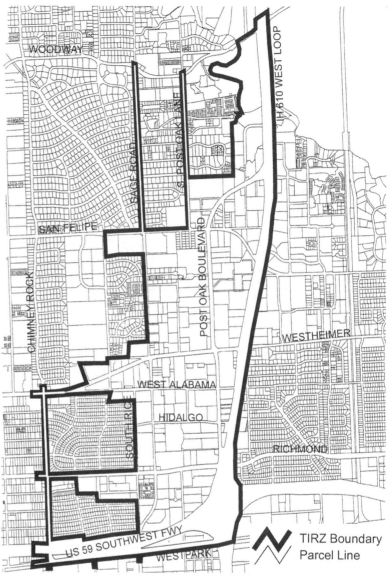

Source: Barton Smith, Vinson & Ellis et al., *Project Plan and Reinvestment Zone Financing Plan* (Houston: City of Houston, 1999).

Lessons Learned

America's suburban business districts can learn two potent lessons from the example of Uptown Houston. The first is that a robust real estate market can be maintained only when it remains in tune with the needs and aspirations of its market demographics. Past performance is no guarantee of future success. The superblock plat of Uptown Houston was simply unable to cope with increasing congestion and was seriously undermining patrons' subliminal habits of repeat visitation. Market share was declining, retail vacancies were increasing, and real estate capital values and the tax base were under threat. The use of a public/private partnership

119

The plaza outside the 790,00-square-foot Valencia Town Center Mall in Valencia, California, connects the 98,000 square feet of retail space and the mixed-use development on Town Center Drive to create the pedestrian-friendly Valencia Town Center.

and TIF funds to create improved access and a more pedestrian-friendly environment within the suburban business district was essential in redressing these problems. The second important lesson is that a unified approach to marketing is the only way to ensure the continued patronage of long-time customers. As patrons took note of the connected offering of the suburban business district, they became the critical mass needed to support a wide range of goods, services, and experiences. Individual projects going it alone can never generate the horsepower that a team of players can muster when they pull together to match their competitors.

Valencia Town Center—
Where the Mall Meets Main Street

Valencia Town Center is an emerging suburban business district located 30 miles north of downtown Los Angeles on I-5. It is the centerpiece of a 36,000-acre master-planned community undertaken in the early 1960s by the Newhall Land and Farming Company. At that time, Newhall had engaged the services of Victor Gruen and worked with Los Angeles County to develop ambitious plans for a new town accommodating 170,000 residents and 45,000 jobs. Gruen's original plan called for a town center that included both a shopping mall and traditional retail-lined main street. In 1992, Newhall opened the 790,000-square-foot Valencia Town Center Mall while the main street, called Town Center Drive, opened in 1998. It was the first retail real estate asset in the United States to integrate a new main street with a mall.

Integrating Main Street with the Mall

Gruen's logic was that the retail main street could provide the pedestrian connectivity to the shopping mall. Instead of traversing a parking lot, residents could stroll down the main street, eat in one of the restaurants, and then shop in the mall. One element would strengthen the attraction of the others. Surprisingly, Newhall met with some strong opposition to its proposal to transform the mall into a traditional town center. The department stores and many of the mall specialty shops were concerned that Town Center Drive would displace mall parking; specialty mall tenants were worried that Town Center Drive tenants would erode their retail sales. Newhall addressed the problems in three ways. It funded the construction of a new parking structure, ensured that all the paseos (walkways) and pedestrian linkages were focused toward the mall, and designed the major public domain space as a huge landscaped plaza that would connect the mall to Town Center Drive.

Newhall paid careful attention to the retail mix so that the retailers along Town Center Drive were not competitors but rather supporters of the mall retailers. Town Center Drive moved slightly upmarket to cater more to the out-of-hours trade. It drew restaurants, high-end fashion retailers, bookstores and entertainment venues, Ann Taylor, Talbots, Zany Brainy, an IMAX and 11 stadium-seating theaters, Paper Mulberry, Java N Jazz coffeehouse, and Borders Books. Finally, Newhall began operating and sponsoring a marketing and promotion program. In particular, the developer created new civic events such as the Santa Clarita Film Festival and the Bella Via—Valencia Italian Street Painting Festival with the express purpose of positioning the town center as the community's desirable and memorable "third place." Public art was placed on the street in the form of "human factor" sculptures—lifelike statues of children looking in a shop window, an office worker on a step reading his newspaper over a cup of coffee, and a family walking to the mall.

The aesthetic design of the entire town center evokes a sense of human scale and history while the visual sense is complemented with the auditory sense through the use of a sound system that serves both the mall and the main street. The result is a pedestrian-friendly place that possesses a critical mass of goods, services, and experiences and, in so doing, induces a subliminal habit of repeat visitation. These strategies extremely very well conceived and brilliantly executed—they remain some of the best-kept secrets in American place making. Valencia

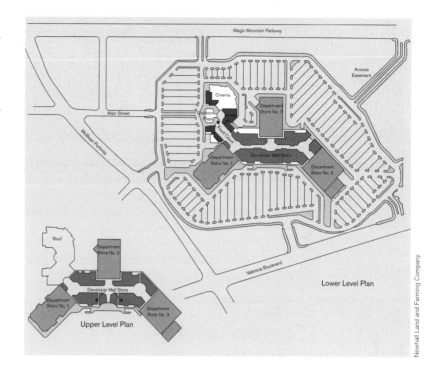

Newhall Land and Farming Company

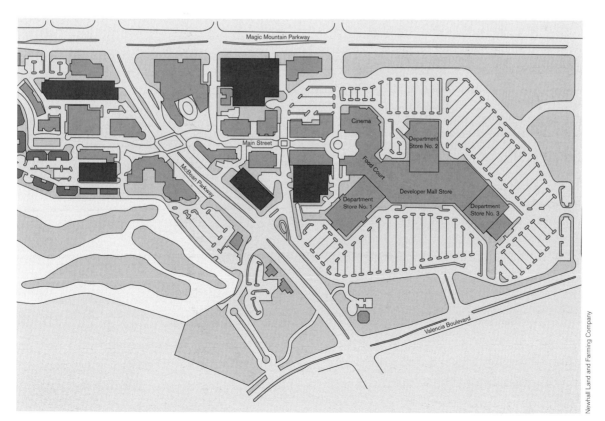

Newhall Land and Farming Company

These plans show the layout of Valencia Town Center both before and after completion of Town Center Drive. The addition of the main street to the shopping mall has transformed the district from just a shopping center to a community focus—a place to live, work, and shop.

One of the keys to Valencia Town Center's success has been the attention to design detail. Newhall insisted that the rear entry and service areas of buildings look just as inviting as the street facades and that all parking structures be located to generate pedestrian linkages.

Town Center is a real estate asset that leverages the mall with a main street to create growing retail sales and increasing retail rents.

Taming the Traffic Engineers

The municipal traffic code mandated the construction of Town Center Drive at a minimum width of 64 feet. Given that a relatively short street (about half a mile) at such a width would attract high-speed traffic at odds with a pedestrian-friendly environment made even friendlier by intimately scaled sidewalks and on-street angle parking, Newhall simply side-stepped the traffic engineers and chose to construct and maintain its own 53-foot-wide Town Center Drive. Tucked away behind the main street buildings are off-street parking garages that accommodate 2,250 cars in a shared-parking arrangement. Over 25 miles of paseos, all of which cross over or under major arterial roads, lead directly from the surrounding residential communities into the town center. The sidewalk widths in Town Center Drive vary from ten to 14 feet. With its newly planted mature shade trees, pedestrian linkages, arcades, plazas, and benches, Town Center Drive is attractive to pedestrians. All Town Center Drive buildings incorporate ground-floor retail uses or restaurants to promote and maintain pedestrian interest. Even the vehicles cruising along the traffic-calmed Town Center Drive provide color, movement, and excitement.

Town Center Drive crosses at grade the six-lane McBean Parkway. While the parkway detracts from the continuity of Town Center Drive and constitutes a pedestrian impediment,

Building facades on Town Center Drive in Valencia are articulated with landscaped garden beds providing separation from on-street parking. Street furniture includes banners advertising town center activities, seating located under shade trees and facing shopfronts, and wide sidewalks that draw pedestrian attention to the retail offerings.

thoughtful design and configuration of development form and land use mix have minimized the roadway's adverse impacts. The 244-room Hyatt Valencia Hotel, 26,000-square-foot Santa Clarita Conference Center, and 55,000-square-foot Spectrum Health Club anchor Town Center Drive on the opposite side of the McBean Parkway. The street retail on the hotel side of Town Center Drive focuses on convenience stores and services targeted to office workers and residents of the 210-unit Montecito apartments and the Avignon luxury dwellings, which surround a small town green.

Mixing Uses to Create a 24/7 Town Center

Newhall used the creation of a compact pedestrian-friendly town center not only to strengthen its residential sales but also to create a whole new portfolio of real estate investments, the synergy of which would never have been realized had it not been for the mixed-use town center configuration. The 98,000 square feet of retail space on Town Center Drive draws patrons and life from the multifamily residential apartments, hotel, convention center, sports and fitness facilities, and six-story office buildings (totaling 275,000 square feet) on Town Center Drive leased to Charles Schwab, Morgan Stanley Dean Witter, Valencia National Bank, KPMG, and Princess Cruise Lines. Over 3,000 people now work in Valencia Town Center. The decision by Princess Cruises to relocate its headquarters to Valencia Town Center underscores how important it is to progressive and competitive employers to secure their office locations in live-work-shop places. With insufficient numbers of college graduates now entering the labor market to fill available positions, employers are coming to realize the importance of providing housing choices, a vibrant working environment, and a range of lunchtime and after-hours activities to retain their employees' services and loyalty.

Lessons Learned

Valencia Town Center provides a valuable model for the transformation of existing shopping malls through the addition of a shop- and restaurant-lined main street. It shows how the two elements —mall and main street—can work together both

Geoffrey Booth

to enrich the financial performance of the real estate asset and to create a sense of place within the suburban business district. The integration of office and residential development and the provision of an extensive network of pedestrian linkages to the surrounding neighborhoods significantly enhance pedestrian access to the town center. The management of Valencia Town Center as a single, integrated place provides an important lesson on how to brand a critical mass of goods, services, and experiences and demonstrates the value of festivals and community activities in the transformation and promotion of suburban business districts. The creative solution to the inflexible traffic regulations governing street width is instructive, as is the importance of mixing uses in a town center format to create new, synergistic real estate investment products.

Mixed-use development on Town Center Drive in Valencia, California, provides retail and restaurant uses at street level and offices above. Over 3,000 people now work in Valencia Town Center.

Washingtonian Center—Proving That Big-Box Retailers Do Not Have to Stand Alone

Washingtonian Center is the town center for the dispersed Maryland Tech Corridor that runs along I-270 for ten to 15 miles northwest of Washington, D.C., to Gaithersburg, Maryland. The original 184-acre site, once part of a golf

The Peterson Companies

course, gained approval in 1984 for development of a 6 million-square-foot office campus. In 1997, the Peterson Companies of Fairfax, Virginia, decided to develop the last 23 acres of the site at the interchange of I-270 and I-370 as a main street town center with a difference—this one would contain big-box retailers—retailers that had traditionally stood alone or formed part of automobile-dominated power-center strips. The completed town center now embraces 575,000 square feet of office space, 460,000 feet of retail space, a 12-screen cinema complex, 576 hotel rooms, restaurants, public squares, a lake, and parking garages for 1,537 cars and surface parking for an additional 629 cars as well as 175 townhouses, 205 high-rise condominiums, and 1,404 rental apartments. The residential density averages 35 units per acre. Washingtonian Center has created a sense of place and a community focal point in a dispersed suburban business district. Plans are well advanced for Washingtonian Center's expansion.

Big-Box Retailers Come to Main Street

Washingtonian Center is modeled on a traditional small-town American main street with one important difference—the Peterson Companies directed architects RTKL to integrate three big-box retailers—Galyan's Sporting Goods (105,000 square feet), Kohl's (103,000 square feet), and Target (153,000 square feet)—into the project.

The centerpiece of the project is the existing ten-acre lake. The concept master plan, which was ultimately adopted, proposed a main street development that originated from a town square on the edge of the lake and ran in a boomerang shape for 800 linear feet. Galyan's, the lakefront restaurants, and the town square would anchor one end of main street, Kohl's would close the vista at the other end, and Target and a small plaza would occupy the apex of the boomerang. A pedestrian bridge would be constructed across the lake to improve pedestrian connectivity to the hotels, entertainment uses, and a yet-to-be-completed final phase of the project.

The innovative nature of the master plan was instrumental in both the county planning commission's and the Gaithersburg City Council's approval of the project. For the big-box retailers, Washingtonian Center represented a dramatically new approach to suburban retailing—Galyan's, Kohl's, and Target developed two-story prototype stores that integrated their offerings into the main street format. Each big-box retailer is treated architecturally as a landmark building within the main street's fabric, creating the diversity and vitality among the individual buildings that give the main street its intimate appeal. Storefront design devices such as distinctive awnings, signage, and store window and entry treatments provide a unique identity to the specialty retailers that line the big boxes at the ground level.

Creating the Sense of Place

The public square at the intersection of the main street and the lakefront is an informal community gathering place, a location for year-round special events. Like many of its small-town precedents, it includes a clock tower. Public art, seating, decorative lighting, specialty paving, and shade trees make the square a pleasant community meeting place. Freestanding restaurants activate and define the public spaces around the lakefront, park, and square.

The lakefront park features a pedestrian bridge and a waterfront promenade. The pedestrian-only arched bridge links the main street to the new office and restaurant plaza that is the final phase of the development's commercial mix. Shade trees, distinctively designed street lighting, benches, flower boxes, landscaping, banner graphics, and flags contribute to the pedestrian-friendly, human-scaled vitality of the street. At 75 feet in width, the main street allows for on-street parking, but careful attention to design and the street's boomerang alignment has made the street both safe and exciting for pedestrians. The street also maintains an intimate scale and provides excellent visibility to all retail tenants, enticing shoppers to cross the street and engage in an enjoyable journey of discovery that leads from retailer to retailer.

Pedestrian Interconnection and Parking

The project is designed around the pedestrian—travel from the parking garages to the main street is via well-lit pedestrian linkages lined with shops. In addition, two pedestrian bridges connect directly from the parking garages to Galyan's and Target. Although shoppers are accommodated in three parking garages located behind the stores and restaurants, one of the biggest challenges was how to make the two additional four-story parking garages compatible with the rest of the project. In response, RTKL incorporated specialty retail tenants to activate the ground-level frontage of the structured parking and created a brick facade, giving both structures warmth and architectural interest. The parking garage built next to the square is sited partially below grade to create a building height compatible with the lakefront buildings. Additional traffic calming in the form of on-street parallel parking is provided off site along both sides of Washington Boulevard to encourage the use of the boulevard's sidewalks as a safe and attractive pedestrian link to the main street. It is anticipated that the residents of the nearly 1,800 homes that are within walking distance of the Washingtonian Center will use this link. In addition, an existing connector street used extensively by residents was extended into the retail project to facilitate pedestrian access.

Lessons Learned

Washingtonian Center was the first town center development in the United States to be anchored by big-box retailers and parking structures integrated into a development format that creates a main street. It has proved that big-box retailers do not have to stand alone. To contribute to the town center's place-making quality, the big-box retailers demonstrated a willingness to adapt their previously rigid store formats to a main street design concept. In agreeing to two-story buildings that would minimize the building footprint and maintain the street's intimate scale,

At Washingtonian Center, the connection of the town square to the main street is a major design feature that allowed the project to be connected across the lake to the entertainment facilities and future development.

Galyan's used a two-story store format to integrate its operation into main street. It sought a location that gave it frontage near streetfront cafés so that patrons would enjoy a clear view of the next retail expenditure opportunity within Washingtonian Center.

125

The Peterson Companies

Target is located at the apex of the boomerang-shaped main street, and the shopfront of Barnes & Noble was designed to draw shoppers down the street. Parallel on-street parking is provided along the main street; parking garages at the rear and on top of buildings are connected by bridge links that add interest and life to main street.

the retailers adopted a model that can have wide application in the development of mixed-use town centers in America's suburban business districts. Galyan's responded to the main street context by opening up large storefronts on all sides of the building facing adjacent streets, creating a more pedestrian-friendly and interesting

sidewalk environment. Kohl's responded by providing two main entrances, one facing main street and the other facing its parking structure. Also facing main street is Target, which anchors the middle of Washingtonian Center with its first two-story prototype store. To facilitate additional access to its stores, Galyan's and Target required their second floors to be connected by pedestrian bridges to their respective parking garages.

In response to the need for a community place, the Peterson Companies took advantage of the existing and underused lakefront and originated the main street project from a town square on the shores of the lake. As a result, the Washingtonian Center incorporates three components that work together to create a sense of place: the main street, the public square, and the lakefront park. Washingtonian Center reflects the trend emerging from America's new demographics toward shopping on a more intimate scale. It provides a vital blueprint to bring big boxes and parking structures onto main street in a way that contributes to the neighborhood and provides for pedestrians. As Peterson Companies President James Todd said, "Washingtonian Center provides many important lessons on how we can transform America's suburban business districts and secure the placemaking dividend."

Careful attention to the streetscape design helps ensure that customers are drawn down main street and enticed by its retail offerings. The pedestrian-friendly nature of the shopping street has played a large part in reinforcing customers' subliminal habits of repeat visitation to Washingtonian Center.

The Peterson Companies

Securing the Competitive Advantage

Richard Longstreth was correct when he said that ". . . retail development is a key indicator of urban form and identity."[12] While some Uptown Houston property owners may still believe that they are domains unto themselves, the smart money in Country Club Plaza, Valencia Town Center, and the Washingtonian Center realizes that both the creation of place and sustained community building reinforce the subliminal habit of repeat visitation. The creation of place expands the range and mix of goods and services on offer, extends the hours of operation, increases retail sales, protects and enhances market share, and increases rents and capital values—all of which add up to the place-making dividend. In essence, the retail real estate asset can be only as strong as the suburban business district of which it forms an integrated and integral part. Big boxes and shopping malls that continue to stand alone limit themselves to a lower level of performance.

Regional shopping malls that realize the importance of integration and interconnectivity and use part of their surrounding surface parking lots to reconnect with their market through mixed-use street retail and infill housing opportunities will not only increase their income streams but will also enhance and reinforce the vitality and attractiveness of their suburban business district. The creation of connected retail environments, which support a critical mass of human activity, can transform the urban form and identity of suburban business districts and, with it, their competitive advantage as real estate investments and community-gathering places. Put bluntly, a dead or dying shopping mall is not good business for surrounding office, hotel, or residential development.

Notes

1. Mark Ruda, "GGP Focusing on Future Shopping Malls," *GlobeSt.com*, May 9, 2001, p. 1.

2. PricewaterhouseCoopers, *Greyfields into Greenfields* (San Francisco: Congress for the New Urbanism, 2001), p. 2.

3. International Council of Shopping Centers, *Shopping Centers Today—May 7, 2001* (New York: International Council of Shopping Centers, 2001), p. 1.

4. Geoffrey Booth's discussions with Dean Schwanke, vice president for development trends and analysis, Urban Land Institute, at ULI offices in Washington, D.C., July 16, 2001.

5. Building Design & Construction, "Malls mutate, breed outdoor, lifestyle concepts—Baby boomers shun bad '80s designs," *Building Design & Construction,* March 2001, p. 12.

6. Paris Rutherford, "The Nature of Main Street," *Shopping Center Business,* May 2001, p. 360.

7. Dean Starkman, "The Mall, Without the Haul," *Wall Street Journal,* July 25, 2001, p. B1.

8. Richard Longstreth, *City Center to Regional Malls* (Cambridge: MIT Press, 1998), p. xvi.

9. Kenneth T. Jackson, *Crabgrass Frontier: The Suburbanization of the United States* (New York: Oxford University Press, 1985), p. 257.

10. Patrick Phillips's various discussions with Howard Biel, Street Retail, Inc., Federal Realty Investment Trust, 2000–2001.

11. Michael Beyard et al., *Developing Retail Entertainment Destinations,* 2nd Edition (Washington, D.C.: ULI–the Urban Land Institute, 2001).

12. Longstreth, *City Center,* p. xvi.

Perkowitz + Ruth Architects

The proposed extension of Washingtonian Center to include entertainment and hotel facilities will draw on the successful pedestrian-friendly linkage that joins the main street and town square.

chapter 7

Making Community Part of the Real Estate Deal

What is community? According to *Webster's Encyclopedic Unabridged Dictionary,* it is "[a] social group of any size sharing common characteristics or interests, and perceived or perceiving itself as distinct in some respect from the larger society within which it exists." Community is human connection and a sense of belonging. It is an identifiable place with a unique character and an active public realm. It is the fulfillment of the human need that goes back to the birth of humanity, and it is reflected throughout the history of human settlement in urban forms such as village greens and town plazas that meet people's need to gather. In suburban business districts, building community is a powerful means of drawing together hitherto disparate, standalone components to create a strong, cohesive whole.

Ten years ago, Schaumburg, Illinois, a post—World War II suburb near Chicago's O'Hare Airport, was the home to many successful real estate projects. Radiating out from a century-old crossroads through former cornfields, Schaumburg boasted the Woodfield Shopping Center (one of the largest malls in the world), 85,000 jobs in the village proper, and nearly 120,000 jobs in the surrounding area in companies including Motorola (its world headquarters) and Zurich American Insurance (then Kemper Life Group). Yet, for all its financial success as a suburban business district, Schaumburg lacked a true public realm and strong sense of community.

To meet that need and give Schaumburg a greater identity amid Chicago's suburban growth, the village government, led by Mayor Al Larson, reached a major decision in January 1989: To build a strong sense of community by constructing a town square near the traditional crossroads at Roselle and Schaumburg roads. The village's land assembly process for what became a 29-acre site required three years of effort, from 1992 to early 1995. "Although we initiated condemnation proceedings on some properties," said Mayor Larson, "we did not go to court. Instead, we ended up negotiating the prices, using $7.5 million from a tax increment financing district to purchase and redevelop the land." The village then worked with Hitchcock Design Group of Naperville, Illinois, to prepare a master plan for its new town square. The plan incorporated many community-creating uses, including a 2.36-acre park with an amphitheater for community events, a public pond, a waterfall, and a 55-foot-tall clock tower, for centuries the traditional icon of town squares.

Construction began in September 1995. Schaumburg celebrated the town square's grand opening in fall 1996. Yet, creating the square itself was only one component of Schaumburg's community-building program. The master plan also required strong anchors along the town

square to generate the necessary pedestrian traffic that would make Schaumburg's community-building program a success. Mayor Larson wanted one of the anchors to be the Schaumburg Township Library, the second-busiest library in the state. Aware that the library wanted to relocate and expand, the mayor convinced the library directors that the town square was the appropriate location. The new library building, which anchors the western side of the square, opened in September 1998 and draws over 1 million visitors to the new town square each year. Dominick's, a 65,000-square-foot grocery store that opened in 1996 just behind the square, is the second anchor. Together, the two anchors activate the square by giving people a reason to visit the town center, thus creating the venue and opportunity for community interaction.

Low-rise commercial buildings for stores, restaurants, and professional offices now flank the other sides of the town square, along with a branch of the Chicago Athenaeum at Schaumburg—Museum of Architecture and Design and an adjacent sculpture garden. Parking is located behind the buildings so that visitors are not greeted by an ocean of asphalt. The internal roadways that serve the square are just 30 feet wide curb to curb to help create a pedestrian-friendly atmosphere. With its carefully planned and integrated uses, the Schaumburg town square is a place in which community

129

life flourishes, and so do property values. From 1991 to 1996, the equalized assessed value for the area hovered around $10.6 million. In 2000, just four years after the square's grand opening, the assessed value had more than doubled to $23 million. In addition to the retail uses, offices, and the library, an open-air European market and special events such as concerts and children's readings draw crowds to the town square throughout the year. Only three retail parcels remained available for development in first-quarter 2001. "It's becoming what we wanted: a public gathering place," said Mayor Larson in 1998.

The Real Estate Value of Community Building

Since their inception, most suburban business districts have followed a development pattern typified by isolated uses in configurations that have failed to capitalize on the place-making dividend. Indeed, municipalities and developers have relied on the standard real estate formula and traditional zoning provisions to create stand-alone buildings surrounded by surface parking lots—a configuration that compartmentalizes

users' work, shopping, living, and entertainment experiences. Moreover, municipalities and developers have not usually integrated community-oriented uses into districts' design and development. Thus, most suburban business districts fail to convey any semblance of community and likewise fail to meet the fundamental needs and aspirations of their users, occupants, and visitors.

Why is a sense of community important to suburban business districts? First, it attracts businesses, residents, workers, and shoppers whose disposable income generates higher property values and higher rents. Town Center Drive, developed by the Newhall Land and Farming Company, is a new $100 million pedestrian-oriented main street in the new town of Valencia, California, 30 miles north of downtown Los Angeles. It features a wide mix of uses, including residential, office, retail, and entertainment offerings and a hotel that together create the public realm for Valencia's almost 40,000 residents and the regional hub for the 200,000 residents in the surrounding Santa Clarita Valley. Town Center Drive, which was 89 percent complete in first-quarter 2001, has attracted national retail tenants (Ann Taylor, Talbots, Zany Brainy, and Borders Books), an IMAX 3-D theater, and numerous regional and local retailers and restaurants. The two-story, 790,000-square-foot Valencia Town Center regional mall (opened in 1992), which anchors the eastern end of Town Center Drive, was fully leased in 2001. At the time of the Town Center Drive's opening in 1996, retail lease rates "on the street" averaged $27 per square foot per year, the highest at that time in the Santa Clarita Valley.

In 2001, the 210-unit Montecito luxury apartment complex anchoring the western end of the street was fully leased at an average $21.60 per square foot per year, the highest apartment rents in the Santa Clarita Valley. At that time, Class A multifamily projects averaged $17.40 per square foot per year. In first-quarter 2001, Town Center Drive's office rents averaged $30 per square foot per year (effective rate averaged over the lease term) full-service gross while office rents for Class A office space in the Santa Clarita Valley averaged $21 per square foot per year (effective rate). One reason for Town Center Drive's success as an office location is its pedestrian-friendly environment and mix of everyday uses that permit employees to walk, rather than drive, to a restaurant, bookstore, dry cleaner, doctor's office, or coffee shop during their lunch hour. Businesses quickly realized the advantages of a Town Center Drive location. Between 1998 and 2001, Princess Cruises, one of the nation's three largest cruise companies, moved all of its 1,500 employees from its Century City headquarters in west Los Angeles to three new mid-rise buildings on and adjacent to Town Center Drive. The new main street offers the built-in amenities, restaurants, shops, and health club that the company needed to retain its employees. Peter Ratcliffe, president of Princess Cruises, said that one reason his company chose Valencia was ". . .the city-center environment being developed along Town Center Drive. It's in our best interest to have our people happy where they work."

Increased Property and Sales Tax Receipts

A sense of community does not just increase real estate values and attract desirable tenants

The human factor sculptures, first developed as a place-making device at World Expo 88 in Brisbane, Australia, are now used throughout the world to enhance community appreciation of art and create a sense of place. Pictured here is one of the human factor sculptures along Town Center Drive, Valencia, California.

to suburban business districts; it also generates higher property and sales tax receipts that help pay for a municipality's schools, police and fire protection, and other vital services. Englewood, Colorado, is a mature and primarily middle-income, blue-collar suburban town south of Denver. In 1997, the city of Englewood bought

By locating its 1,500 employees in Valencia Town Center's live-work-shop place, Princess Cruises gave its labor force amenities such as housing choice, a less stressful commute to work, restaurants, shops, entertainment venues, and a health club–all within walking distance of the office.

the failed Cinderella City mall, which it demolished a year later. In 1999, the city began redeveloping the 55-acre site into CityCenter Englewood, a pedestrian-friendly, transit-oriented village with civic uses (library, courts, administrative offices), a public plaza, a cultural and performance center, 438 residential units, and 350,000 square feet of retail space. The civic center, transit station, and first-phase retail development opened in 2000. Unlike the case of many modern transit systems, the station location was central to CityCenter's development, fostering pedestrian movement and opportunities for interaction within the heart of the business district. Residential construction started in 2000. The entire project is scheduled for completion in first-quarter 2002.

Even though only 25 percent of the CityCenter project was completed in 2001, that portion was already generating strong sales tax revenues. In 1999, the city collected just $6,839 in sales taxes from the site. By contrast, between January 1 and May 1, 2001, the city collected $301,189 in CityCenter sales taxes, an amount substantially greater than the Cinderella City mall generated in its last two years of operation ($180,240 in 1996 and $78,694 in 1997). The city estimated that, at buildout, the 430,000 square feet of CityCenter's commercial space will generate $2.4 to $2.58 million annually in sales taxes.

The community-oriented revival of Northwest 23rd Avenue in Portland, Oregon, once home to biker bars and drug dealers, has brought about an enormous increase in the immediate area's market and retail sales activity. Since the 1980s, private investment led primarily by developer Richard Singer has fostered a new sense of community supported by distinctive, locally based retailers, restaurants, offices, a branch library, and housing that has become a regional draw in its own right and is generating considerable pedestrian activity. Sales activity along Northwest 23rd Avenue (Portland does not have a sales tax) rose to $500 to $800 per square foot per year in 2000 compared with a national average of $207 per square foot per year. Housing prices on and near Northwest 23rd Avenue have also benefited from the development of this new

Communities such as Old Town Alexandria have remained strong because the opportunity to interact has been nurtured by the physical form of the place and reinforced through the weekly market held in the town square.

community-nurturing environment. For example, a 5,000-square-foot house one-half block from the avenue that was purchased in 1989 for $250,000 sold in 2001 for $1 million.

Not only does a sense of community generate higher property values and greater sales tax returns, but it also prevents a town from locking into the "throw-away suburb" syndrome. In look-alike suburban business districts across the country, buildings and retail centers suffer from built-in obsolescence that, if not addressed, leads to their eventual demise and abandonment.

Community Building Means Sustainability

Park Forest, Illinois, an inner-ring suburb outside Chicago, was once a boomtown of cookie-cutter, post–World War II housing in the 1940s and 1950s. It eventually became home to one of the country's first regional shopping malls. In the 1970s, however, a new shopping mall in the newer suburb of Matteson, two miles to the west, drew shoppers away from Park Forest. Subsequently, Park Forest evidenced other signs of decline. Between 1980 and 1990, for example, its population decreased by 14 percent to 24,656, and its median household income fell by 3 percent while income rose nationally by 10 percent. Between 1977 and 1997, Park Forest lost 2,400 jobs at a time when the Chicago metropolitan area was experiencing strong employment growth. Census 2000 indicated that Park Forest has been undergoing a long-term population decline, from 24,656 in 1990 to 23,462 in 2000. Park Forest was not alone in facing decline. Outside Chicago, an arc of declining inner-ring suburbs, some little more than 25 to 30 years old, stretched over 60 miles from just south of O'Hare Airport into northwestern Indiana. To a large degree, it is their standalone configuration and lack of integration and synergy in their use patterns that have spelled obsolescence and decline for these Chicago-area communities.

Genuine communities seldom become obsolete, and they are rarely abandoned. Decade after decade, they endure and evolve as desirable places to live, work, and shop. Among the towns established before the 20th century, Old Town Alexandria, Virginia; Charleston, South Carolina; and Savannah, Georgia, stand out as examples of enduring communities. J.C. Nichols's Country Club Plaza in Kansas City was one of the first live-work-shop places of the suburban age and continues to be a vibrant community. The late 20th century has witnessed the creation of mixed-use communities at Mizner Park in Boca Raton, Florida, and Reston, Virginia, and the transformation of Bethesda, Maryland, into a compact pedestrian- and transit-friendly suburban business district—all communities that exhibit a sense of place and in which visitors and residents can literally live, work, and shop. The effort to introduce greater community and cohesion into suburban business districts is in its infancy. However, effective strategies can be drawn from other real estate models, such as thriving downtowns, main streets, and new town centers, that offer suburban business districts a set of important lessons and abiding principles related to sustaining the value of community.

Community Building through Public/Private Partnerships

Often, the public sector must jump-start community-building activity by making infrastructure improvements, assembling and/or rezoning properties, and developing one or more civic or cultural facilities to initiate the transformation process in suburban business districts. Typically, public investment attracts and leverages substantially increased investment from the private sector. In some cases, it is the private sector alone—particularly one or several large property owners in a suburban business district—that initiates community building. However, the most potent examples of community building emerge when the public and private sectors work together in a public/private partnership that brings together the city, developers, businesses, and residents to work toward a common goal.

The city of Aurora, Colorado, outside Denver, partnered with the University of Colorado Health Sciences Center to redevelop the decommissioned one-square-mile Fitzsimons Army Medical Center into a mixed-use development that

Creating the Live-Work-Shop Place–Bethesda, Maryland

Bethesda, Maryland, is a compact suburban business district in the Washington, D.C., metropolitan area. The catalyst for the district's transformation was the construction of the Washington Metro rail system, which made Bethesda a major transit interchange. Montgomery County developed a strategic plan that guided Bethesda's transformation into a pedestrian- and transit-friendly live-work-shop place that, through several formal and informal public/private partnerships, established the multifamily residential housing stock, high-rise offices, a transit station, and, finally, the retail project known as Bethesda Row, which rounds out the mix of uses in this suburban business district.

Bethesda Row is a multiphase main street, mixed-use redevelopment project undertaken by Federal Realty Investment Trust to create the retail heart of Bethesda. Covering five contiguous city blocks, the site was largely in the hands of one private landowner. Previous uses on the site included warehouses, an automobile wrecking yard, a cement plant, medical office buildings, and "mom and pop" retailers. In Phase I, Federal Realty renovated and re-tenanted several existing retail facilities while constructing a new building to house Barnes & Noble. It also undertook major streetscape improvements, including the addition of brick sidewalks and a fountain. The developer paid close attention to small details, going so far as to custom design attractive manhole covers for the sidewalks.

When Phase I opened in June 1997, the community enthusiastically received Bethesda Row; since then, the development has become a neighborhood focal point and gathering place. Phase II involved the renovation of existing retail space while Phase III consisted of new construction. In both of these latter phases, Federal Realty continued its successful streetscape improvements. The company also sought to make the buildings appear less like superblocks and more like city blocks that had evolved naturally over time. The design process for both phases involved multiple architects (with Atlanta-based Cooper Carry as the primary architect) and a conscious effort to differentiate various components of the buildings. The result, in all phases, has been an outstanding streetscape of great visual interest with a genuinely urban ambience.

Mixed-Use Development

The multiple uses at Bethesda Row contribute to the project's success by mutually supporting each other–local office workers patronize the restaurants while people from the larger community who make a special trip to Bethesda Row restaurants also shop at the stores. By providing a variety of people with a host of reasons to come to Bethesda Row at different times of the day and evening, the mix of uses contributes to the project's vitality and sense of place. Federal Realty has reinforced this mix of uses with each new phase. Phase IV, for example, will include entertainment uses, and the developer is considering mixed-density residential uses for Phase V.

Transit- and Pedestrian-Oriented Design

Federal Realty went beyond Montgomery County's planning requirements to create an outstanding urban environment for pedestrians. For example, the company planted larger street trees than required by the code and put considerable effort into ensuring that storefronts and building facades were differentiated from each other, significantly improving the streetscape's attractiveness. One of Federal Realty's biggest accomplishments was convincing regulators to permit the placement of restaurant patios next to the curb with sidewalks adjacent to

Bethesda Row in Maryland, developed by Federal Realty Investment Trust, has created a popular neighborhood focal point and gathering place within this suburban business district.

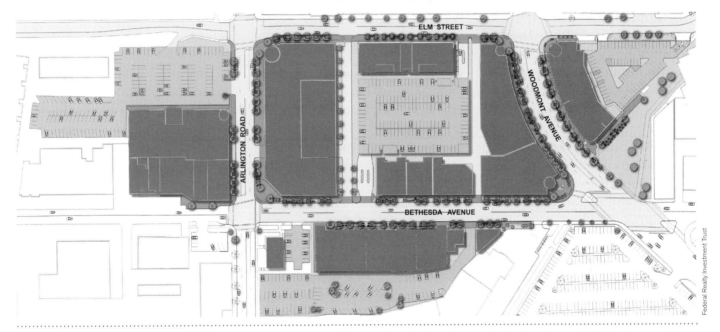

To the casual observer, Bethesda Row does not look like a community shopping center. Designed as an infill development along the streets of Bethesda, Maryland, it is being built block by block in line with demand. The parking garage shown in the center of the block was built by Montgomery County and is operated and managed as shared parking.

the storefronts, rather than the other way around. This configuration not only does a better job of supporting the retailers, but it also creates a pleasant pedestrian environment. The arrangements required a reciprocal easement with the county to allow a public easement next to the stores and an easement for Federal Realty to use the space next to the curb.

The pedestrian environment is supported by a 922-space, county-built park-ing structure located in the middle of the Bethesda Row project. This, along with on-street parking, provides visitors with convenient parking without creating the un-pleasant "moonscape" of parking lots com-monly found in suburban areas. Finally, Bethesda Row's pedestrian environment is designed to facilitate easy access to Metro rail and public transit through the use of the Bethesda 8 shuttle, an initiative of the Bethesda Urban Partnership.

Public/Private Partnership

One unusual feature of Bethesda Row is its parking facilities. Nearly all of the parking for the project is provided in the county-owned garage and in county-owned sur-face lots, with some metered street park-ing. Many years ago, Montgomery County established a parking lot district for the Bethesda business district in which the county builds parking facilities that users

continued on next page

then pay for on an hourly or daily basis. The facilities are supported by a surcharge on property tax assessments for properties that do not provide their own parking. This arrangement means that owners of smaller buildings do not have to provide their own on-site parking and ensures that the area's parking spaces are efficiently operated and managed as shared parking.

In 1994, Montgomery County established the Bethesda Urban Partnership, which is a public/private partnership charged with marketing and managing the suburban business district. Funding for the partnership comes from a special property tax, fees from parking lots, and sponsorships for special events. In 2000 alone, over 500 community volunteers contributed to the success of these special events, which are designed to engage the community; they include the Literary Festival, Summer Concerts, European Market, Children's Street Festival, Cycling Grand Prix, the Tastes of Bethesda, Holiday Lights, and the Arts Festival. The partnership initiated the Bethesda 8 bus shuttle, directional signage, and the Art Discovery Trail. All of the efforts played a major role in securing Federal Realty Investment Trust's commitment to invest in Bethesda Row.

Regulatory Barriers
While the county's strategic plan for Bethesda did establish the framework within which Bethesda Row could be developed, it also created some barriers, particularly

with regard to transportation and streetscape improvements. According to the county's traffic models and standards, capacity was insufficient to support the proposed project despite the fact that the county's strategic plan called for the development of mixed-use infill projects on the site. As a result, Federal Realty spent considerable time addressing traffic standards. Similarly, the county had developed a specific streetscape concept for the downtown area, which regulated everything from paving materials to trash containers. Again, Federal Realty had to convince the regulators that its development concept would provide an attractive streetscape that would meet the needs and aspirations of the community. The lesson that emerges is that local development regulations do not need to be rigidly calibrated and applied to ensure top-quality development. Instead, they must inspire but not emasculate innovative infill development projects.

Public Opposition
When Federal Realty first proposed Bethesda Row, many local residents were concerned about the project's impact on their community. They were particularly worried that Bethesda Row would drive local retailers out of business and replace them with the same national retailers that can be found at any suburban mall. Federal Realty responded to neighbors' concerns by meeting with local residents to discuss their ideas for the development and by

demonstrating through its leasing strategy that the residents' fears were unfounded. Indeed, Federal Realty has managed to attract a balanced mix of local, regional, and national retailers that has generated considerable customer traffic while still providing a unique shopping experience. Residents now appreciate the fact that Bethesda Row is a major improvement on the uses that previously existed on the site, and they continue to reward the project with repeat visitation.

Lessons Learned
The transformation of the Bethesda suburban business district and the Bethesda Row project demonstrates the importance of public/private partnerships in securing a live-work-shop asset for the community. While the public sector clearly needs a strategic plan to guide development, the plan provisions must be truly inspirational rather than just rule-book regulations. For its part, the developer must be prepared to go beyond the code to create a place that delivers a strong and sustainable placemaking dividend. In managing and marketing the suburban business district, a public/private partnership drawn from the community and meeting the community's needs and aspirations ensures that the suburban business district creates and sustains life. ●

Source: David J. O'Neill, *The Smart Growth Tool Kit* (Washington, D.C.: ULI–the Urban Land Institute, 2000), p. 83.

provides vital community amenities and services and hundreds of new jobs. The city renovated several buildings for use as the Aurora Police and Fire Department Training Complex, built a child development center, and created several parks and considerable open space. For its part, the University of Colorado Health Sciences Center constructed a new medical center to anchor the property. Together, the city and the University of Colorado Health Sciences Center are developing a 160-acre bioresearch park adjacent to the site. This public/private partnership has taken the potentially devastating economic impact of a base closure and created a vital and profitable community-oriented district that serves the entire town.

In Bethesda, Maryland, Montgomery County has played a major role in undertaking strategic

The provision of community parks located along pedestrian linkages that allow people to meet and greet and to rest and reflect are a vital component of place making in suburban business districts. Pictured here is a pocket park in Rockville Town Center, Maryland.

planning, providing a library and county offices, creating and beautifying parks, encouraging and providing public transit, constructing a parking garage, and forging public/private partnerships to transform Bethesda into a live-work-shop place that the community embraces and supports.

Transforming Suburban Business Districts through Community Building

In 1992, Schaumburg (Illinois) Mayor Al Larson requested participants in a Mayors' Institute on City Design seminar to critique a preliminary plan for Schaumburg's town square. That plan would have redeveloped the 29-acre site as a traditional shopping center. "They handed me my head on a platter," said Larson several years later. "They told me that if you are going to have a true village center, you must have more than a place to shop . . . and a wishful-sounding name." According to *Emerging Trends in Real Estate 2001*, a study prepared by Lend Lease Real Estate Investments and PricewaterhouseCoopers, "The best opportunity for suburban investments appears to lie in urbanizing suburban commercial nodes—subcities—[that] feature smaller-scale, multifaceted core environments—attractive neighborhoods, office centers, excellent

shopping, parks and entertainment amenities, and in some cases, alternative transportation to the core. People can live and work in these places—they will be golden." In short, people drive community, and therefore people drive the uses that build a community. Most fragmented and dispersed suburban business districts are dominated by geographically proximate but physically separate office parks or retail centers and, in many cases, both. To build a vibrant community, those products must be integrated and supplemented with an expanded range of community uses that, through careful programming and locational decisions, help knit together the physical fabric and activity of the suburban business district into a true community.

An excellent example of a new suburban business district that integrates a range of land uses into a pedestrian-friendly live-work-shop place is Reston Town Center in Fairfax County, Virginia. Opened in October 1990, this suburban business district includes 530,000 square feet of office space, 240,000 square feet of specialty retail uses and restaurants, a 13-screen cinema, a 514-room Hyatt Regency Hotel, a post office, a one-acre central plaza with a fountain, and the Equity Office Skating Pavilion, which is used for ice skating from mid-November to mid-March and for community events, festivals, and

The 5,400-square-foot Equity ice-skating pavilion located in Fountain Square in Reston Town Center, Fairfax County, Virginia, is the setting for community concerts during the summer and ice skating in the winter. These activities enliven the suburban business district and create community gathering opportunities.

a concert series during the rest of the year. Parking structures and surface lots are sited behind the buildings. Each use was located and configured so as to add value and patronage to its companion uses.

Built in a single stage, the first 20-acre phase of Reston Town Center has been a great success since completion. Not only does it serve the function of a typical downtown that brings together Reston's 60,000 residents, but it has also become a regional center for residents, workers, and shoppers from throughout Northern Virginia. The Old Dominion Trail, which links several historic Virginia sites, including Mount Vernon, runs past Reston Town Center, bringing joggers, cyclists, and even horses (and their riders) to the town center for a meal or refreshment. In mid-2001, commercial and residential properties enjoyed a 10 to 15 percent rental premium (and sometimes higher) over comparable buildings in other Northern Virginia locations. The key to Reston Town Center's strength is that each component contributes to the experience of a seamless whole. The town center has tapped into the power of community building rather than following the path of least resistance and randomly providing isolated, standalone land uses.

The Essential Elements of Community Building

The successful community-building programs at Suisun City, California; Schaumburg, Illinois; Valencia Town Center, California; Country Club Plaza, Kansas City; CityPlace, Florida; Bethesda, Maryland; and Reston, Virginia, highlight a number of lessons that can guide the transformation of suburban business districts into pedestrian- and transit-friendly live-work-shop places that meet the needs and aspirations of the communities they serve.

Ensure a 24-Hour/Seven-Day Mix
Programming must provide daytime and nighttime uses and activity. The country is already littered with civic plazas and office districts that become ghost towns every night after 5:00 and on weekends. Community exists 24 hours a day/seven days a week, and the suburban business district should be its epicenter. As part of its reclamation of its historic main street as a community hub, Suisun City, California, located 44 miles east of San Francisco in sprawling, fast-growing Solano County, transformed a long-closed supermarket into a community college that includes a performance space for its theater group. The school and theater bring students and audiences to a town center day and night as well as on weekends. Suisun City's downtown redevelopment also includes a new marina, a public plaza, a waterfront promenade, and an adjacent neo-traditional residential neighborhood. The people drawn to Suisun City's downtown enjoy its public spaces and facilities and patronize its restaurants, shops, and other venues morning to evening, seven days a week.

Monitor and Meet the Community's Needs
Before deciding what daytime and nighttime uses are appropriate for a suburban business district, developers and the municipality should study local demographics and emerging trends and then determine how best to respond to them. "We planned CityPlace [in West Palm Beach, Florida] as a retail-driven, mixed-use destination," said Kevin Ryan, a senior vice president at the Palladium Company, one of the CityPlace development partners. "That gave us a broader demographic of 1 million people within a 30- to 40-minute drive of City-Place, plus 300,000 seasonal visitors. That market could support 500,000 to 600,000 square feet of retail, restaurant, and cinema space.

"That market also had an unsatisfied demographic profile hungry for a more urban residential experience, which CityPlace fills [with its 600 housing units]. The mix of uses also gives CityPlace a competitive advantage over local office developments, which will generate higher lease and absorption rates for our office towers."

Retailing is one of the catalysts in the trend toward suburban place making. As Arthur E. Lomenick, formerly senior executive vice president of the western division at Post Properties, Inc., noted at the Urban Land Institute's second Place Making Conference in September 2000, "Retail developers are . . . trying to appeal to a market that likes the immersive district experience, as opposed to malls and big boxes." In short, major retailers such as Banana Republic, Victoria's Secret, the Gap, and even Nordstrom and Sears are expanding beyond traditional standalone shopping centers to community-oriented districts. "We open stores where the consumer is," said Beverly Butler, director of corporate external communications for the Gap, "and work to become part of the fabric of the community. A significant portion of our future sites will be off the mall." With the absence of common-area management charges, with rental structures that need not embody anchor tenant subsidies, and with the flexible store hours that suit local demographics, main street locations enjoy lower occupancy costs and thus are highly attractive to a wide range of retail operations.

Achieve a Balanced Mix of Uses

To even out the economic ups and downs of various property sectors, developers and municipalities must carefully program a balance of space and uses to create the broadest possible market for suburban business districts. When Newhall Land was programming the half-mile-long Town Center Drive in Valencia, California, some executives and outside consultants wanted the retail sector to function as the street's sole driver. Others pushed for office uses. But the street was built with a balance of uses to weather the ups and downs of various market segments. Thus, if the retail market were to experience a downturn, Town Center Drive still would have its office, entertainment, residential, hotel, and professional uses to keep it active and profitable.

In CityPlace, retailing, multifamily housing, restaurants, enticing public squares and fountains, and the Harriet Himmel Gilman Theater have been brought together to create a place that the community could not resist making its own.

To create community in a suburban busi-ness district, a selection of uses should be pro-grammed to complement and support one another. Office uses, for example, feed retail operations by supplying customers for stores and restaurants both during the day and after work. At the same time, retail uses within a ten-minute walk of work locations reinforce the desirability of office development by providing amenities—such as restaurants, bookstores, cloth-ing stores, gift shops, and coffee bars—that per-mit and even encourage employees to go out to lunch or run errands without getting into their cars. Each office building on Town Center Drive incorporates ground-floor retail space and/or restaurants. Many more stores, restaurants, a hotel, cinemas, and other uses are all within easy walking distance along the street's land-scaped, tree-shaded sidewalks.

Incubate Local Tenants

A real community includes a number of locally based establishments such as hobby shops, used bookstores, and coffee shops, along with the offices of local professionals and a range of personal services and convenience uses such as beauty parlors, dry cleaners, and veterinari-ans. Local uses help strengthen a community's

sense of place by generating discretionary visits from both residents and workers and by giving the town or district a distinctive character not found elsewhere. Suisun City has encouraged local entrepreneurs to remain in or move to its reinvented downtown by setting aside small sites for new buildings. None of Solano County's complement of traditional suburban malls, for example, can claim Babs' Delta Diner, a one-of-a-kind Suisun City institution now located in a new two-story waterfront building where regulars hang their personalized coffee mugs on peg boards and owner Babs Curless makes most dishes from scratch for her family-oriented clientele.

Integrating Uses to Create Community

When the real estate assets in a suburban busi-ness district cater to all the facets of people's daily lives, they succeed in accommodating the live-work-play dimensions of community life. Apart from the office buildings that are tradition-ally identified with suburban business districts, a range of other land uses should be integrated into suburban business districts. These uses in-clude civic facilities, cultural venues, multifamily housing, hotels, educational institutions, student housing, shops, restaurants, entertainment facilities, and parks and public spaces. With these uses woven into the suburban business district in a pedestrian-friendly manner, they create a place in which the various facets of our private and community lives can be satisfied.

Civic Facilities

Civic facilities—a library, post office, or town hall—are essential building blocks in a genuine community. They attract strong pedestrian traffic that becomes the basis for a range of other uses. They reinforce a subliminal pattern of visitation to a business district. Both municipalities and developers increasingly recognize the community-building value of civic facilities. The new 130-acre Southlake Town Square, which broke ground in February 1998 in Southlake, northwest of Dallas, will have 2.5 million square feet of retail, restaurant, office, cinema, and hotel space at its initial buildout around 2020. The first phase was completed in 1999. By mid-2001, the town square already had a town hall that houses county offices, the city council chambers, the constable's office, and a public library, the first for the Southlake community. The town square also features a 22,000-square-foot post office that anchors an eight-acre retail, restaurant, and services center.

In Rockville Town Center, the city of Rockville, Maryland, has used municipal offices, a library, and the courts as the anchor for its redevelopment. The transformation process had several false starts as most retail activities were drawn to the adjoining commercial strip along Rockville Pike. However, a moratorium on further major retail development along the pike has refocused attention on Rockville Town Center. With the city currently preparing a new strategic plan for the town center's redevelopment and the county confirming its commitment to locate the new regional library in Rockville, the town center has seen a resurgence of multifamily housing and hotel development. Federal Realty Investment Trust recently announced that it will seek to redevelop its landholdings within the suburban business district by way of several integrated mixed-use projects consisting of street retail with residential apartments above—all wrapped around internal parking garages.

Cultural Facilities

Cultural facilities, such as live theaters, museums, and art galleries, put people on the street both day and night and increase activity in suburban business districts. A suburban business district is obviously unable to support a large, costly facility like Carnegie Hall, but it can benefit from smaller performance and studio spaces for actors, artists, dancers, and musicians. Similarly, a branch of a major museum can generate considerable activity. The redevelopment of downtown Silver Spring, Maryland, includes a new satellite facility of the American Film Institute while Schaumburg Town Square boasts the Chicago Anthenaeum at Schaumburg—Museum of Architecture and Design. The International Museum of Cartoon Art makes its home in Mizner Park in Boca Raton, Florida. And downtown San Jose, one of the largest suburban business districts in the San Francisco Bay Area, claims an impressive range of cultural facilities that include the Center for Performing Arts, the San Jose Repertory Theater, the Montgomery Theater, the San Jose Museum of Art, and the Children's Discovery Museum. Together, these facilities attracted over 4 million visitors to the suburban business district in 2000. Clearly, the integrated provision of several cultural facilities within a suburban business district can generate increased levels of community and pedestrian activity and provide a powerful driver for the development of multifamily housing.

In October 2000, the Arlington County Council granted Federal Realty Investment Trust permission to transform the Village of Shirlington in Arlington, Virginia, into a pedestrian-friendly live-work-shop place. The Shirlington suburban business district currently includes the television studios of WETA (the local Public Broadcasting Service outlet), but will soon encompass additional street retail, multifamily housing, offices, and a county library as well as the Signature Theater, home of Arlington's nationally recognized local theater group. In conceptualizing the extended main street, architects Cooper Carry provided the library and Signature Theater

Multifamily residential units, when integrated into the fabric of the suburban business district, provide a constant customer base for shops, restaurants, entertainment venues, and local businesses.

with their own 110-foot by 75-foot plaza to close the vista down main street. Robin Mosle, vice president of development at Federal Realty, said the cultural facilities at Shirlington will make the suburban business district the focus of community activity and secure a strong place-making dividend. It will bring life to the suburban business district after hours, support the street-front restaurants, and afford residents a rich diet of cultural activity within walking distance of their homes. It will also provide office workers with entertainment choices close to their place of work, thereby relieving peak-hour traffic congestion.

The $750 million Rio Nuevo project in Tucson, Arizona, which won city approval in March 2001, is planned as downtown's public center for the city's 496,139 residents and surrounding Pima County's 864,067 residents. A 125,000-square-foot amphitheater, a 60,000-square-foot aquarium, the 50,000-square-foot Arizona State Museum, and a 40,000-square-foot children's museum are to be integrated into the Rio Nuevo development. The city estimates that the facilities will draw 4.6 million visitors to downtown Tucson annually.

Residential Uses

As discussed in chapter four, America's changing demographic profile is creating demand for multifamily housing in suburban business districts as residents increasingly embrace the opportunity to live in a more urban, pedestrian-oriented environment. Despite changing demo-

graphic and consumer preferences, many developers have been caught short by the growing market demand for multifamily apartments in urban-type living environments. In August 1997, the Winmar Company opened Redmond Town Center, a 1.38 million-square-foot mixed-use project arranged around a new and attractive five-block-long main street on a 120-acre site in Redmond, a suburb of Seattle. The project initially included retail uses, offices, a cinema, a hotel, a community center, parks, and open space, but no housing. Nevertheless, it quickly generated significant housing demand. So, in 2001, the new developer, Macerich Company of Santa Monica, California (which in 1999 acquired the town center in a joint venture with the Ontario Teachers Pension Fund), initiated a program to add multifamily units to Redmond Town Center to meet community demand. The addition of a significant and growing resident population within a suburban business district makes the environment more secure and creates a sense of community ownership and pride in that place.

Hotels

A hotel is a destination in itself. However, it also generates an important spillover effect that puts people, particularly business travelers, on the streets of suburban business districts, especially in the evening. In addition, for companies that need to host out-of-town clients and employees, a hotel makes a suburban business district more attractive as an office location. A 124-room Hampton Inn anchors Phillips Place in Charlotte, North Carolina, at one end of its main street. The suburban business districts of Tysons Corner and Pentagon City in the Washington, D.C., metropolitan area both include Ritz-Carlton hotels as part of their regional shopping mall developments.

In Redmond Town Center, a 180-room Residence Inn by Marriott anchors 164th Street, which is one of the two roadways leading into the town center. Thanks to AT&T, which moved 2,500 employees into six buildings totaling 600,000 square feet of office space in Redmond Town Center, and to Microsoft, which is headquartered a few miles away, the hotel enjoys one of the highest occupancy rates in Washing-

Legacy Town Center–The Ultimate Amenity for 36,000 Employees

The 155-acre Legacy Town Center in Plano, Texas, is undergoing development as the community focal point of a fragmented low-density suburban business district that currently includes the corporate headquarters of Electronic Data Systems (EDS is the developer of the suburban business district and Legacy Town Center); JCPenney, Dr Pepper/7-UP, Ericsson, Countrywide Funding, and Frito-Lay. The Leddy Company, based in San Antonio, Texas, opened its four-star, 405-room Doubletree Hotel and conference center in Legacy Town Center in March 2001. The hotel entrance overlooks the town center's three-acre park and adjoins the west side of the shopping district. As the first luxury hotel to open in the 2,665-acre (36,000-employee) Legacy suburban business district, the Doubletree includes 52,000 square feet of meeting and banquet space and 15,000 square feet of fine restaurants.

According to Marilyn Kasko, director of asset management at EDS, "The 9:00-to-5:00 workday isn't the standard anymore –workers can't spend hours in their cars each day. This town center is the ultimate amenity for the employees in Legacy. . . . The town center is already having a positive impact on corporations looking at campus sites in Legacy." This live-work-shop place is a collaborative effort of Post Properties, the city of Plano, and EDS. On completion, the town center, modeled on a traditional downtown, will include 2,500 multifamily apartments, 345,000 square feet of main street retail, 2 million square feet of office space, and five acres of civic space. The development is centered on a three-acre park that features a lake and an extensive network of pathways designed to promote pedestrian activity and community interaction. The pathways link to the town center's narrow tree-lined streets with their sidewalk cafés. Buildings are built to the street alignment instead of behind acres of parking lots.

Store facades vary dramatically from merchant to merchant to provide urban character, vitality, and street appeal. Loft-style living spaces, daycare facilities, fitness centers, dry cleaners, and restaurants

The view from the Doubletree Hotel takes in Bishop Park and the 384-unit Post Properties multifamily housing development. The town center is based on a grid plat, with buildings built to the street alignment instead of behind acres of surface parking lots. Sidewalk cafés are used to create interest and vitality in the streets of the town center.

are all integrated with retail and office space to create a live-work-shop amenity designed to give Legacy employers a strong competitive advantage in attracting and maintaining increasingly scarce high-quality employees. According to Post Properties's chair and CEO John Williams, who opened the first apartments in the firm's 384-unit Legacy project in summer 2000, "Our goal is to build live-work-shop communities–Legacy Town Center will feature a unique character that provides a more interactive mix of uses than the typical suburban model." Compaq Computers has leased the larger (eight-story) of the two office buildings now under construction. Put simply, "They want this amenity [the Legacy Town Center live-work-shop place] for their employment base," says Marilyn Kasko. ●

Source: Adapted in part from Brian Brodrick, "Hometown on the Edge," *Urban Land,* June 2000, p. 79.

The four-star, 405-room Doubletree Hotel and conference center in Legacy Town Center opened in March 2001. The entrance to the hotel overlooks the town center's three-acre Bishop Park and adjoins the west side of the shopping district.

The incorporation of a hotel into a shopping mall as shown in this photograph of the Ritz-Carlton Hotel at Tysons Galleria in Tysons Corner, Fairfax County, Virginia, allows hotel patrons access to a wide range of shops, restaurants, and entertainment facilities and injects life outside normal working hours into a suburban business district.

ton state. "In my last dozen trips to Redmond Town Center, I could only get into the hotel once," said Chuck Davis, vice president of real estate for the Macerich Company. "We are actively looking at a new hotel and other uses to strengthen what's there and provide longer-term viability."

Educational Facilities

Schools, particularly community colleges, college or university branches, and vocational institutes, serve resident and worker needs. They are used both day and night, often seven days a week, bringing more life and energy to a place. Most suburban business districts, however, have yet to recognize the value of educational facilities. They could learn much from the example of downtown Chicago, which has developed an education corridor with more than a dozen major educational institutions along State Street and nearby blocks. In 2000, those institutions put more than 57,000 students of all ages on the street day and night. San Jose State University, integrated into the suburban business district of downtown San Jose, is an employment center in its own right, catering to 29,000 students and staff. It is a valuable education and labor force

resource for firms located in Silicon Valley and is a major retail, housing, and entertainment driver for the suburban business district.

The suburban business district of Stamford, Connecticut, redeveloped a former Bloomingdale's department store into the $58 million satellite campus of the University of Connecticut. Designed by architects Perkins Eastman, the 225,000-square-foot academic center includes the Connecticut Information Center. Stamford Mayor Dannel P. Malloy explained at the inception of the project why it had the city's support. "We want to glue our employers to Stamford by providing a specialized workforce. The campus will supply the workers for the growth sectors of our economy. It will also bring a wide variety of people downtown at all hours of the day and night."

Student Housing

Student housing is another still largely overlooked strategy for community building in suburban business districts. Students bring vitality and interest to the district, and, while they do not always command high disposable incomes (although America's changing demographic profile is changing even this stereotype), they do patronize entertainment establishments, cultural facilities, restaurants, and service retail establishments. They also are significant users of public transit and usually do not adopt 9:00-to-5:00 working hours. In Chicago's Loop, historic buildings have undergone conversion into student residences. The School of the Art Institute renovated an old office building and constructed an adjacent 17-story tower at State and Randolph streets to accommodate 490 dormitory rooms. The student housing, along with retail uses, restaurants, and a new home for the Art Institute's Film Center, all provide a built-in market for businesses throughout the Loop. Even though Chicago is obviously a big-city example, it does indicate the potential role of student housing in the transformation of suburban business districts.

Community Retail Uses

Suburban business districts transforming into live-work-shop communities should not encourage the development of standalone strip retail centers, shopping malls, big boxes, or power centers. Because of their size and associated surface parking lots, standalone structures erode the community fabric and discourage pedestrian activity. Retail uses can, however, be the glue that holds a suburban business district together if the plan for retail programming specifies a careful mix of local and national retailers, particularly the "mom and pop" stores, restaurants, and services that lend a distinctive personality to a place. Grocery stores, for example, are often an ignored but important component in community building. As community gathering places, they generate daily activity for nearby uses. In addition, they provide a vital service for nearby residential developments, making a district's housing more desirable to buyers and renters. They are also attractive to office workers who must buy groceries on their way home at the end of the day.

The Publix grocery store frames the vista at one end of Mizner Park's main street in Boca Raton, Florida. A 30,000-square-foot Safeway supermarket sits on top of a four-level basement parking garage with 12 floors of multifamily residential apartments above in Bethesda, Maryland. The Dean and Deluca grocery store is a

major draw in Phillips Place in the SouthPark suburban business district of Charlotte, North Carolina. Simon Property Group's new main street 556,000-square-foot shopping center in Bowie, Maryland, includes a 101,000-square-foot grocery component anchored by a Safeway. Clearly, grocery stores are becoming a major component in the transformation of suburban business districts when they are properly integrated into the pedestrian fabric of town centers and not just created as standalone buildings in a sea of parking spaces.

In the 3,200-unit traditional neighborhood community of King Farm in Rockville, Maryland, a 54,000-square-foot Safeway supermarket

The revitalization of State Street in downtown Chicago has created a distinctive place. The addition of the Art Institute's Film Center and student housing has activated this area, making it a favorite community gathering place that is both aesthetically pleasing and enticing with its rich mix of live-work-shop uses.

145

The incorporation of the Safeway supermarket into the King Farm town center in Maryland required careful siting to provide access on one side of the building for parking and service vehicles.

On another side of the building, the Safeway supermarket at King Farm, Maryland, presents an attractive face to the main shopping street.

The main shopping street at King Farm in Maryland connects to the village square and residential apartments that are constructed above the ground-floor shops, all of which benefit from the Safeway supermarket's proper integration into the town center.

anchors the mixed-use town center. The supermarket and its large parking lot are located at one end of the town center and are integrated into the center by shop-lined streets leading to the town square, creating a pedestrian-friendly main street shopping environment. All truck servicing and vehicular access to the supermarket parking lot is via roads other than the town center's shopping streets. Patrons can park on the street or in the supermarket parking lot and walk along the shop-lined pedestrian linkages to other establishments in the town center. From the front, the supermarket looks like a conventional suburban store—it is its integration into a pedestrian-friendly town center that makes the difference.

Entertainment Uses

Venues such as cinemas, indoor and outdoor skateboard and roller blade rinks, dance clubs, interactive game centers, and indoor children's play areas such as Discovery Zone help transform suburban business districts solely from work or shopping destinations into balanced communities that attract new residents who in turn draw new employers. The important cinema component of the entertainment mix can, however, challenge community building. Cinema complexes are big-box structures with long, blank walls that create dead zones in the streetscape and undermine the pedestrian environment. In an innovative move, Reston Town Center has located its cinemas on the second floor of retail buildings, with shops and restaurants still occupying the traditional ground-floor streetfront. This arrangement creates a more vibrant streetscape and protects the town center fabric from huge dead zones if a cinema closes. At the Avenue at White Marsh, a town center development in suburban Baltimore in Maryland, the cinema foyer was treated as a shop front, but the cinemas were set back behind a row of main street retailers.

Layout and Mix

Programming a full mix of uses is only half of the community-building equation for suburban business districts. Where different activities locate is just as important. For example, a cinema and adjacent bookstore reinforce one another. Pet shops with their unique aromas are not generally good neighbors for outdoor restaurants. The proper location and configuration of major uses can help foster the transformation of a suburban business district by creating pedestrian movement up and down shop-lined pedestrian linkages. To draw pedestrians up and down its main street, Newhall Land placed cinemas at one entrance to Town Center Drive (in Valencia, California) as well as in the middle of the half-mile-long street. In programming a community-building mix of uses, the key to success is to anticipate change. Entertainment preferences evolve; shops and restaurants evolve. So, to protect and strengthen community-building efforts, uses should be enduring in their popularity and balanced with cultural, civic, office, hotel, and educational facilities.

It is important to remember that change is an asset, not a liability. It creates important opportunities to meet shifting market demand and further strengthen the community appeal of the suburban business district. Cinemas, like any real estate product, are prone to cyclical ups and downs. From 2000 to 2001, the overbuilding crisis in the theater sector and the rise of the stadium-style megaplex led to declining ticket sales at older, less comfortable, and out-of-date multiplexes. Fortunately, standalone cinema complexes with their acres of parking—and even streetfront cinemas—are large enough to be redeveloped into a wide variety of community-building uses, such as performing arts centers, schools, or even a small mixed-use town center.

The Need for a Strategic Plan

To strengthen community, a strategic plan is essential to hasten the transformation of any suburban business district. The plan should encourage the development of adaptable or flexible buildings in several major locations so that retail space, for example, can be transformed into office space, or office space can become retail space, an entertainment venue, or housing, depending on market demand. Such strategies will help a suburban business district adapt to chang-

The main street at The Avenue at White Marsh is boomerang in shape, and the vista is closed at each end by major store locations. The sidewalks are generous in width, and careful attention has been paid to streetscaping. On-street parking provided along the main street is complemented by large parking lots located out of sight behind the buildings.

Southlake Town Square in Dallas/Fort Worth, Texas, incorporates a town square, town hall, and municipal offices framing the vista down the square, with parking areas provided at the rear. The strategic plan for Southlake Town Square allows the town center to grow to meet the needs and aspirations of America's changing demographic profile.

Creating Parkland in Bellevue Suburban Business District

Public parks are an important community asset missing from many of today's suburban business districts. The provision of such facilities will play a vital role in the transformation of suburban business districts into distinctive and attractive live-work-shop places. Downtown Park is a 20-acre oasis in the heart of downtown Bellevue, a suburban business district ten miles east of Seattle. The park's design was the product of a juried competition and features a grassy meadow at its center surrounded by a canal and 20-foot-wide walkway lined with plane trees and obelisk-shaped light standards. The park's formal entry is located along a boulevard on the site's north side, offering views of the park itself and the city beyond. Situated at the western fringe of Bellevue's central business district and just north of historic Old Bellevue, Downtown Park is a major component of Bellevue's downtown master plan. It also provides a highly valued amenity for the people who work in nearby offices and for residents of the area.

Community Leadership to Create a Community Asset

Under the leadership of then-Mayor Cary Bozeman, the city acquired most of the park site (17.5 acres) in 1983 from the Bellevue School District after the school district had declared the land surplus. It purchased the remainder of the site in 1988 and made a few additions since then. Acquisition did not occur without controversy over the park's siting and high cost. Some citizens questioned the wisdom of developing a downtown park at all. At the time, downtown Bellevue was largely a nine-to-five office core, but Bozeman saw the park as an investment that would help encourage the development of higher-density housing in the area.

Financing the park became something of a roller-coaster ride. The proceeds of councilmanic bonds paid for park acquisition, but a 1984 general obligation bond issue to cover the park's development failed to gather sufficient voter support. In response, a coalition of the city's civic and business leaders formed a nonprofit corporation that leased the site from the city and then raised $1.8 million to begin park development. The effort generated significant publicity and support from major corporations and, eventually, from the general public. Voters subsequently approved bond issues to cover the park's further development costs. The addition of the park to round out the offering of the suburban business district has been a huge success. Land values in the immediate vicinity have more than doubled, and the park has become a catalyst for new, higher-density residential development. Downtown Park provides an attractive open space in the heart of the suburban business district by encouraging public and private interest in park development and by serving as the keystone of the city's park system.

The Advantages of a Public/ Private Partnership

The creation of Downtown Park would have been impossible without the unprecedented partnership between the city and the private sector. As noted, a coalition of citizens and businesses contributed their time, effort, and money to create the park. Their cooperation began with the sponsorship of the design competition and continued with the lease arrangement for the parkland and a massive—and successful—fund-raising effort. The partnership arrangement caused some tensions along the way, particularly with respect to determining the locus of authority for planning and implementing the park's design. However, partnership members learned to trust each other and to cooperate. As a result, the process of developing Downtown Park became a community-

The 20-acre Downtown Park in the heart of the Bellevue suburban business district in Washington state was the result of a public/private partnership. Public parks are important community assets missing from many suburban business districts.

building effort as many groups were brought together to achieve a common goal.

Open-Space Protection

Before the development of Downtown Park, downtown Bellevue was deficient in open space. Moreover, if the area around what is now Downtown Park was to develop as the city hoped, with a greater intensity and variety of land uses, it would need a significant open space. In the early 1980s, Mayor Bozeman realized that it would be many years before the park would achieve its potential but that any delay would result in prohibitively high land costs This farsighted development now serves as a valuable place for reflection and recreation while enhancing downtown's pedestrian system and fostering a sense of place.

Downtown Revitalization

New residential development is now underway in the area around Downtown Park. In 1994, a 97-unit condominium project—among the first downtown housing projects built in Bellevue in years—opened on the edge of the park and sold out almost immediately. The park, along with the other amenities recently developed in downtown (including a regional library and new retail stores), has strongly encouraged the development of hundreds of additional residential units in the surrounding area. As one residential developer has said, a site next to Downtown Park is "a blue-ribbon location."

Overcoming Public/ Political Opposition

Initially, not everyone in Bellevue was convinced that the site of today's park should be dedicated to open space. Some thought the site was inappropriate for a "central" park; others felt that the acquisition cost was too high and that voters should have had a say in approving the bonds that paid for the land acquisition. To win citizen en-

Downtown Park, along with other amenities recently developed in the Bellevue suburban business district, including a regional library, new shops, and office buildings, has encouraged the development of hundreds of multifamily apartments. As one residential developer has said, a site next to Downtown Park is "a blue ribbon-location."

dorsement, both city and business leaders had to work together to establish a convincing case. Moreover, phasing development of the park helped demonstrate the benefits provided by an attractive public park in the suburban business district. Since the project began, park development has become popular in Bellevue. Downtown Park has spurred additional investment in other parks in the city of Bellevue.

Overcoming Financing Complications

Putting together the financing for Downtown Park was no easy matter. Indeed, the initial public resistance to financing development of the park forced the city's leaders to search for novel solutions. One reason for the success of the fund-raising campaign was its reliance on the creation of a private entity to develop the park; many contributors believed that the group would manage the funds and the park's creation more efficiently than would city government. The professional marketing efforts that supported the fund-raising campaign generated favorable results but would have been impossible if the city had undertaken the project on its own. By combining the strengths of the public and private sectors,

the coalition raised sufficient funds to make Downtown Park a reality.

Lessons Learned

The public/private partnership model used to develop Downtown Park has proven itself highly effective and is now a commonly used technique for the provision of open space in Bellevue. Such partnerships can be difficult to manage, however. Both sides need to have confidence in one another and must be willing to compromise. The example of Downtown Park proves that the creation of public parks in suburban business districts can be an effective technique for promoting development and livability. One successful park project can foster political support for the development or acquisition of additional parks and open space. Downtown Park has helped tremendously in the creation of a network of parks and in the process has contributed to the transformation of the Bellevue suburban business district into an attractive live-work-shop place. ●

Source: David J. O'Neill, *The Smart Growth Tool Kit* (Washington, D.C.: ULI–the Urban Land Institute, 2000), p. 53.

Creating a Community Entertainment Focus in a Dispersed Suburban Business District

The Avenue at White Marsh in the northeastern suburbs of Baltimore is a lifestyle retail and entertainment center structured around cinemas, restaurants, lifestyle retail stores, a Barnes & Noble bookstore, and outdoor community-building spaces that promote community interaction and deliver an upscale ambience in a middle-income market. Over the past 20 years, Towson-based developer Nottingham Properties has been transforming a 2,000-acre site into the White Marsh suburban business district—a dispersed residential, retail, and business district. The Avenue at White Marsh is the district's main street town center located on the opposite side of a major road leading to the 1.2 million-square-foot White Marsh regional shopping mall. About a half-mile away across I-95 are a 350,000-square-foot power center and several small neighborhood-oriented commercial projects. The Avenue at White Marsh was designed to fill a void and serve as the town center for the surrounding suburban business district. Modeled on the 1950s ideal of a main street town center, the project integrates generous landscaping, streetside cafés, plazas, fountains, and public art to create central public gathering places and allow restaurants and shops to open onto the sidewalks and the development's open space. The center hosts a seasonal farmers' market and a summer concert series at the main plaza.

A Community Entertainment Center

Six restaurants, a 16-screen stadium-seating movie theater (4,000 seats), and a mix of local, regional, and national retailers round out the main street retail/entertainment mix. The community has embraced this 295,000-square-foot project as the focal point and meeting place for White Marsh and the surrounding community. The first Christmas parade held at The Avenue at White Marsh drew a crowd of 6,000 people; the second and third parades each drew 15,000 people. Workers from the nearby office community frequent the town center for shopping, dining, and evening entertainment.

On-street parking is provided along the main street, with large parking lots located out of sight behind the buildings. This arrangement maintains the development's main street appeal. The pedestrian environment is distinguished by wide, tree-lined sidewalks, attractive sidewalk furniture, and

The Avenue at White Marsh in Baltimore is a lifestyle and entertainment center that uses cinemas, restaurants, lifestyle retail stores, a Barnes & Noble bookstore, and outdoor community-building spaces to promote community interaction and deliver an upscale ambience in a middle-income market.

ing markets in the coming decades. Perhaps even more important, the strategic plan should accommodate future growth and changing uses through infill development. "Southlake Town Square can grow for the next 500 years," declared Frank L. Bliss, executive vice president with Cooper & Stebbins LP, the project owner and developer. The town square can grow down with underground floors, up from low-rise to high-rise buildings, and out on infill parcels such as surface parking lots. Its strategic plan allows it to change as demand changes to ensure that it continues to meet the needs and aspirations of America's new demographic profile.

Why Community Matters to Suburban Business Districts

When a suburban business district embraces community, it becomes more than a collection

sensitive use of finishes to create a cohesive, walkable environment. Landscaping and attractive gateway features enhance the pedestrian linkages that lead from main street to the parking areas.

Regulatory Barriers

The existing zoning precluded the mix of uses originally planned for the project; moreover, given Baltimore County's quadrennial zoning cycle, the property could not be rezoned for four years. To remedy the situation, Nottingham Properties worked with county officials and other landowners to craft Planned Unit Development regulations for commercial developments (PUD-C). After the approval of the regulations, it took 15 months to obtain the PUD-C approval. The final plan permits great flexibility in project layout and design—helping ensure the long-term viability of the project and allowing it to change to meet the community's evolving needs and aspirations.

Lessons Learned

The Avenue at White Marsh demonstrates that a sense of place and social connection can be created with new retail shops lining an open pedestrian and vehicular street. The project delivers an upscale ambience in a middle-income market and thereby constitutes a prototype for middle-income projects, demonstrating that main streets are not just the preserve of high-income com-

The Avenue at White Marsh in Baltimore demonstrates that a sense of place and social connection can be created with new retail shops lining an open pedestrian street enlivened with tamed vehicular movement and parking.

munities. Although White Marsh has fulfilled a social vision for a shopping center, it is not a real town center in that it lacks a library, town hall, post office, church, or fire department. In addition, the absence of residential uses in the center prevents a 24-hour/seven-day environment from developing. Finally, the Avenue at White Marsh missed a golden opportunity to integrate with the regional shopping mall as was achieved at Valencia Town Center in California. The center would benefit from improved pedestrian linkages to the adjoining regional shopping mall, office parks, and residential areas. The flexible zoning that now applies to future development of the site allows the center to meet changing community aspirations and demands. The tighter regulatory controls applying to other centers will protect the Avenue at White Marsh from competition that may remove some of its incentive to innovate to meet community needs.

of aging, standalone office buildings and retail facilities competing with now-resurgent central business districts and other suburban business districts. Community transforms a suburban business district into a vibrant and enticing *place* —a place where people can live, work, and play. Town Center Drive in California, Reston Town Center in Northern Virginia, Addison Circle in Texas, and CityPlace in Florida are only a few examples of places that have harnessed the power

of community building to create real estate value and a secure tax base in their suburban business districts. Their respective communities have rewarded them with repeat visitation. Without doubt, community building is an essential component of place making and a potent strategy in the transformation of America's suburban business districts.

chapter 8

Place Making to Enhance Real Estate Returns

Thomas L. Lee, former chair and chief executive officer of Newhall Land and Farming Company, opened ULI's first Place Making Conference in Chicago in May 1999 with these words: "Place making is the very essence of a real estate development. As people choose one place over another, the place of choice attracts a higher valuation and sells at a premium. Desired places are ones that appeal to all of the senses—sight, sound, smell, taste, and touch. It is a rich mix of aesthetic design, the activities offered, the quality of providers, and price. Successful place making is therefore about meeting the demand from the local community. It is not a formulaic real estate product or the latest fad. Therefore, developers should exercise a high level of conceptualization and market matching in their place-making activities."[1] Place making is all about community building, about creating special places that the community values and rewards with repeat visitation, pride of ownership, and a sense of belonging. As America launches into a new century, with a new demographic profile and a new appreciation of how it can transform its suburban business districts into live-work-shop places reflective of our needs and aspirations, the art of place making will increasingly become the focus of development opportunities while innovative real estate development and investment will become the tools through which place making is achieved.

"There is no there there." With this reference to Oakland, California, in 1937, Gertrude Stein launched what has become an ongoing discussion of "place," its meaning, and its relevance to contemporary development forms, including suburban business districts. The perception of "place making" varies from descriptions of physical places to the dynamic impacts of human activity, historic context, the natural environment, and the recognition that "places" develop and evolve over long periods of time. The word "place" derives from the Latin *platea* (broad street).[2] *Webster's Dictionary* defines place as ". . . physical surroundings, a building or locality used for a special purpose . . ." and cites examples of a "square or court in a city, short narrow street, a space or room, a particular area, a city, town or village." Dennis Pieprz, internationally noted urban designer, says that ". . .memorable places have a physical dimension by virtue of extraordinary physical position, by being rooted in the form of the land, or through a beautiful man-made composition of buildings and open spaces. You will personally experience the place. You will know when you are there."[3]

The one thing we *all do*—apart from eating, sleeping, and breathing—is to assess place. Every facet of our daily lives occurs in a place. There-fore, it is not surprising that during every waking hour, even arguably while we sleep, we are involved in a subliminal assessment of place. Our senses are constantly assessing: deciding whether we like a place; whether we want to change it; escape from it; or reward it with repeat visitation. When we reward a place with repeat visitation, we create value. In suburban business districts, the creation of a place that people want to return to produces three tangible impacts. It is easier to draw and retain tenants because customer attraction translates into increased sales, increased rents, and capital value.

- The quality of a place ensures a market share premium over the competition.
- A place is more adaptable to demographic and market changes over time, allowing it to grow, develop, and change without forcing tenants to relocate to another business district.

Our response to place owes much to how we "fit into" a particular place: whether we find it welcoming, engaging, stimulating, or exciting. Does it have a character that suits us? Our perception of how we fit into a place relates to

- form;
- balance;

The word "place" derives from the Latin *platea* (broad street). *Webster's Dictionary* defines place as "... physical surroundings, a building or locality used for a special purpose ..." and cites examples of a "square or court in a city, short narrow street, a space or room, a particular area, a city, town or village." Pictured here is CityPlace in West Palm Beach, Florida.

- synergy;
- proportion; and
- symmetry.

Placemaking by Lynda H. Schneekloth and Robert Shibley[4] introduces the dynamic relationship of people to place. The authors define place making as "... the way all of us as human beings transform the places in which we find ourselves into places in which we live. It includes building and tearing buildings down, cultivating the land and planting gardens, cleaning the kitchen and rearranging the office, making neighborhoods and mowing lawns, taking over buildings and understanding cities. It is a fundamental human activity that is sometimes almost invisible and sometimes dramatic. Place making consists both of daily acts of renovating, maintaining, and representing the places that sustain us, and of special celebratory one-time events such as designing a new church building or moving into a new facility."

Historically, place has been associated with extraordinary natural features or constructed environments that use traditional elements in compositions of squares, streets, buildings, and objects. In Europe, for example, natural features would include the Rock of Gibraltar and the Tuscany region of Italy. Constructed places would include the Piazza Navona, the Spanish Steps, and the Trevi Fountain in Rome. In the United

States, place has been associated with natural features such as the Grand Canyon and Niagara Falls while constructed places would include Quincy Market in Boston, Times Square and Central Park in New York, Wrigley Field in Chicago, and even the pattern of streets and public open spaces in the historic districts of Charleston and Savannah. One of the most striking examples of place making occurs when a natural phenomenon and the built environment interact, as dramatically demonstrated by Australia's Sydney Harbour, Opera House, and the Sydney Harbour Bridge.

Place Making in Suburban Business Districts

Place makers and community builders in the pre–World War II period attempted to use

Our perception of how we fit into a place relates to its form, balance, synergy, proportion, and symmetry. This photograph of a retail street in Celebration, Florida, shows how these elements can be brought together to create a place that is rewarded with repeat visitation.

The Essence of Place Making

Place making involves the development of places designed, constructed, and maintained to stimulate and please the senses, to encourage community use, and to promote civic and personal pride. Besides allowing people to perform essential functions, such as employment and shopping, places should be enjoyable, entertaining, and educational. Success in place making lies in configuring spaces and structures, and the connections between them, in a way that facilitates and encourages human activity and interaction within the context of the community. Encouraging human interaction requires comprehensive forethought and highly developed design skills. Successful place making is not necessarily achieved by erecting architectural monuments or building with expensive materials and elegant finishes. Rather, it is the essence of best-practice urban planning; it creates an integrated vision of what people consider most desirable in terms of opportunities for social integration, economic return, and environmental sustainability.

Place making is about creating an environment that uplifts our spirits—an environment that people want to be part of because it has been designed, built, and maintained with the goal of satisfying human needs and aspirations, from the mundane to the spiritual. A successful place appeals to the senses, engaging visitors and inhabitants alike in a voyage of discovery of enticing sights, sounds, and scents. •

A successful place appeals to the senses, engaging visitors and inhabitants alike in a voyage of discovery of enticing sights, sounds, and scents. Pictured here is one of the famous town squares in Savannah, Georgia.

Source: Geoffrey Booth, "The New Sensory Law," *Urban Land*, October 2000, p. 14.

---

the traditional palette of streets, public open spaces, and mixed uses to create a place-making framework for the first suburban business district prototypes at Country Club Plaza in Kansas City and Highland Park Shopping Village in Dallas. In the post–World War II period, some of the nation's planned suburban business districts such as Crown Center in Kansas City; Reston Town Center in Reston, Virginia; Las Colinas in Dallas; and Mizner Park in Boca Raton, Florida, likewise turned to the traditional elements of streets, open spaces, and mixed uses to create place. The most distinctive nontraditional form that has evolved in the post–World War II era is the enclosed suburban mall, which proved to be the catalyst for many suburban business districts.

Problems Facing Suburban Business Districts

As they age, suburban business districts throughout the country find themselves grappling with a wide range of planning and design issues. Primary among these issues is dysfunction due to obsolete facilities, irrational traffic and parking patterns, and the restrictions imposed on districts by communities seeking to remedy a district's adverse effects on the larger jurisdiction. The most intractable of the functional problems, both from the developer's and the community's perspective, are traffic congestion and parking accommodation. Another significant issue relates to a district's underlying land use patterns whereby each property stands apart from its

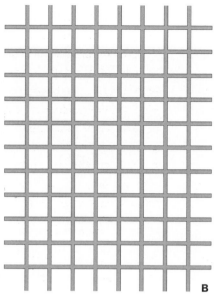
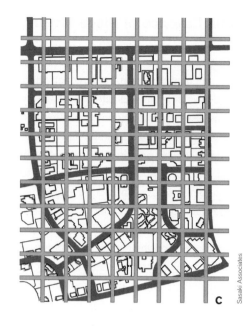

A   B   C

Sasaki Associates

A – The supergrid plat in Irvine Business Complex, California, that is typical of many suburban business districts throughout America.

B – The traditional grid plat of streets and blocks on a 400-foot centerline to centerline.

C – A superimposition of the grid over the superblock plat shows that some superblocks can cover an area of up to 12 grid blocks, making them difficult and unattractive for pedestrians to navigate, thereby promoting otherwise unnecessary vehicle trips and traffic congestion.

neighbor—isolated by parking lots, freeways, stormwater management facilities, or service roads. The dominant land use in suburban business districts is pavement. In *Streets and the Shaping of Towns and Cities,*[5] Michael Southworth and Eran Ben-Joseph note, "An amazing amount of land is devoted to roads, parking lots and other vehicular infrastructure, particularly in post-World-War-II development. On the average, the automobile consumes half the land area in cities in the United States, and in some cities such as Los Angeles, it approaches two-thirds."

The challenge in transforming suburban business districts centers on the liberation of surface parking lots' real estate value for infill development. Instead of functioning as a place-making liability, a surface parking lot can be transformed into a place-making asset. Mixed-use pedestrian-friendly forms of development can take shape on parking lots in a way that will transform America's suburban business districts into desirable live-work-shop places. In realizing this potential, our communities will have to craft new regulatory tools that focus on the creation of places rather than on the segregation of land uses.

Regulatory Response

The regulatory tools applied during the 20th century to mandate and control place making have been woefully inadequate and in most

cases counterproductive in vesting suburban business districts with a sense of place. In concentrating on legally prescriptive and exclusionary zoning codes, we have come to rely on a flawed mechanism to convey the vision of the places we wish to create. Black-letter law and legal terminology do not evoke the full power of the visual sense, and they certainly do not trigger the companion senses of sound, smell, taste, or touch. The literal interpretation of the law, with its limited and limiting vocabulary and legal style, fails to evoke a sense of place or capture the imagination in the way good writing or a film can. Indeed, our regulatory scheme is pedantic and restrictive and, as such, is the complete antithesis to place making that is creative, engaging, and inspirational.

The advent of "sensory law" is one approach that can equip us with new regulatory tools to "virtually" create places so we can experience them *before* we approve and construct them. We will be able to use our senses to assess the quality of a proposed project and its contribution to place making. Using this approach, the city plan, in digital form, can use real-time interactive models synchronized with sound to evoke the senses of taste, touch, and smell. The Gold Coast City Council in Queensland, Australia, is adopting a new sensory-focused approach to planning in its Place Making Code. And it is not alone. Arlington County, Virginia, is developing Virtual Arlington, a real-time, nearly photographically realistic, interactive computer model of the Rosslyn suburban business district.

Metropolitan Dade County, Florida, became the first jurisdiction in the nation to apply visualization techniques to zoning reform when it formulated the zoning ordinance for the Downtown Kendall Urban Zoning District. In response to both the real and perceived impacts of a suburban business district, Metropolitan Dade County approved creation of an overlay zone, called the Downtown Kendall Urban Center District, for an area that includes the Dadeland Mall in the Kendall area of south Miami. The Dadeland Mall is one of the largest and most financially successful malls in the southeastern United States, with 1.5 million square feet of space, sales exceeding $550 million each year, and 15 million visitors annually.

The new ordinance requires any future growth or expansion of the mall to take the form of a street-fronted, new urbanist, traditional town center. It mandates the introduction of open public streets through the existing enclosed mall.

From a community perspective, the ordinance is designed to address a serious traffic problem, to remedy an unattractive wall of high-rise parking garages, and to help create a desired downtown pedestrian environment. From the Dadeland Mall owner's perspective, however, the ordinance bears little relationship to the requirements for a successful mall operation and the owner's master plan for mall expansion. The ordinance is also inconsistent with the mall owner's long-term tenant leases and operating agreements. The clear mismatch between regulators and property owner needs to be resolved if the ordinance is to be readily implemented. Otherwise, the conflict will frustrate the county's place-making objectives.

The Value in Place Making

For the developer, the value of place making in suburban business districts such as Dadeland lies in creating a sustainable economic and physical environment in which businesses can respond to

The visualization of place through real-time, near-motion picture-quality interactive computer modeling provides the platform to move beyond zoning to place making. Shown here is a frame from the Virtual Arlington computer model developed by Arlington County, Virginia.

Arlington County Mapping Center and Department of Economic Development

market requirements. One district that is noted for changing with the times is Country Club Plaza in Kansas City, which, in addition to its other attributes, has sustained its market position over the decades. It has undergone renewal and expanded in response to its location, shifts in market demand, and the desire for a high-quality place. Similarly, traditional New England town centers as well as main streets throughout the country are exhibiting a renewed pride of place as they assume new functions and roles within their communities.

Mizner Park—Transforming a Decaying Business District through Place Making

Mizner Park in Boca Raton, Florida—a 398,000-square-foot mixed-use town center—pioneered the postsuburban renaissance of place making in American real estate development and now exhibits many of the elements essential to the creation of place. The project's first phase included four mixed-use buildings surrounding a public park. The buildings house 156,000 square feet of specialty retail space, 106,000 square feet of office space, 136 over-the-shop rental apartments, and a performing arts amphitheater. The second stage of the project included development of the International Museum of Cartoon Art, a Jacobson's department store, an additional

136 apartments, an office building, and parking structures lined with apartments. The project is especially noteworthy because of its careful attention to urban design issues and the creation of a sense of place through its mix of uses and town-center configuration. Restaurants and streetfront retail facing the central public park have stimulated a vibrant, 24/7 mosaic of activity that brings new life to this business district and creates the ambience that drives apartment demand.

Demolishing the Mall to Create a Main Street

The 30-acre Mizner Park site is located on Route 1 at the heart of downtown Boca Raton. It was occupied by a failing 15-year-old, 420,000-square-foot regional shopping center called Boca Raton Mall. Laid out in a dumbbell configuration with two anchors, the center was suffering from inordinately high vacancy rates and had failed to keep pace with the needs and aspirations of the community it served. Moreover, it had gone into significant decline following the opening of the 1.3 million-square-foot Town Center at Boca Raton shopping mall, about a half-mile away.

The Boca Raton Community Redevelopment Agency (CRA), established in 1980, provided the impetus to redevelop the mall site by uniting business leaders, private citizens, and cultural groups through the formulation of a strategic plan for downtown revitalization. The CRA later designated the site and its vicinity as blighted and proceeded to formulate a redevelopment plan for the mall and the surrounding area. The agency then took two important steps toward redevelopment; first, it approved a $50 million program to update downtown infrastructure, and, second, it secured state approval in 1986 for a downtownwide development of regional impact (DRI) plan. The DRI plan is a requirement of Florida law for projects likely to have regional road and infrastructure impacts. Once approved by the state, the DRI plan triggers an obligation on the part of the developer to fund works to mitigate the regional impacts of the development.

After inviting input from numerous consultants, the CRA recommended in 1987 that the city council redevelop Boca Raton Mall and re-

Geoffrey Booth

Mizner Park pioneered the post-suburban renaissance of place making in American real estate development and now exhibits many of the elements essential to the creation of place. Two public streets border the central park shown in this photograph. The park is well landscaped and provides a major visual and recreational amenity for residents and visitors alike.

place it with a mixed-use complex. Crocker & Company, aware of the CRA's desire to redevelop the site, bought the mall in June 1988 and subsequently entered into negotiations with the CRA to forge a ground-lease deal and redevelopment plan for the site. The CRA was to purchase the land through a $58 million bond issue that would be paid back through tax-increment financing. Twelve acres of the site, on which the new buildings now stand, were to be leased back to Crocker & Company for $280,000 annually for ten years following completion of the development. The city also was to provide $3.4 million to the developer for clearing the land.

A small but vocal group of citizens began voicing opposition to the redevelopment plan. Thus, in January 1989, at Crocker & Company's request, the city held a referendum to determine whether the community supported the proposed redevelopment, which was to be called Mizner Park. When the referendum indicated an overwhelmingly favorable reaction, the developer and the CRA signed a contract in February 1989, using the major deal points outlined above. Two years later, in mid-January 1991, the first stage of the project opened.

Creating the Place

The project is configured as a village-within-the-city that encompasses two city blocks on either side of a central public park/open space. Conceived as a traditional downtown, the nucleus of the project is organized around four mixed-use buildings facing each other across the park and public space, creating a visually uninterrupted ambience that visitors often compare to that of a charming European city. The plan did not call for any single-use, standalone buildings; moreover, any use that could be located on an upper floor—such as offices, housing, or cinemas—is located there. All ground-floor space is used either for retail establishments or pedestrian interconnections. While later development stages have not followed the plan slavishly, the synergistic value of the mixed-use approach has not been lost.

The innovative design did not evolve without the benefit of an arduous planning process. Indeed, it represented a good deal of risk because the return to street retail was a new concept in the late 1980s—and untested on such a grand scale—in a southern Florida market. In developing the concept, the developer and architect

159

To generate additional real estate income to offset the upfront cost of the parking structures and to contribute to Mizner Park's streetscape and place-making excellence, the parking structures were faced with residential buildings that front onto the streets.

looked to many other models, including East Hampton on Long Island; Old Town Alexandria, Virginia; Worth Avenue in Palm Beach, Florida; South Street Seaport in New York; and Cross Keys in Baltimore.

The project's central space is bordered by two public streets designed with pavers and plaza details to provide vehicular and pedestrian access and on-street parking. In this way, needed circulation elements are combined with open-space amenities, furthering the traditional main street atmosphere. One advantage of a central open space bordered by two streets is that ample on-street parking is available in front of the stores and restaurants, as cars can park on both sides of both streets. Additional parking is provided in parking structures located behind the main street mixed-use buildings. To generate additional real estate income to offset the upfront cost of the parking structures and to contribute to Mizner Park's streetscape and place-making excellence, the parking structures were faced with multifamily residential buildings that face onto the streets.

In fact, the project's parking requirements were primary determinants in the overall sizing of Mizner Park such that a mix of uses would support a shared-parking scheme. In a strategy that reduced the number of parking spaces by more than 25 percent, the parking structures are located to maximize the shared-parking potential associated with Mizner Park's cultural and entertainment venues. The accommodation of shared parking means that two-thirds of the site is devoted to public areas—the amphitheater, broad arcade walkways, and the park/village green, which is dotted with gazebos, benches, and fountains. Outdoor dining plazas and apartment balconies overlooking the activities contribute to a buzz of activity that delights area residents and visitors alike. The central public space is well known as the "living room" of Boca Raton. The architecture reflects a strong, appropriate style and sense of place by building on Boca Raton's well-known design traditions and adapting the fanciful, highly articulated style of 1920s architect Addison Mizner to the demands of the 1990s and early 21st century.

Reaping the Place-Making Dividend

The retail component of the project was 90 percent preleased before its 1991 opening. In the first few weeks after their debut, shops sold out of inventory and restaurants ran out of food.

Over the past decade, retail sales have continued to set new benchmarks, underpinning strong growth in rents and capital value. Interestingly, the developer's initial retail leasing strategy was to start by targeting local tenants and then move on to regional and then national prospects (the exact opposite of most retail leasing campaigns). Most of the tenants, though not national chains, were already operating out of other locations and opened an additional establishment in Mizner Park; some relocated existing businesses into the project while a few others saw an opportunity and created businesses anew. Five tenants were carried over from the previous mall—a bookstore, delicatessen, movie theater, and two office tenants.

In choosing retail tenants, the developer focused on high-end specialty retailers, primarily fashion stores and art galleries drawn from the Palm Beach/Broward County area. Within a few months of opening ten years ago, Mizner Park has enjoyed a virtual zero vacancy rate. Its reputation both nationally and locally was such that retailers wait for retail vacancies so they can locate in the center. Entertainment facilities and restaurants anchor the retail component of the project with support from the Jacobson's department store, which was a later addition. The six restaurants represent three levels of pricing and appeal to a broad range of markets. Generally, the restaurants were the first spaces to be leased. AMC Theaters' eightplex cinema and the L&N Seafood and Ruby Tuesday restaurants are among the top-grossing outlets in their respective national chains.

The office space has also leased well, attracting not only local credit tenants but also national firms such as La Salle National Bank (11,000 square feet), Pantry Pride Grocery Company (12,500 square feet), and Bear Sterns Investment Banking. All leasing was handled in house as Crocker & Company enjoys a considerable presence in Boca Raton's office leasing market. Half of the initial 136 apartments rented before construction—even before furnished models were available for tours—and all of the apartments leased before opening day. The press generated not only by the redevelopment effort but also by the referendum gave the residential

units tremendous visibility in the marketplace, necessitating only a minor marketing effort. Additional stages of development have added to Mizner Park's apartment stock but, again, have failed to satisfy demand. The apartment manager reports a significant list of tenants waiting to rent apartments as vacancies occur.

Mizner Park's grand opening drew 20,000 people. Since then, the project has hosted several community events, including an annual arts festival, symphonic and jazz concerts, and a circus. The city-owned park, whose management follows the rules and regulations of other parks in Boca Raton, has become a significant gathering place for retirees and other community residents.

Lessons Learned

Crocker & Company's early strategy was to emphasize Mizner Park's cultural offerings as a means of selling the project concept—a cultural/commercial village—to the public. However, the cultural elements were slow to develop in that they depended on arts institutions' ability to finance their own programs. Without doubt, the developer was too far ahead of the curve with its cultural arts strategy, but it witnessed the realization of that strategy in the late 1990s as the economy continued to grow and America's changing demographic profile demanded leisure-time cultural pursuits. The most important lesson to be learned from Mizner Park is that the mixed-use town-center environment can unearth an undiscovered market for multifamily apartments—a market that the developer just cannnot satisfy at this location. The innovative use of shared parking in structures that have been fully integrated into the district and screened by apartments and mixed-use developments (also offsetting the cost of the parking structures) has made parking provision a place-making asset rather than a liability of this transformed business district.

A main street, mixed-use town-center design was a risky approach in the late 1980s. It broke with the proven retail and office formulas that until then had been embraced by lenders and developers. In defiance of conventional wisdom, the retail uses faces inward, with no visibility from the adjacent arterial road; the residential component is located above the retail stores; and the early office space lacked a distinctive identity. However, the project proved that a well-conceived mixed-use project can add up to more than the sum of its parts. The sense of place created at Mizner Park helps the project overcome the downside risks of what was at the time considered a novel approach, and the project has continued to deliver a healthy place-making dividend.

The Essential Elements in the Creation of Place

Place making transcends the simple streetscape, the introduction of a park, or even reversion to yesteryear's main streets. It brings together the

figure 8.1 **The Essential Elements of Place Making**

Element	Example
Composition of physical form(s)	The French Quarter in New Orleans is a unique and memorable urban district by virtue of its intensity of use and density, spatial order, distinctive architectural continuity, and clearly defined edges and entrances. Reston Town Center in Reston, Virginia, through its physical configuration featuring a traditional main street, plaza, and fountain, has created a memorable place of distinction.
Distinctive open spaces	Memorable cities possess great public spaces, for example, Boston's Public Garden, London's Piccadilly Circus, and New York streets such as Fifth Avenue.
Pedestrian scale and connectivity	It is reasonable to expect pedestrians to walk distances of up to four blocks (1,600 feet) depending on climate and the quality of the pedestrian environment. Despite the dominance of the automobile and the Internet, the physical and social characteristics of people and their interest in walking, gathering, celebrating, and eating have not changed significantly in our contemporary society.
Access	Suburban business districts grew as a consequence of location, highway access, and ease of parking. These factors represent the underlying requirements for the economic feasibility of suburban business districts and are principal elements in the perception of the quality of modern places. Desirable places can surmount poor or weak vehicular circulation and limited parking.
Mixed land uses	Memorable urban environments and the perception of place are characterized by intense pedestrian activity in attractive settings for the better part of the day and evening. Historic centers such as Boston, with its in-town residential neighborhoods, and new business centers such as Reston Town Center, which has introduced housing within its center, are highly regarded places. While planners and designers can create the stage or framework for place, only mixed land uses, including residential uses, will bring the actors to the stage on a 24-hour/seven-day basis.
Landscape environment	Climate, topography, water, and plants play important roles in the creation of place. The late James Rouse, developer of Columbia and the festival markets, found through his experience that "people seek beauty and delight." Alan Ward, author of *American Designed Landscapes,* suggests that ". . . elements of the natural environment, including climate and landscape, are a powerful part of place" and that ". . . meaningful landscapes are narrative and tell you about place."[1]
Connectivity to adjoining neighborhoods	Connections to adjoining neighborhoods can lend strength to a suburban business district by drawing on the attributes of neighboring businesses and residents.
Partnership	The creation of place in suburban business districts requires a partnership between the public and private sectors. Both CityPlace in West Palm Beach and downtown San Diego brought together the expertise and financial resources of the public and private sectors in a winning formula to create enduring, inviting, and valuable places.

[1]Interview with Alan Ward, principal, Sasaki Associate, author of *American Designed Landscapes* (Washington, D.C.: Spacemaker Press, 1998), November 2000.
Source: Richard Galehouse, Sasaki and Associates, 2001.

Elements of the natural environment, including climate and landscape, are a powerful part of place. Well-conceptualized landscapes are narrative and tell about a place. Pictured is a pocket park in Buckhead in Atlanta, Georgia.

realities of contemporary real estate development and the values of the host community to create a place of enduring value by drawing on several essential elements. Figure 8.1 summarizes the essential elements of place making.

The Prospects for Place Making in Three Suburban Business Districts

Tysons Corner in Fairfax County, Virginia; Irvine Business Complex in Irvine, California; and Buckhead in Atlanta are three of America's best-known and largest suburban business districts. The following case studies explore how each of these suburban business districts has addressed both the functional and qualitative issues of place. They represent typical, though not necessarily best-practice, examples of place making in contemporary suburban business districts. All three suburban business districts encompass vast acreage. Tysons Corner and Buckhead evolved into their current form through the incremental but not integrated development of individual real estate projects approved on a project-by-project basis in conformance with the two areas'

respective zoning ordinances. In essence, development was geographically proximate but rarely integrated or interconnected. Planning was confined to the boundary of the site and not to how the various projects could work together to create a place. The Irvine Business Complex, by contrast, developed under a districtwide plan but was initially conceived as an industrial subdivision. Of the three suburban business districts, Buckhead is the one most advanced in its planning to transform itself into a live-work-shop place that will meet the needs and aspirations of America's new demographic profile.

Tysons Corner—Who Needs Place with a Market as Strong as Ours?

Eight miles west of Washington, D.C., Tysons Corner in Fairfax County, Virginia, began its life as a commercial real estate subdivision encompassing 6,000 acres between State Routes 7 and 123, the Capital Beltway (I-495), and the Dulles Toll Road. The Tysons Corner suburban business district now embraces 5.6 million square feet of retail space, 23.2 million square feet of office space, 1 million square feet of in-

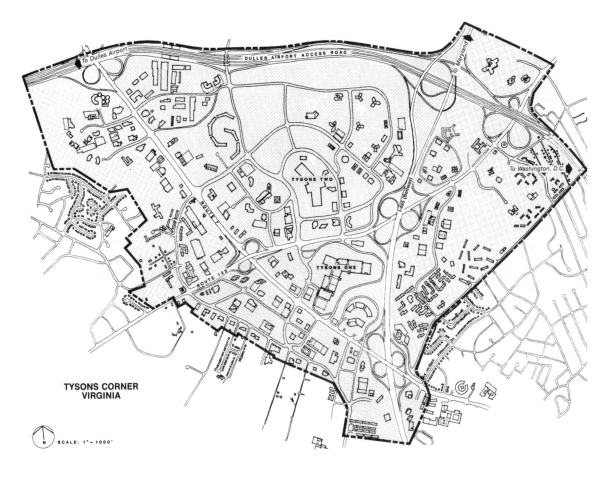

TYSONS CORNER
VIRGINIA

SCALE: 1" = 1000'

dustrial and hybrid space, ten hotels accounting for 3,300 rooms, and a population of more than 10,000 residents.[6]

The favorite target of journalists, urban designers, and architects as the quintessential example of what is wrong with today's suburban business districts, Tysons Corner is the 16th-largest business district in the United States, with the 14th-largest daytime office population in the country. In the 1960s, construction of the Dulles Airport access road and I-495 encouraged the development of strip malls and automobile dealerships in the area. Initially the location of large corporate back offices, Tysons Corner in particular soon became Northern Virginia's business district and a regional shopping destination. Today, Tysons claims the greatest concentration of retail activity on the East Coast outside New York City.

Development Form, Governance, and Transportation

Land use in Tysons is dominated by retail and office development. Two regional malls—the

Tysons Corner Shopping Center (1.9 million square feet) and Tysons Galleria at Tysons II—are located on opposite sides of a major arterial road. In addition, the area encompasses six strip shopping centers and several freestanding retail operations. Office space is housed in standalone mid- and high-rise office buildings. Tysons Corner is an unincorporated area of Fairfax County, with governance split among three county planning districts, three county supervisory districts, and two postal addresses (McLean and Vienna). The public sector has undertaken few projects, and public improvement initiatives in transportation—normally the purview of the public sector—have fallen to private corporations and associations. Private sector interests within the district have created a transportation management association to address traffic problems. Despite the framework of modern highways that gave birth to Tysons Corner's explosive growth, transportation and traffic congestion is now a major problem. The Dulles Corridor Transportation Study, completed in 1997, explored different public transportation alternatives along the Dulles Toll Road. It identified rail as the preferred transit alternative, with additional bus service aiding in the transition. In July 1998, bus service more than doubled, completing the first phase of the expansion. In accordance with Fairfax County's development standards, most roadways in Tysons Corner have sidewalks, but those sidewalks are little used. Clearly, sidewalks and street furniture cannot compensate for the expansiveness and discontinuous pattern of development parcels and the width of area roadways. Pedestrians face eight or more lanes of traffic at intersection crossings of major arterial roads.

The Dominance of the Superblocks

Despite the associated transportation issues, Tysons Corner is a significant district by virtue of both its size and the range of services it offers. Its two large shopping malls are two of its principal destinations. Tysons's weaknesses as a place, however, stem from a pattern of superblocks and arterial roads that promotes separation and accords the automobile prominence over the pedestrian—a pattern that is reinforced by Tysons Corner's relatively low density. Moreover, even with its acres of woods, lobbies, entry courts, and malls, Tysons lacks a defining public open space or community focus.

The development of place at Tysons requires a synergistic configuration of use patterns that supports the

- infusion of more in-town housing;
- development of a defining public open space;
- introduction of community facilities;
- development of a pedestrian network to connect parcels;
- achievement of higher densities to ensure the cost effectiveness of alternative methods of transportation; and
- provision of choice in transportation mode.

Creating Place in Tysons Corner

Place making in Tysons Corner faces three hurdles. The first is community leaders' and property owners' failure to recognize the potential increase in real estate values that comes

Pedestrian-friendly places are found only within the buildings at Tysons Corner and do not connect with each other to promote walking between buildings. Shown here is the Starbucks Court in Tysons Galleria shopping center.

Geoffrey Booth

The extension of the Metro rail system to Tysons Corner and provision of a station on vacant land (on the right in this photograph) between Tysons Corner Shopping Center and Tysons Galleria could link the two shopping centers with a mixed-use transit- and pedestrian-friendly town center.

with creating a sense of place. The second is the threat posed by unbridled traffic congestion to the area's continued prosperity. The third is the absence of a progressive public/private partnership that can undertake the strategic planning necessary to ensure Tysons Corner's transformation into a transit-oriented and pedestrian-friendly live-work-shop place. More specifically, development in Tysons Corner is fragmented and inextricably linked to the automobile, which merely exacerbates the traffic congestion associated with an already low development density. To counter the congestion problem, Fairfax County decided to limit development densities; the net effect has been an increase in the separation between buildings and the continuing necessity to drive between buildings.

The Tysons Corner Urban Center Plan approved by the Fairfax County supervisors in 1994 was supposed to address Tysons Corner's lack of cohesiveness and identity by promoting a pedestrian-friendly environment with tightly clustered buildings—close to sidewalks and close to a future Metro station and ancillary uses. It was said that workers would be able to run everyday errands or meet a friend for dinner and a movie without relying on their car. In administering the plan, the county has brought about

the exact opposite by approving new office developments located an unreasonable distance from the proposed Metro station and the existing shopping malls.

Seizing the Opportunity

It is the extension of the Metro rail system to Dulles Airport via Tysons Corner that provides the catalyst for place making in this suburban business district. One station location is proposed for vacant land between Tysons Corner Shopping Center and Tysons Galleria. The proposed station would provide the opportunity to link the two shopping malls with a mixed-use transit- and pedestrian-friendly town center similar in form to Reston Town Center or Mizner Park. Such a development pattern would consolidate a critical mass of multifamily residential, office, retail, civic, and cultural uses around a high-capacity rapid transit station. But capitalizing on the opportunities associated with the new Metro station will require Fairfax County to become an active financial partner in the project, not just an observer and reactive regulatory approval authority. The Centre City Development Corporation established by Pete Wilson, former mayor of San Diego, provides an excellent model of the public/private partnership needed to realize Tysons Corner's full potential and the protection of the county's tax base. As the spokesperson for the Fairfax County Chamber of Commerce said prophetically in 1999, "If you can provide people with opportunities to live-work-shop all in Tysons Corner without getting in their cars . . . that's the way you maintain the viability of Tysons Corner in the long run."[7]

Irvine Business Complex—A Place-Making Solution in Need of Political Leadership

The Irvine Business Complex is a 2,500-acre mixed-use suburban business district in the planned city of Irvine, California, in southern Orange County. It is located 40 miles south of Los Angeles and is bounded by the city of Tustin on the north, the residential villages of Irvine on the east, the city of Newport Beach on the south, and John Wayne Airport and the city of Santa Ana on the west. Originally a master-planned industrial park, the complex grew in importance as a business address in the 1970s, triggering the redevelopment of industrial uses into high-rise office buildings.

Regulatory Barriers to Mixed-Use Development

Not surprisingly, with its emergence as a suburban business district and shift to higher-density business uses, Irvine began to experience significant traffic congestion. In 1982, to remedy the traffic problem, the Irvine City Council approved a rezoning of the business complex. The new zoning scheme introduced an elaborate bonus system aimed at encouraging developers to construct dynamic mixed-use developments that would locate housing and services near jobs. The goal of the ordinance was to create walk-to-work and service opportunities. Community-building elements eligible for bonuses included high-density housing, atriums and public art, retail uses, hotels, and road improvements. Irvine's original zoning ordinance and private covenants, conditions, and restrictions prohibited mixed-use developments that incorporated residential and retail uses.

Unfortunately, the new zoning scheme and bonus program failed to work together to deliver the desired multifamily housing and mixed-use development. Instead, the regulatory system permitted virtually unlimited development—development far in excess of the capacity of the

The aerial view of the Irvine Business Complex shows the dominance of road and parking space within this suburban business district that in turn increases the separation between buildings and promotes additional vehicle trips. Those trips further drive demand for additional road space and parking areas.

Sasaki Associates

167

The use of the superblock plat rather than a traditional grid reduces the number of roads within the suburban business district but increases their width and capacity, which leads to increased vehicle speeds, making the Irvine Business Complex pedestrian-unfriendly.

transportation system planned for both the complex and the surrounding community. In 1988, the city appointed a task force—the Urban Village Steering Committee—to look for alternatives to the then-current development type and configuration. The committee's first goal was to develop a plan that would locate people closer to jobs by providing housing and services needed for daily life within the Irvine Business Complex, thereby reducing automobile dependence. Second, the committee sought to develop alternative methods of transportation in lieu of reli-

ance on the single-occupant automobile. Despite the size of the suburban business district, its dispersed development pattern had denied the district a sense of place and a town center that could function as a community focus.

Identifying the Place-Making Problem

The city of Irvine retained a professional consultant to develop a plan that would address and remedy the district's several problems.[8] The consultant found that the business complex had been developed on a superblock plat in the form of a modified grid—the largest of which measured 1,200 by 1,600 feet; the smaller blocks measured 600 by 1,200 feet (the traditional block within a grid framework typically averages 400 by 400 feet). As a consequence of the superblock configuration, freestanding low- and high-rise structures with landscaped setbacks and courtyards sat on large parcels with self-contained parking in open lots or structures. This pattern undermined pedestrian interconnectivity and contributed substantially to automobile use and traffic congestion. Accordingly, while some of the new high-rise office and hotel buildings were architecturally significant and endowed with attractive landscape, sculpture, and water elements, the business district did not constitute a single, unified place but rather a collection of disjointed real estate developments. Furthermore, excellent regional highway access limited the use of public transit and explained why only limited bus service was provided to the suburban business district and why its infrequent service was proving a less-than-attractive option to commuters.

The original plan for the complex accorded highest priority to the movement of automobiles on a network of avenues and roads. Roadways were typically six to eight travel lanes in width, with additional turning lanes at major intersections. The pedestrian network consisted primarily of unattractive sidewalks adjacent to the arterial roads. In 1990, the business complex embraced more than 37 million square feet of building space. In terms of acreage and square footage, office uses, primarily research and development firms and some corporate offices, dominated the Irvine district. More than 1,600 of the

The typical intersection design in a superblock-platted suburban business district carries significant volumes of traffic at speed and constitutes a major barrier for pedestrians and cross-street activity. Due to their width and volume of traffic, such streets are incapable of serving as main streets for a mixed-use town center.

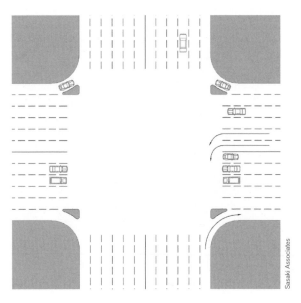

2,500 acres of land and 20 million of the 37 million square feet of building space were dedicated to office use. Industrial/warehouse use accounted for 15 million square feet of the remaining space and a series of business hotels for another 1.5 million square feet. In 1990, the complex included only 403 residential units.

Two serious structural flaws continue to undermine any sense of place within the Irvine suburban business district. First, the dominance of office development means that peak traffic flows occur during the morning and evening rush hours, thereby restricting district activity to the nine-to-five workday. Second, the superblock plat is designed to accommodate formulaic real estate products and encourage automobile use —to the near exclusion of pedestrian movement.

Although superficially cost-efficient from the perspective of Irvine's initial development, the superblock configuration dictates exceptionally wide arterial roads such that two or three major streets carry the business complex's total traffic load. Consequently, the traffic problems are exacerbated, and what little pedestrian movement is possible is both unsafe and unpleasant. For this reason, pedestrian circulation and interconnectivity within Irvine's superblocks remain significantly underdeveloped.

Failing to Implement the Solution

To address the above problems, the consultant developed an innovative urban village plan for the Irvine suburban business district. The plan addressed the area's functional problems and its less-than-outstanding quality of place. Its overall land use concept recognized that the 2,500-acre suburban business district was beginning to organize itself naturally into a series of distinct precincts corresponding to freeway access, visibility, and relationships to adjoining urban areas. The urban village land use concept defined the precincts and proposed a zoning change to support a mixed-use approach. It provided for the creation of two new residential neighborhoods containing a full range of community facilities and services adjacent to the office core. A principal design tenet was the provision of smaller block sizes within the residential districts to improve pedestrian interconnectivity. In particular,

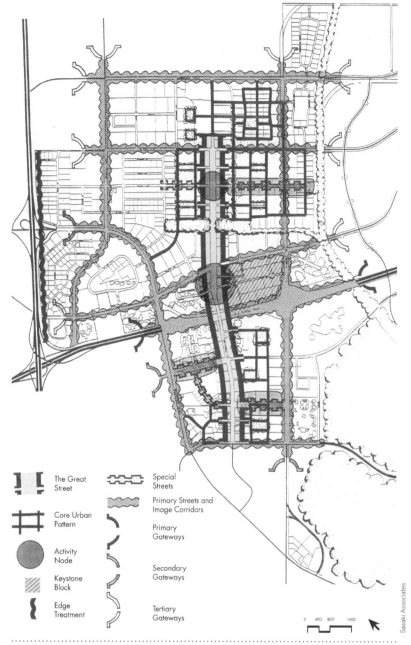

Sasaki Associates

The Great Street

Core Urban Pattern

Activity Node

Keystone Block

Edge Treatment

Special Streets

Primary Streets and Image Corridors

Primary Gateways

Secondary Gateways

Tertiary Gateways

0   400'   800'   1600'

An innovative urban village plan was devised for the Irvine Business Complex that involved the creation of boulevards and the breaking up of the superblocks with a grid plat. Pedestrian spines and mixed-use development opportunities laid the framework for the introduction of a sense of place, but a change in community leadership saw the plan abandoned in the early 1990s.

the plan proposed the redesign of Von Karman Avenue, an arterial road within the complex, as an attractive boulevard with high-density mixed uses served by public transit. It also set the basis for redrafting land development regulations to support mixed-use development. Further, the plan reclassified the entire road network into a hierarchy of five street types, from local streets

One of the successful innovations of the Irvine Business Complex urban village plan was the introduction of multifamily apartments that for the first time allowed office workers the choice of living within the suburban business district and walking to work.

to primary arterial roads, to guide the development of streetscape standards.

After a change in community leadership in the early 1990s, the city abandoned the urban village plan. As a result, intensive new commercial development over the ensuing years has mimicked earlier patterns. Since 1990, another 4.5 million square feet of office space have entered the market, along with an additional 1,700 residential units.[9]

Nonetheless, the addition of the residential units and some remedial work on improving pedestrian connections within and between the superblocks has been welcome, although the lack of political leadership ensured that the Irvine suburban business district entered the 21st century and a rapidly changing market without the implementation of a strategic plan that would have created a sense of place and would have vested the Irvine suburban business district with a competitive advantage.

Buckhead—Seizing the Competitive Advantage in Place Making

The Buckhead suburban business district is located four miles north of central downtown Atlanta and encompasses an area of 28 square miles. Buckhead's core is one of the nation's

largest suburban business districts, combining major offices, retail outlets, hotels, restaurants, an entertainment district, and high-rise residential condominiums and apartments. The commercial core encompasses approximately 15 million square feet of office space, more than 5,000 hotel rooms, 1,400 retail establishments, 200 dining places, and 16,500 multifamily units.[10] Buckhead has been characterized as "the Beverly Hills of the East" because of the quality of its commercial and neighboring high-end residential developments.

Capitalizing on Access and Governance Infrastructure

Lenox Square, the largest shopping center in Buckhead, was developed in 1959. It proved to be the catalyst development for a series of high-rise office, hotel, and residential developments. Buckhead is well served by both transit and interstate highways. Atlanta's AMTRAK station is located in Buckhead, and the district includes three stations on two of Atlanta's transit lines (MARTA). The area is framed by two of the South's most important interstate highways, I-75 and I-85. Even though Buckhead lies within the city of Atlanta, several professionally staffed nonprofit groups, including the Buckhead Coalition, Inc., headed by former Atlanta mayor Sam Mas-

170

sell, and the Buckhead Business Association represent the district's interests, planning for its future and self-taxing in order to carry out improvements within the district. The mission of the Buckhead Coalition is "to improve the quality of life in the suburban business district."[11] In 1994, the Buckhead Coalition carried out a major economic and physical planning effort that resulted in the formulation of the Buckhead Blueprint,[12] which called for a series of transportation, open-space, and streetscape improvements. The Buckhead Blueprint also recommended a long-range implementation program. In 1998, the Urban Land Institute conducted an Advisory Services panel on Buckhead's core area with a focus on transportation and zoning.[13]

Focusing on Place Making in the Urban Core

From an urban design perspective, Buckhead's core presents two sharply contrasting yet adjoining districts: the Buckhead Village district and the Piedmont-Lenox district. Historic Buckhead Village is a pedestrian-scaled area composed of street-fronted low-rise buildings dominated by restaurants and bars. The village has maintained a significant degree of architectural continuity by requiring little or no setback in the siting of buildings, maintaining a low-rise building configuration, and specifying brick as the dominant building material. When retail establishments in the village vacated their properties after development of Buckhead's shopping malls, the city of Atlanta, in an effort to stimulate reuse of the properties, relaxed its liquor licensing and parking requirements. As a result, the village evolved into a center of nightlife for the Atlanta metropolitan area. However, the success of the village as an entertainment district has created other problems. Sam Massell characterized the area as "bumper-to-bumper traffic, seedy and ugly,"[14] so much so that the city has tightened its licensing and parking requirements as well as code enforcement practices in order to regain control of the area. As a further response to conditions in the village, the Buckhead Blueprint proposed clearance of a four-block area in the heart of the district to accommodate a major public open space.

In contrast to the Buckhead Village district, the Piedmont-Lenox district has developed as an automobile-oriented suburban business district replete with standalone shopping malls, high-rise office buildings, hotels, and residential condominiums. The skyline presents a random picture of high-rise towers of varying architectural styles and materials. As with the village, no overall plan guided the initial development of

Sasaki Associates

The aerial view of the Buckhead suburban business district shows high-density pods clustered amid low-rise residential and commercial development dispersed over a wide geographic area. Three MARTA transit stations were required to accommodate the transit needs of this form of development.

The size of the resident population in hotels and high-rise condominiums complements the large daytime population of office workers, providing a significant dimension to the 24/7 live-work-shop environment. Buckhead's primary weakness as a place is its lack of significant central open space, which is desirable as both a symbolic focus and place for public celebration. Historically, the district has used the Lenox Square Shopping Center parking lot for its Fourth of July fireworks display. In fact, the Buckhead Blueprint proposed clearance of almost four blocks in the heart of Buckhead Village as a central park. However, because of concerns about the demolition of buildings in the village, the city square has never been developed, and the city is still considering the ULI Advisory Services proposal to replace the Lenox

The concentration of traffic on wide arterial roads that serve as circulators and through-traffic arteries for the Buckhead suburban business district dissects the district and makes the creation of one place difficult.

the district. Each property within the Piedmont-Lenox district features a green landscaped forecourt facing Peachtree Road, and, while individual properties convey a sense of quality, the overall concentration still lacks a sense of place. On-site parking takes the form of a random collection of dispersed open lots or parking structures. Recognizing the current practice among urban designers to build with little or no setback from the street, Massell retorted, "We like our building setbacks with their small gardens and fountains." The overall effect is that of a high-quality, high-rise commercial suburban subdivision, with each property standing alone and designed primarily for automobile access.

Underlying both the Buckhead Village and Piedmont-Lenox districts is a street pattern and system of platting that follows Atlanta's dendritic pattern of ridges and ravines and endows Buckhead with appealing and interesting views. Unfortunately, the major arterial roads such as Peachtree ride the city's ridgelines and are a dominant feature that bisects the suburban business district, impeding pedestrian connectivity.

Two Steps Forward and One Step Back

Overall, the Buckhead suburban business district demonstrates place-making opportunities and pitfalls. Massell was emphatic in his assessment of Buckhead. "I refuse to see us as a fragmented suburban business district."[15] Buckhead's strength of place includes its extraordinarily high quality, its densities, and its mix of land uses.

In contrast to the pedestrian-unfriendly nature of the road network are the beautifully landscaped but disconnected pocket parks and building setback areas around what are some handsome, architecturally designed buildings in Buckhead.

Square open parking lot on Peachtree Road with a large new central park atop a parking deck.

In general, the quality of the pedestrian environment throughout Buckhead is poor. Many sidewalks are narrow and in poor condition and lack street trees and street furniture. Pedestrian crossings in the high-rise Piedmont-Lenox district require a pedestrian to cross as many as ten to 12 lanes of traffic at major intersections. In September 1999, in response to the poor quality of the pedestrian environment, Buckhead's commercial property owners formed the Buckhead Community Improvement District (CID). Their objective was to raise $12 million over the next six years to leverage federal and state transportation funds for a major streetscape program. While recommendations in the Buckhead Blueprint for narrowing Peachtree Road and permitting on-street parking are unlikely to be implemented, the Buckhead CID is looking at options for developing new streets, planting street trees, installing street lighting, and reconstructing intersection crossings to make them more pedestrian-friendly. The CID is also evaluating a people-mover system or shuttle bus loop to improve connectivity within the suburban business district and relieve traffic congestion.

Another significant weakness in Buckhead is the relationship of the high-rise commercial core in the Piedmont-Lenox district to neighboring residential uses. In several areas, the commercial core turns its back to its neighbors with blocky garages, retail service areas, and open parking lots that present an unwelcome face to adjoining single-family residential areas. Despite its weaknesses, Buckhead can point to a foundation for transforming itself into a series of transit-oriented and pedestrian-friendly live-work-shop places that meet the needs and aspirations of America's new demographic profile. To its credit, it has put in place the strong leadership and governance structures needed to address its physical development and to work toward the creation of a sense of place. It used the ULI Advisory Services program to lay the basis for its strategic plan. Key strategic planning and development initiatives have included the provision of transit and the establishment of a business improvement district. As it moves to

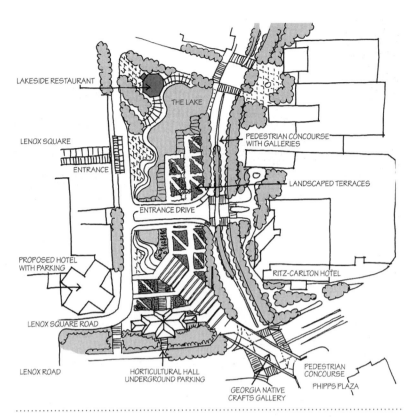

The ULI Advisory Services panel proposed a scheme to link the pocket parks and create a civic square from the open parking lot along the Peachtree Road frontage of the Lenox Square Shopping Center. The road corridor was to be enhanced with planting and the provision of safe and attractive pedestrian sidewalks that were designed to integrate the district. The proposal is still under consideration by the city.

acquire some of the traditional elements of place, such as a central park and a high-quality pedestrian environment, Buckhead is incrementally implementing a new design form that seeks to reconcile the spatial demands of the automobile with the need for a transit-oriented and pedestrian-friendly live-work-shop place.

The Place-Making Targets

The shopping mall, which is perhaps the most distinctive contemporary urban form that has developed in the post–World War II period, tends to be the focus of many suburban business districts. However, it satisfies only one limited dimension of our need for place. Its weakness lies in its insular form and its isolation from adjoining development. Recognizing the limits of a mall's ability to contribute to community building, some projects such as Valencia Town Center in Valencia, California, and the Mall of Georgia

in Atlanta are helping the mall meet main street. Our lives are not just about shopping—work and home are fundamentally important and this is why mixed use plays a critical role in the transformation of suburban business districts.

Most suburban business districts would benefit from an emphasis on mixed uses, particularly the addition of multifamily housing and an increase in densities to support a choice in transportation options. Desirable, too, would be the use of voids such as open parking lots to accommodate the development of more attractive pedestrian-friendly environments. Place making is something we all understand. It is rooted in the form of the land, the quality of the landscape, climate, and history. It is supported by patterns of property ownership, framed by its community context, governed by its institutional framework, and given life by its social and cultural dimensions

The creation of place in the nation's suburban business districts is essential to the districts' sustained real estate value. In the short term, suburban business districts will not achieve an overall quality of place akin to town centers and downtowns. Their sheer size, underlying suburban real estate plats, and scale, all designed to serve the demands of the automobile, make the achievement of place difficult, but not impossible. What we are likely to see is the development of more attractive and accommodating places within suburban business districts. The importance of these places, however, should not be underestimated, as over time they can actively transform suburban business districts into live-work-shop places.

Notes

1. Thomas L. Lee, "Place Making in Suburbia," *Urban Land,* October 2000, p. 113.

2. Jean McKechnie, ed., *Webster's New Universal Unabridged Dictionary, 2nd ed.* (New York: Simon & Schuster, 1979), p. 1,370.

3. Interview with Dennis Pieprz, principal, Sasaki Associates, Inc., November 2000.

4. Lynda H. Schneekloth and Robert G. Shibley, *Placemaking: The Art and Practice of Building Communities* (New York: John Wiley & Sons, 1995), p. 1.

5. Michael Southworth and Eran Ben-Joseph, *Streets and the Shaping of Towns and Cities* (New York: McGraw-Hill, 1997), pp. 4–5.

6. Fairfax County Economic Development Authority, *Area Business Report: Tysons Corner* (Vienna, Va.: Fairfax County, April, 2000), pp. 1–4.

7. Michael D. Sheab, "New Town Center Planned to Put a 'Heart' in Tysons—Design Aims to Appeal to Pedestrians," *Washington Post,* February, 24, 1999, p. B1.

8. Irvine Business Complex Urban Village Project (1989), Hellmuth, Obata & Kassabaum, Inc. (architects); Sasaki Associates, Inc. (planners); Barton-Aschman Associates (transportation); Keyser Marston Associates (economic); Sedway Cooke Associates (legal); the Keith Companies (environmental).

9. Information provided by Stephanie Keys, senior planner, city of Irvine, January 2001.

10. Sam Massell, ed., *Buckhead Guidebook* (Atlanta: Publication Concepts, 2000).

11. Ibid.

12. Buckhead Blueprint, plan prepared for Buckhead Coalition, Inc., by EDAW, Inc., 1994.

13. ULI Advisory Services Panel Report, *Buckhead Community, Atlanta, Georgia* (Washington, D.C.: ULI–the Urban Land Institute, 1998), p. 7.

14. Interview with Sam Massell, president, Buckhead Coalition, November 2000.

15. Ibid.

chapter 9

Embracing Strategic Public/Private Partnerships

F ew suburban business districts elect a mayor or a city council, and their boundaries seldom match political boundaries. In suburban business districts, it is predominantly the federal and state governments that fund transportation. However, it is local governments that largely control land use. While the role and function of federal, state, and local government is relatively well defined in a constitutional sense, the nation is only now coming to understand the magnitude of the impact of transportation policies on land use. Regrettably, the various policies and expenditure priorities of the federal, state, and local governments are often "out of sync" with one another, and no effective mechanism has yet surfaced to integrate policies and spending priorities in the interest of community building. Yet, the function of government is to carry out community-building endeavors that are beyond the legitimate scope and resources of individuals. In the case of suburban business districts, community building relates to

- the provision, maintenance, and protection of infrastructure, including schools, water supply, sewerage disposal systems, public parks and gardens, libraries, cultural facilities, and so forth;

- the provision of services required by the community, such as police, criminal justice, and social services; and
- the planning and integration of real estate development projects to maximize the place-making dividend flowing to the community.

Despite the overall function of government, many U.S. metropolitan areas are typified by "fragmentation in service delivery and revenue collection and disparities in tax burden and service quality."[1] U.S. metropolitan areas encompass large numbers of local governments. "In 1997, the average metropolitan area consisted of 114 local governments: two counties, 42 municipalities or towns, and 70 special districts, of which 21 were school districts. There were 18 local governments for every 100,000 people in metropolitan areas."[2]

School boards and city and county councils aside, the range of local governments includes the following forms:

- special districts created to finance and operate region-serving facilities such as airports, transit systems, water supply and sewerage disposal systems, and air and water pollution control;

- redevelopment agencies created by municipalities and counties to undertake development and tax base enhancement in parts of their respective jurisdictions. These agencies are often granted the power of eminent domain; and
- metropolitan planning organizations and two-tier councils established to coordinate government funding allocations or service delivery either pursuant to federal or state legislation or by formal and informal agreement of local governments and other entities in metropolitan areas.

These types of local governments provide a suite of government implementation vehicles and instruments for private and public developers who are about to embark on a program to facilitate the transformation of a suburban business district.

Many forms of local governmenst are premised not on reasons of efficient public administration but rather on financial imperatives. While states control the types of taxes that municipal governments can levy, the predominant form of local taxation is linked to real property; nonetheless, some states permit local governments to levy a sales tax, and a few allow an income tax levy. California's Proposition 13 (approved

Caroline Freeland Park in the suburban business district of Bethesda, Maryland, is typical of the types of community parks that governments can provide and maintain to round out the attractiveness of suburban business districts as desirable live-work-shop places.

in 1978) and Proposition 218 (approved in 1996) are the best-known examples of property tax–expenditure limitations; however, only 13 states do not impose limits on local government property taxes.[3] In addition, most states place some restrictions on local government borrowing, and some circumscribe service responsibilities. Under these circumstances, the delivery of services, access to intergovernmental financial transfers, and growth of the property tax base under *other* forms of local government allow the circumvention of many state financial restrictions.

By adopting a form of government that it deems, for the time being, to be appropriate, each community exercises its right to match the level of local taxation it considers reasonable to the level of community services it is willing to provide. At the local level, choice in government is highly valued. "Because citizens can migrate from jurisdiction to jurisdiction, municipalities (and other local governments) offer competitive bundles of services for a certain price (or tax)."[4] If fragmentation is the price of choice, the American people willingly pay for it.

There is, however, one constant in matters of government jurisdiction—local governments' jealously guarded prerogative to regulate land use. Land use control is central to real estate development and valuation. Without an entitlement, there is no right to develop, no potential income stream, and therefore no bankable development project. For the transformation of suburban business districts, the government body authorized to exercise control over land use is all-important.

Partnering with Government— Tools of the Trade

Community building involves mobilizing public and private capital to create assets that engender community use, pride, and value. Laying the foundation for successful community building requires the activation and growth of community support. Unlike downtowns, suburban business districts are not currently the centerpieces of their community. In fact, some local governments have more than one suburban business district within their jurisdiction. Given that many of these districts are to date "uncut jewels," their potential value to the community often goes overlooked.

Astute Leadership and Investment of Public Funds

In the early 1990s, Nancy Graham took office as mayor of West Palm Beach, Florida. A strong mayor, Graham earned accolades for the transformation of West Palm Beach's business district, made possible by an innovative combination of public and private finance and expertise.

The transformation began with the construction of a new fountain in Centennial Plaza near city hall and significant public investment on Clematis Street—the city's historic but then-dormant retail spine. The fountain became a popular gathering spot and site for special community events and street entertainment while Clematis Street evolved into a vibrant oasis of small local retailers and cottage industries. With community use and pride reestablished in West Palm Beach, Mayor Graham next set out to create value and secure the tax base.

Accordingly, the mayor issued a Request for Proposals (RFP) for redevelopment of a nearby 72-acre downtown site. The city ultimately awarded a contract to a consortium led by Ken Himmel's Palladium Company of New York. The result was Palladium at CityPlace, a $500 million public/private partnership investment project that demonstrates what is possible in transforming an underperforming business district into an exciting live-work-shop environment.

CityPlace is a mixed-use development that brings together 68 national and regional specialty retailers in a European-style village setting. It offers open-air shopping plazas, handsome tree-lined esplanades that invite strollers, and winding walkways that lead to sidewalk dining establishments, entertainment venues, and family-friendly activities such as free concerts and dancing fountains. Retail rents in CityPlace now average $35 per square foot, and several restaurants are achieving monthly turnovers in excess of $1 million, positioning them in the top 1 percent of the industry. CityPlace includes 600,000 square feet of retail space and nearly 600 condominium units and rental apartments.

CityPlace in West Palm Beach, Florida, is the result of a $500 million public/private partnership investment project that demonstrates what is possible in transforming an underperforming business district into an exciting live-work-shop place.

CityPlace is a mixed-use development that brings together 68 national and regional specialty retailers in a European-style village setting. It offers open-air shopping plazas, handsome tree-lined esplanades that invite strollers, and winding walkways that lead to sidewalk dining establishments, entertainment venues, and family-friendly activities such as free concerts and dancing fountains.

Three office towers, totaling 770,000 square feet, will round out the mix, along with a 400-room hotel and the Palm Beach County Convention Center, which is scheduled to open in 2003. The cultural infrastructure of CityPlace, which currently includes the Kravis Center for the Performing Arts, is being expanded to include the new home of the Palm Beach Opera and the Norton Museum of Art.

The city was a financial partner in the transformation of West Palm Beach's business district. It borrowed the $20 million required to acquire the CityPlace site and leased the parcel to Palladium for 75 years, with payments tied to the debt service on the loan. The city also raised $53 million through a public infrastructure bond issue floated by the community development district. The bond proceeds were invested in parking deck construction, landscaping, fountains and artwork, lighting, and public space improvements. CityPlace represents an astute investment of public funds not just in terms of community building but also with respect to

building and securing the local tax base. The city paid on average $10 per square foot to acquire the site, which is now valued at ten times that amount.[5] While CityPlace is obviously located in a traditional downtown, it nonetheless offers lessons for the transformation of suburban districts, particularly as related to the importance of strong civic leadership and the use of public funding to support an effective public/private partnership.

Matching Style with Substance

Public/private partnerships have long played a role in the revitalization of downtown areas. The early pioneers—Ernest Hahn on the West Coast and James Rouse on the East Coast—turned to public/private partnerships to tackle some major challenges. One of the most notable projects was the 1970s transformation of San Diego's "porno" district into Horton Plaza. Hahn's style was a major factor in mobilizing and generating community support for that project. "Hahn was willing to start projects without resolving every issue in advance. . . . His readiness to live with open-ended and uncertain situations made it possible for cities to start projects without having all the answers in hand. Once a project was underway, Hahn's confidence worked like a self-fulfilling prophecy. As city officials and his company invested more and more energy and resources, both became increasingly committed to completing the project. When the stakes were large enough, both were eager to strike workable bargains."[6]

Adapting to Local Sensitivities

Relying on public/private partnerships to expedite the transformation of suburban business districts requires an understanding of and sensitivity to local circumstances. While models of success offer important lessons for future projects, they cannot and should not be adopted on a wholesale basis, as is evident from the recent experience in Walnut Creek and Pleasant Hill in Contra Costa County, California.

In the late 1950s, plans called for developing Walnut Creek into a major employment center in the San Francisco Bay Area. However, realization of the plans could come only with completion of the Bay Area's interstate highways, an improved Caldecott Tunnel, and construction of the Bay Area Rapid Transit (BART) system. The city's motivation, like that of many other local California governments, was to secure its tax base.

When the original plans envisaged office development in Walnut Creek's downtown, local businessmen limited their investments to that area. However, for reasons of cost, the BART alignment followed the I-680 corridor and bypassed downtown Walnut Creek, thus creating a "golden triangle" of land immediately adjoining BART's Walnut Creek station and the interstate interchange. As a result, downtown Walnut Creek lost its appeal as the focus of office development. Not surprisingly, much of the planned office development occurred in the golden triangle on land assembled by national office developers, outside the holdings of local developers.[7]

As local businessmen watched the initial round of development opportunity shift location, the city council changed its attitude toward development of the golden triangle from one of support to one of opposition. The council threw its resources and support behind the Citizens for a Better Walnut Creek, an organization that ultimately saw its members elected to the city council. The new council then sponsored a series of measures that culminated in the passage of Measure H.

Measure H was a voter initiative that amended the Walnut Creek plan by limiting commercial development on any downtown parcel to 10,000 square feet until peak-hour–volume-to-capacity ratios at downtown intersections fell below 0.85. In short, Measure H halted development in the golden triangle. The trigger for the successful passage of Measure H was traffic congestion. Patrick McGovern astutely observed, "While some evidence suggests that residents, particularly in Walnut Creek, were stunned by the scale of the new centers, the real measure used by residents to gauge changes in the city and the quality of their life was traffic congestion. . . . Movement within these communities, and the experience of its urban form, is overwhelmingly from inside an automobile."[8] The Walnut Creek experience stresses that understanding and adapting to local sensitivities are vital to the successful transformation of suburban business districts.

Building Consensus and Developing Community Ownership

Just one BART station away from Walnut Creek lies the community of Pleasant Hill. The Contra Costa Redevelopment Agency is trying to bring a close to many years of controversy that have prevented the redevelopment of 18 acres of surface parking lots around the Pleasant Hill BART station. Earlier proposals by Millennium Partners to develop a 24-cinema megaplex and a later proposal for a community college met with intense community opposition. The primary concerns revolved around the loss of commuter parking, traffic congestion that would result from any proposed development, the loss of community recreation facilities, and the fear that a project would not be tailored to the needs of the community but rather follow an "anywhere USA" formula.

According to the vision promoted by the local redevelopment agency, "The Pleasant Hill BART station area can be a part of our community that we can be proud of. It can have interesting uses, attractive architecture, and a welcoming, safe, walkable and bicycle-friendly design. But to get there, WE NEED YOUR HELP!"[9] Thus, the redevelopment agency has invited more than 6,000 people to participate in an innovative charrette process that will be structured to give everyone a voice in deciding how a group of unattractive parking lots can be transformed into a community asset. To bring participants together in a series of workshops aimed at crafting a community-based solution, the redevelop-

ment agency has engaged the services of Peter Katz and the Portland-based Lennertz Coyle and Associates design group. With the design solution in hand, the redevelopment agency will then shepherd its proposal through the county and BART approval processes.

In such a highly charged environment, it is not surprising that some participants are portraying the process as a charade rather than a charrette. However, the initial round of meetings has succeeded in building community consensus. As Katz says, "We need to settle on a strategic plan that allows the project to evolve with changing community needs rather than a fixed entitlement that would require on-going approval."[10]

Adapting the Public/ Private Partnership

The problems facing the nation's suburban business districts have yet to command the attention or the massive injection of public money that was required to bring central business districts back from the brink. In fact, the earlier that districts are transformed, the less public investment they will need. Nonetheless, the embryonic signs of decline are already evident in some suburban business districts—degenerating and dead shopping malls, aging and obsolete office buildings, traffic congestion, a dearth of parks and pedestrian places, and a nine-to-five persona. These conditions prompted then-mayor of San Diego Pete Wilson to call for ". . . housing, and for cultural, educational, and recreational facilities to provide diversity of texture and experience among the office towers. . . . We must commit to aggressively seek major retail activity downtown. We must in short, do whatever we can to make our downtown livable, rather than a place to flee at day's end to the suburbs."[11]

While public/private partnerships have traditionally focused on downtown regeneration, the public/private partnership established by Mayor Wilson to develop, finance, and implement the Horton Plaza strategic plan holds valuable lessons for those seeking to transform the nation's suburban business districts. With the mayor's leadership and the concerted efforts of San Diegans, Inc., an organization of business

In an innovative charrette process in Pleasant Hill, California, Peter Katz and the Portland-based Lennertz Coyle and Associates design group have been brought together by the Contra Costa Redevelopment Agency to run a series of community workshops to achieve a consensus on how to transform the Pleasant Hill suburban business district. The community vision is to embrace mixed uses, attractive architecture, and a welcoming, safe, walkable, and bicycle-friendly design in this suburban business district's transformation. The Internet is being used to convey images of the design solutions and inform the community of dates and venues for future community meetings.

The transformation of the Pleasant Hill suburban business district revolves around the redevelopment of the surface parking lots adjoining the Pleasant Hill BART station. The suburban business district has kept development in a compact form, but at its center there remains a void of wasted surface parking. Commuters, angry at the prospect of losing their parking, have joined with residents to oppose development on the basis of increased traffic congestion, despite the fact that a seven-level parking garage has been constructed immediately adjoining the station.

owners, developers, and downtown property owners, the Horton Plaza Redevelopment Project gained approval in July 1972. A nationally advertised Request for Proposals (RFP) led to a partnership between the city of San Diego and the Hahn Company, a national retail developer.

In January 1975, the city council adopted a proposal advanced by the mayor and San Diegans, Inc., to create the public nonprofit Centre City Development Corporation (CCDC) that would focus solely on downtown redevelopment. The mayor and the city council appointed CCDC's seven-member board of directors for three-year terms. Under an operating agreement, the CCDC would act as sole negotiator between the city and developers. It also assumed responsibility for strategic planning, urban design, property acquisition, relocation of affected residents and businesses, public improvements, and public financing for all downtown redevelopment projects. Its primary source of revenue was to be tax-increment financing (TIF).

In 1978, the CCDC adopted its first strategic plan, which called for the revitalization of downtown through redevelopment projects in four areas, each with a specific, synergistic objective as follows:

- Horton Plaza was to bring large-scale retailing back downtown;
- projects in the Marina area aimed to create a residential community downtown;
- projects in the Columbia area were to extend the city's traditional central business district

Understanding Tax-Increment Financing (TIF)

When a redevelopment causes property values to rise, the difference between the old assessed value and the new assessed value leads to a change in property tax revenue. In the case of San Diego, the increases were the tax increment to be paid to the Centre City Development Corporation. In 1972, the Horton Plaza Redevelopment Project area was assessed at $18.7 million. New construction within the redevelopment area increased the assessed valuation to $467.5 million in fiscal year 1992–1993. Property taxes due in that fiscal year, calculated at the standard rate of 1 percent of assessed valuation, equaled $4.7 million. To cover its share of redevelopment costs, the development corporation received the difference between the 1972 tax payment of $187,720 and the 1992–1993 payment of $4.7 million, which amounted to $4.5 million. The CCDC, working through the local redevelopment agency, then used the increment to underwrite bond issues as part of an investment program to create continued increases in property value. While not a universal practice across all states, tax increments under TIF are not generally shared with county government, school districts, and special districts. •

westward to the bay and were to include a major convention facility; and

- work in the Gaslamp Quarter was expected to reclaim and rehabilitate historic structures along Fifth Avenue to showcase downtown's Victorian heritage.

Importantly, the strategic plan was not a static document but rather responded to new opportunities as they presented themselves. This flexibility was important in delivering the turnaround that is today's downtown San Diego.

The CCDC now has a 39-member staff led by Peter J. Hall. It continues to

- initiate projects through the public Request for Proposals process;
- review development proposals to ensure their conformance with redevelopment law and redevelopment project plans;
- develop financial programs to assist in the rehabilitation of properties;
- review project designs for compliance with the strategic plan and local ordinances; and
- assist developers in assembling sites for all types of new development or in reconstructing or rehabilitating low- and moderate-income housing.

A project area committee advises the CCDC. Annual elections select committee representatives from the six neighborhoods within the redevelopment area. Representatives include residents, business and property owners, and members of community groups. On average, the committee meets once a month and reviews matters relating to the planning and provision of replacement residential units, relocations, and other issues affecting residents within the project area. To ensure that all stakeholders have a continuing voice in the redevelopment of downtown San Diego, all committee recommendations are referred to the CCDC board, the local redevelopment agency, and the city council.

Using Special Districts

Special districts, which account for just over one-third of the nation's 83,000 local governments, are a form of local government created pursuant to state legislation. Their powers and characteristics vary from state to state, depending on a state's particular needs. They offer an alternative to higher communitywide taxes in that they reflect the public's willingness to approve the establishment of districts that impose special tax levies, assessments, and charges for defined services delivered in a carefully prescribed area. Special districts are generally created for a single function such as

- education and social services—school buildings, libraries, hospitals, and health facilities;
- transportation facilities—highways, airports, parking facilities, transit, and ports;
- environment and housing—natural resources protection, parks and gardens, sewerage and other sanitation services, and housing and community development;
- utilities—water supply, electric power, and gas supply; and
- public safety and fire protection.[12]

In a few cases, special districts deliver a combination of services. One suburban business district that has turned to a special district is Dublin/Pleasanton, California. The North Pleasanton Improvement District (NPID) issued its first tax-exempt bonds, worth $24 million, in 1985. A city of 50,553 in 1990, Pleasanton experienced a dramatic increase in office, commercial, high-tech, and light industrial development during the 1980s. The development necessitated new and improved freeway interchanges and ramps, additional lanes, and major access roads. Established with the support and consent of area developers, the improvement district imposes a fee on about 894 acres within North Pleasanton in accordance with the benefits received from district improvements. The district has used the fee not only to cover the improvements occasioned by rapid growth but also to provide synchronized traffic signals and pay for the required feasibility studies, specifications, design, initial signal timing, and signal maintenance. Before the creation of the district, developers spent over $25 million on roadway improvements; however, they received a credit through a redistribution of assessments. Increasingly, special districts can be expected to fund public

Using TIF to Break Up Superblocks

The Uptown Houston suburban business district is the 15th-largest business district in the United States. It embraces over 23 million square feet of office space, more than 4 million square feet of retail space, over 5,300 hotel rooms, and more than half of Houston's high-rise residential condominiums. However, over the last 15 years, Uptown Houston has experienced stagnant and declining property values and retail sales.

An increase in traffic congestion and the absence of transportation infrastructure have undermined Uptown's future competitiveness relative to other suburban business districts in the metropolitan area. More specifically, no new office buildings have been constructed in the past 16 years, and no new full-service hotels have been built in the past 15 years. A 1999 survey of Houston residents found that traffic congestion was the least desirable feature of the Uptown area. Moreover, a study undertaken for the district found that new office, retail, hotel, and residential development projects would not proceed until Uptown Houston remedied its traffic and access problems.

In response to a petition signed by more than 50 percent of the district's property owners, in 1999 the city of Houston created the Uptown Houston Tax-Increment Reinvestment Zone (TIRZ), which is slated for a 30-year life. The goal is to fund a $235 million local mobility improvement program that will involve

- the upgrading of existing streets ($67 million);
- the creation of a street grid network ($33 million);
- the improvement of intersections ($26 million);
- the development of a parking management program ($50 million);
- the creation of a pedestrian network ($53 million); and
- the administration of both the TIRZ and the mobility improvement program ($6 million).

The Uptown Houston district will issue tax-increment bonds as necessary to fund the improvements.

Significantly, the Uptown Houston Tax-Increment Reinvestment Zone includes the city of Houston, the Metropolitan Transit Authority of Harris County, Harris County, and the Houston Independent School District. It is important to note that the Texas legislature created the Uptown Houston district in 1987. In the 1999 fiscal year, the district levied an ad valorem tax of $0.14 per $100 of assessed value for services and improvements within its boundaries. Over the life of the TIRZ, Uptown Houston is projected to contribute tax revenues of $144 million to the transformation of the Uptown Houston suburban business district. •

Source: Adapted from Barton Smith, Vinson & Ellis et al., *Project Plan and Reinvestment Zone Financing Plan* (Houston: City of Houston, 1999).

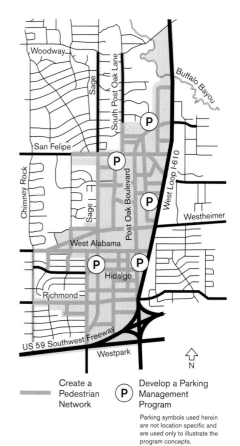

Create a Pedestrian Network

P Develop a Parking Management Program

Parking symbols used herein are not location specific and are used only to illustrate the program concepts.

The Uptown Houston Tax-Increment Reinvestment Zone has raised capital not only to provide needed pedestrian linkages within this suburban business district but also to locate shared parking as part of a districtwide parking program. The parking facilities and the new pedestrian linkages work together to reduce traffic congestion by decreasing the need to drive from one suburban business district establishment to another. They also optimize retail sales by creating pedestrian linkages that connect and expose patrons to retail establishments.

---

facilities, transit, and place-making investments in suburban business districts.

Creating Business Improvement Districts

Business improvement districts (BIDs), or community improvement districts (CIDs) as they are sometimes called, are a type of public/private partnership that manages business districts in much the same way that a shopping center manager undertakes the promotion and maintenance of a shopping mall. BIDs differ from traditional government by bringing under the aegis of a single organization both public financing and private management. "A Business Im-

Geoffrey Booth

provided by BIDs was largely determined by the size of their budget.

- Small BIDs (annual budget $40,000 to $250,000) tend to focus on retail areas, offering services such as promotions, special events, joint advertising, seasonal lighting, and business attraction and retention programs, including marketing and sometimes incentive financing.

- Large BIDs (annual budget $1 million to $30 million) tend to concentrate on improvement and maintenance of the public environment, making major outlays for labor-intensive sidewalk cleaning and supplementary security as well as for streetscape capital improvements.

In his survey of BIDs, Houstoun found that the main appeal of business improvement districts among business leaders was what he called the "turf factor." No matter how disillusioned business leaders may be with how municipal and county governments do or do not work, the stakeholders viewed the BID as an important management tool for enhancing business districts.

Using Government Tenants to Create Value

An important component of any strategic plan for transforming a suburban business district is the securing and retention of government tenants and services. Recently, the Federal Trade Commission and the Securities and Exchange Commission signed leases for, in aggregate, 850,000 square feet of office space in the Union Station area of Washington, D.C. At a notional rent of $38 per square foot per year and a notional capitalization rate of 10 percent, these two government leasing deals created $323 million in real estate value, which will play a major role in reinvigorating the Union Station area.[15]

By comparison, the loss of government tenants erodes capital value and can undermine government policy. The Georgia Department of Revenue is reportedly relocating from downtown Atlanta to an office development eight miles to the northeast of the city in DeKalb County. The deal involves a ten-year lease for 199,176 square feet of office space at a cost of

provement District (BID) is an organizing and financing mechanism used by property owners and merchants to determine the future of their retail, commercial and industrial areas. The BID is based on state and local law, which permits property owners and merchants to band together to use the city's tax collection powers to 'assess' themselves. These funds are collected by the city and returned in their entirety to the BID and used for purchasing supplemental services (eg., maintenance, sanitation, security, promotions and special events) and capital improvements (eg., street furniture, trees, signage, special lighting) beyond the services and improvements provided by the city. In essence, the program is one of self-help through self-taxation."[13]

In 1965, Alex Ling, a merchant in Toronto's Bloor West Village, organized local business interests to counter the threat from a new shopping mall. When he promised local government that business owners would tax themselves and make the commercial area succeed, Ling effectively created the first BID in North America. In *Business Improvement Districts,*[14] Lawrence O. Houstoun, Jr., found that the range of services

Ten Typical BID Functions

1. Maintenance—collecting rubbish, removing litter and graffiti, washing sidewalks, shoveling snow, cutting grass, trimming trees, and planting flowers in public places.
2. Security—hiring supplementary security and street "guides" or "ambassadors" and buying and installing electronic security equipment or special police equipment.
3. Consumer marketing—producing festivals and events, coordinating sales promotions, producing maps and newsletters, launching image enhancement and advertising campaigns, and erecting directional signage.
4. Business recruitment and retention—conducting market research, producing data-oriented reports, offering financial incentives for new and expanding businesses, and marketing to investors.
5. Public space regulation—managing sidewalk vending, street performances, street furniture, code compliance, and vehicle loading and unloading.
6. Parking and transportation management—managing the public parking system, maintaining transit shelters, and operating ridesharing programs.
7. Urban design—developing urban design guidelines and managing facade improvement programs.

One of the main purposes of the business improvement district program is to market the suburban business district to the community. By producing festivals and events, coordinating sales promotions, producing maps and newsletters, launching image enhancement and advertising campaigns, and erecting directional signage, the business improvement district seeks to create and reinforce a subliminal pattern of repeat visitation to the suburban business district. Pictured is Valencia Town Center's Bella Via Art Festival.

8. Social services—creating or assisting with help-the-homeless, job training, and youth services programs.
9. Visioning—developing a vision or strategic plan.
10. Capital improvements—installing pedestrian-scale lighting and street furniture and planting and maintaining trees. •

Source: Richard Bradley, International Downtown Association.

$22.74 per square foot per year. The determining factor in the relocation decision was the provision of 400 free on-site parking spaces for the 800 employees who will be relocated from downtown. "The move is all the more ironic since Governor Roy Barnes has made 'smart growth' and mass transit among the key issues of his administration."[16] In addition to the associated erosion in property values, such leasing deals exact a high opportunity cost in the form of forgone pedestrian traffic, retail sales, entertainment patronage, and general enrichment of a live-work-shop place.

Moving from Zoning to Place Making

As noted, the power most jealously guarded by local government is land use control. Why? For the fundamental reason that land use determines property value, which in turn is critical to a local government's fiscal health. In his *Guide to California Planning,* William Fulton refers to the land use/property value connection as the "fiscalization of planning"[17] whereby cities and counties use their zoning schemes to encourage some types of development and discourage others in accordance with fiscal considerations,

including a land use's impact on the local tax base. Provided that a locality's zoning regime facilitates the mixed-use consolidation of suburban business districts, the fiscalization of planning can hasten the transformation of suburban business districts. Unfortunately, many zoning schemes are obsolete and restrictive. Frequently, their administration accords greater weight to the precise meaning of the words with which they are expressed rather than to the rationale that led to their formulation.

In many cases, contradictory provisions in the zoning scheme subvert the policy outcome, often specified in the comprehensive plan, that a planning agency is seeking to achieve. Furthermore, in a majority of cases, judicial precedence rests with the zoning plan. In Hillsboro, Oregon, the innovative strategic plan for Orenco Station was delayed for two years while a new zoning code and design guidelines were developed, negotiated, and finally approved to replace the obsolete zoning regime that prohibited the proposed development. Only the most financially robust projects can sit by idly for two years and absorb the added costs associated with the reformulation of local development regulations.

To promote best-practice development, a planning document should be inspiring. In the case of downtown Kendall near Miami, Dade County redrafted the zoning ordinance to increase its visual content and place less emphasis on precise and unevocative language. A vocabulary limited to precise legal terms inevitably thwarts the imaging of places that could and should be created. Although the common wisdom holds that developers demand certainty, the achievements of Hahn and Rouse owe more to flexibility and the developers' ability to seize what was desirable than to a slavish adherence to what the zoning laws prohibited. In a stimulating article in *ULI on the Future—Cities in the 21st Century*,[18] Peter Katz argues for the replacement

The Orenco Station town center provides ground-floor shops with residential apartments above and live-work-shop establishments with parking at the rear of the building. The development is compact, includes an excellent standard of streetscaping, and is pedestrian- and transit-friendly.

of zoning with typological codes that show desired instead of prohibited development forms and types. He draws on computer-aided graphics to create pictures of the place-making outcomes that plans aim to achieve.

More and more, the role of computer modeling in urban planning is gaining recognition for its importance and value. By combining its geographic information system with the latest software, similar to that used by the U.S. Department of Defense for simulation, the Arlington County (Virginia) Department of Economic Development and the Arlington County Mapping Center have developed a virtual, near-photographic–real motion picture of the Rosslyn suburban business district. While Virtual Arlington is not immersive, the model does provide the user with the ability to walk through Rosslyn and observe everyday events, such as planes flying overhead as they approach Washington National Airport. Significantly, the program has the capacity to simulate the precise visual impact created by any new development.

Potentially, Virtual Arlington provides the platform for a new type of planning code called "sensory law," which has been pioneered by the Gold Coast City Council in Australia. Sensory law is predicated on the logic that responses to place depend on all five senses. Accordingly, a truncated vocabulary of printed legal terms is inadequate to guide place making. Under sensory law, the planning document would encompass a digital representation of the desired place by using Virtual Arlington—type near-photographic–real visual imagery combined with sound to evoke all the senses. The virtual plan shows the desired place while the developer then generates the project in similar form for approval. The decision-making or appellate body's response to the virtual places created by both parties determines whether an entitlement to the development will be granted. In time, sensory law can allow for preapproval of development projects and the replacement of zoning with planning instruments understood by everyone in the community[19] while innovative imaging tools will improve development conceptualization and place-making skills in the transformation of suburban business districts.

Applying Federal Government Programs and Responsibilities

The power of the federal government to intervene in city development derives not from the U.S. Constitution but rather from the government's allocation of federal funds to a wide variety of development-related programs and policies. Even though the federal government has retreated from its 1960s and 1970s level of close involvement in the nation's cities, it nonetheless continues to play a significant part in urban development through

- the allocation of federal funds for transportation pursuant to the Intermodal Surface Transportation Efficiency Act of 1991, which was reauthorized with the enactment, on June 9, 1998, of the Transportation Equity Act for the 21st Century;
- the allocation of community development block grants pursuant to the Housing and Community Development Act of 1974;
- the setting of environmental standards pursuant to federal environmental legislation, including the Clean Air Act; and

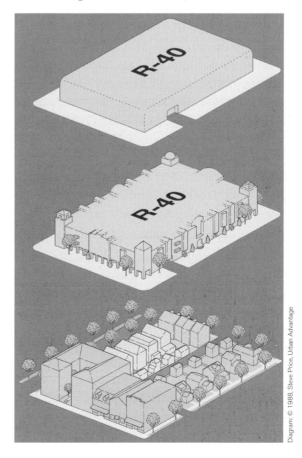

Diagram: © 1988, Steve Price, Urban Advantage

One solution proposed for bringing zoning codes into the 21st century is Peter Katz's typological zoning code that seeks not just to control land use entitlement but also to dictate building type and location. This is a prescriptive but inflexible form of zoning amendment that may be difficult to change as community needs and aspirations change.

- the ability and, in some cases, obligation (enforceable by the courts) to withhold federal funding when federal standards or laws are breached.

When the City Planning Commission of New York was established in 1938, its charter mandated the preparation of a comprehensive city plan. It was not until 1969, however, that the plan was prepared and adopted. One of the primary motivations for its completion was a threat from the federal government to cut off New York's housing and urban renewal subsidies if the city failed to meet the statutory prerequisite for adoption of a comprehensive plan.[20] Thus, the use of the "federal financing carrot" to encourage American cities to undertake land use and transportation planning has a long tradition.

Transportation and Air Quality

A more recent example of the link between local planning activities and federal involvement in land use occurred in January 1998 in Atlanta, when the U.S. Environmental Protection Agency classified Atlanta as a serious nonattainment zone for ozone. Because the region had failed to prepare a plan that adequately addressed air quality concerns, it lost $600 million in federal funding for transportation assistance. In response, Governor Roy Barnes and the Georgia General Assembly created, in 1999, the Georgia Regional Transportation Authority (GRTA). Its mission was ". . . to provide the citizens of Georgia with transportation choices, improved air quality, and better land use in order to enhance their quality of life and promote growth that can be sustained by future generations."[21] The regional authority is empowered to

- veto major highways and major developments of regional impact;
- create and operate mass transit; and
- deny state funds to local governments unwilling to cooperate with state policies.

This bold attempt on Georgia's part to coordinate land use and transportation planning is unusual in the United States. While federal transportation and air quality programs are both administered on a regional basis, the in-

tegration of transportation, environmental control, and land use is usually lacking at all levels of government.

The relationship between transportation planning and urban form and land use is evident from the catalytic effect of the interstate highway system on the growth and development patterns of suburban business districts. As every trip has an origin and a destination, land use is the major determinant of travel demand. Hence, it is not surprising that many planners and environmentalists share the belief that traffic congestion and air quality problems can and should be addressed through land use planning and controls. In fact, the 1991 Intermodal Surface Transportation Efficiency Act granted metropolitan planning organizations (MPO) the authority to allocate transportation funding across modes; MPOs do not, however, exercise control over land use entitlements.

Metropolitan planning organizations are made up of representatives appointed from state and local governments; the representatives therefore are not directly elected by the citizens of an MPO's region. In addition, the performance of MPOs differs dramatically from one metropolitan area to another depending on the extent to which local planning bodies are integrated with implementing and operating authorities. In 1999, the Committee on Improving the Future of U.S. Cities through Improved Metropolitan Area Governance found that ". . .there is a long history of thinking and acting regionally in the realm of metropolitan transportation, but in the United States land use planning, zoning, subdivision regulation and land taxation remain jealously guarded prerogatives of local governments."[22] The local response to major transportation infrastructure investment, much of which will continue to be federally and state-funded, will nonetheless have a major impact on the transformation of suburban business districts. To secure their share of transportation funds, developers—either public or private—engaged in suburban business district development will need to develop a sound working relationship with the appropriate MPOs and transportation agencies involved in transportation decision making and operation.

Community Development Block Grants

Apart from transportation funding, the federal government provides financial assistance through a range of other urban development programs. The Housing and Community Development Act of 1974 provides community development block grants to state and local governments and neighborhood-based non-profit organizations. In fiscal year 2001, a total of $4.9 billion in federal funds flowed into the block grant program.[23] Of these funds, 70 percent must be used to benefit low- and moderate-income persons. The funds can be used to promote neighborhood revitalization, economic development, or the provision of improved community facilities and services. Specific activities that can be carried out with block grant funds include

- the acquisition of real property;
- relocation and demolition;
- rehabilitation of residential and nonresidential structures;
- direct assistance to facilitate and expand homeownership among low- and moderate-income persons; and
- the provision of public facilities and improvements, such as water and sewer facilities, streets, and neighborhood centers.

Each year, the U.S. Department of Housing and Urban Development undertakes a comparative review of its grants and through the John J. Gunther Blue Ribbon Practices initiative recognizes those programs that have set benchmarks in community development.[24] The award-winning programs provide a useful guide to those who wish to apply for a block grant. Award recipients with some relevance to suburban business district development include the following:

- Place-Based Community Planning, Baltimore County, Maryland, which participated in the preparation of a countywide plan that, among other things, addressed private sector employment and business opportunities, the revitalization of business districts, and creating safe communities in which to live, work, play, and raise a family;[25]

- Nassau Urban County Consortium, Nassau County, New York, which participated in a coordinated approach to development that focused on revitalizing an existing business district through infrastructure improvements, including upgrades to sidewalks, curbs, and street lighting; tree planting; and improvements to building facades;[26]
- Redwood City Redevelopment Agency, Redwood City, California, which participated in the development of an "urban village" consisting of 81 affordable housing units above 20,000 square feet of retail space as well as a community space, a child care center, and a secure parking garage. Located adjacent to Redwood City's new city hall and library, this landmark project is a model mixed-use, transit-oriented development. The site is located two blocks from a light-rail station, which is also a major bus transfer station. The central paseo, or walkway, provides a direct pedestrian connection from main street businesses to the new city hall;[27] and
- City of Englewood Redevelopment Project, Bergen County, New Jersey, which involved the acquisition of residential buildings subjected to code enforcement, followed by re-sale of the buildings to a private developer who renovated the buildings and then sold them to low- and moderate-income owner-occupants.[28]

Other Federal Government Grants and Transfers

Federal funds and transfers are also available under a variety of other programs, including the Homeownership and Opportunity for People Everywhere (HOPE VI) program, the Urban Revitalization Demonstration Program, Urban Enterprise Zones, the Community Reinvestment Act of 1977, and tax credits available for the rehabilitation and renovation of certified historic structures. In fiscal year 2001, the federal government funded the most significant of these programs—HOPE VI and the public housing programs—at a total of $3.2 billion in operating funds and $2.96 billion in capital funds.[29] Not every federal program may have funds that can

Montgomery County, Maryland–Smart Growth for Suburban Business Districts

Montgomery County, Maryland, lies on the northwestern boundary of the District of Columbia and is bordered on its western edge by the Potomac River. Once primarily agricultural, the county began suburbanizing in the 1890s with the development of Chevy Chase and other communities linked by trolley lines to Washington, D.C. The tremendous expansion of the Washington metropolitan area following World War II quickly spread into Montgomery and other close-in counties in Maryland and Virginia, turning sedate older communities such as Bethesda and Silver Spring into suburban business districts. The county's population currently numbers 855,000 and continues to grow by 1 to 2 percent a year.

Today, Montgomery County is as much urban as it is suburban in character. The county has attracted significant economic growth, much of it in high-tech industries. Almost 60 percent of its residents work in the county, and development is intensifying in its suburban business districts. The county government (Maryland's counties act much as municipalities do in other states) is funding a new conference center and several arts centers, both of which will be located at Metro rail stations. The county's excellent education and park systems continue to make Montgomery one of the most desirable residential areas in the Washington, D.C., metropolitan area.

Smart Growth Strategy

Montgomery County has earned a reputation for more than 60 years of comprehensive and imaginative land use planning. The county's planning process began in 1927 with the formation of the Maryland-National Capital Park and Planning Commission, a bicounty planning, zoning, and park acquisition agency. The county adopted a home rule charter in 1948 and designated a county planning board as part of the park and planning commission.

County planning is grounded in the general plan approved in 1964, which lays out a development pattern commonly referred to as "wedges and corridors." The wedges were to be reserved as low-density rural lands, with development corridors centered on I-270 and U.S. 29. In the 1970s and 1980s, the 18.5-mile extension of Washington's Metro rail system reinforced development along the red line rail corridors in Montgomery County. In 1980, the designation of a farmland preservation area in the northern third of the county helped conserve Montgomery's green wedges. The county's basic development strategy remains focused on intensifying development along the corridors and increasing the use of public transit while conserving substantial areas of open space.

The county has adopted an integrated set of public policies to ensure smart growth, including adequate proof of public facility provision as a prerequisite to development approval, a transfer of development rights (TDR) program to compensate landowners in the farmland preservation area, an inclusive housing program that complements other housing programs for low- and moderate-income families, a redevelopment program for reviving the Silver Spring suburban business district, incentives for transit-oriented development and transportation demand management, and increased attention to providing the cultural infrastructure central to the livability of an urban community.

The successful redevelopment of Silver Spring as a transit-oriented suburban business district office and multifamily housing location is now being rounded out by a public/private partnership between Montgomery County and the Peterson Companies to create the suburban business district's retail heart.

Montgomery County is working with the Washington Metropolitan Area Transit Authority and private developers to plan the proposed transit-oriented mixed-use town center for the White Flint suburban business district at the White Flint Metro station. The artist's rendering shows how this town center will provide a needed sense of place for this dispersed suburban business district.

Integrated Public Policy for Suburban Business Districts

Since the launch of the Washington Metro rail system in the 1970s, Montgomery County has encouraged transit-supportive development in response to mounting traffic congestion in rapidly growing areas. The county has consistently supported higher-density development and redevelopment around rail stations and along major highways, sometimes over the objections of nearby residents. Two manifestations of the county's commitment to promoting compact, pedestrian-friendly suburban business district development around rail stations are its support of the transformation of Bethesda and the current redevelopment of Silver Spring. County officials, working collaboratively with the transit authority and private developers, established design parameters and approved density increases for mixed-use development over Bethesda's

centrally located rail station. The county followed up with an aggressive density-bonus/mixed-use zoning program that produced significant public amenities during a period of strong office and commercial development. County-financed parking garages, pedestrian bridges, and streetscape improvements funded through a business improvement district have encouraged private development, which in turn has totally transformed Bethesda into a model live-work-shop place.

At the other end of the Metro rail's red line, in the eastern part of the county, the county is sponsoring the transformation of Silver Spring, a rail-centered suburban business district long in decline. County officials pushed redevelopment efforts by assembling land, offering infrastructure improvements, and sponsoring a ULI Advisory Services panel to recommend a feasible redevelopment process. After several

false starts and considerable controversy, the county selected the Peterson Companies as the developer; the first phase of the project has been completed, with future phases to include a mixed-use retail, office, and entertainment center. James Todd, president of the Peterson Companies, and County Executive Douglas Duncan both confirmed that ". . . the transformation of the Silver Spring suburban business district would not have been feasible without a genuine public/private partnership."

The county has initiated a similar redevelopment program that involves Federal Realty Investment Trust in the creation of a pedestrian-friendly live-work-shop town center in the county seat of Rockville, which is also served by a Metro rail station and bus transfer station. ●

Source: David J. O'Neill, *The Smart Growth Tool Kit* (Washington, D.C.: ULI–the Urban Land Institute, 2000), p. 31.

The reconstruction of Lexington Terrace in Baltimore is being undertaken by a public/private partnership using funds from the federal government's Homeownership and Opportunity for People Everywhere (HOPE VI) program. The availability of selected federal financing tools can be an essential element in triggering the transformation of a suburban business district.

be used for enhancing suburban business districts, yet the availability of selected federal financing tools can be an essential element in triggering the transformation of a suburban business district.

Understanding the State Government Role

State laws and regulations set the framework in which local governments operate. While the states have responsibility for highway provision, income support, social service provision, education funding and equalization, and major infrastructure, the preferred locus of government is the local level. "In political terms, . . . government authority should be exercised at the very local level, where elected officials are close to the people and understand their needs and concerns and where individuals can engage in meaningful political participation and hold their elected officials accountable."[30] This explains

the state deference to local governments with regard to

- land use;
- state laws permitting the ready incorporation of municipalities; and
- a fiscal system that requires municipal governments to finance most services from their own tax base.

State governments provide general grants for local government operations and categorical grants for specific purposes. State aid for local governments, especially for general-purpose local governments, tends to decline during periods of poor state fiscal performance. The recession of the early 1990s and the particularly severe recession of the early 1980s saw states adjust their budgets by holding the line or cutting state aid to local governments even though local governments were in need.

In the late 20th century, a few states adopted state and metropolitan land use planning and smart growth acts. In 1996, Maryland adopted a nationally recognized smart growth program that directs state investments such as funding for roads, sewers, schools, and other public investments to "designated growth areas." Such smart growth programs effectively create state partnerships with counties and municipalities to direct development in ways that promote fiscal responsibility and community livability. With the exception of Oregon, these programs to date have had a limited impact on the exercise of land use controls and local discretion. Even the two-tier metropolitan councils, such as the Twin Cities Metropolitan Council established in 1976 in the Minneapolis-St. Paul area, have rarely required amendment of individual municipal plans as a consequence of their review processes. The implication for suburban business districts is that, in most states, a district is unlikely to be subjected to metropolitan planning controls. In fact, given that municipalities and counties are heavily dependent on property tax revenues, they have a strong fiscal incentive to strengthen their tax base through the transformation of suburban business districts and thus are unlikely to cede any authority to another level of government.

Governing Suburban Business Districts

The American palette of government form and finance plays and will always play a major role in transforming suburban business districts. To harness government processes and structures in furtherance of desired development outcomes, a community must understand and endorse a clear vision of what is required to realize its vision. A concise strategic plan is an essential prerequisite to those vital public/private partnerships that truly embrace government as a strategic partner. To be most effective, the strategic plan must become the vehicle to coordinate the policies, programs, and fiscal priorities of each level of government so as to transform suburban business districts into new live-work-shop places.

Notes

1. Alan Altschuler, ed., *Governance and Opportunity in Metropolitan America* (Washington, D.C.: National Academy Press, 1999), p. 253.

2. Ibid., p. 23.

3. Ibid., p.278.

4. Ibid., p. 271.

5. Kenneth A. Himmel, "Entertainment-Enhanced Retail Fuels New Development," *Urban Land,* February 1998, pp. 42–46.

6. Bernard J. Frieden et al., *Downtown, Inc.— How America Rebuilds Cities* (Cambridge: The MIT Press, 1989), p. 126.

7. Patrick S. McGovern, *Edge City Development and Local Environmental Mobilization Walnut Creek and San Ramon, California* (unpublished, 2000), p. 3.

8. Ibid., p. 8.

9. Contra Costa County, *Imagine a Better BART Station Area,* March 23, 2001, http://www.co.contra-costa.ca.us/depart/cd/charette/.

10. Geoffrey Booth's discussions with Peter Katz at ULI offices in Washington, D.C., May 29, 2001.

11. Pamela M. Hamilton, "The Metamorphosis of Downtown San Diego," *Urban Land,* April 1994, p. 32.

12. Douglas R. Porter et al., *Special Districts—A Useful Technique for Financing Infrastructure* (Washington, D.C.: ULI–the Urban Land Institute, 1992), p. 2.

13. Department of Business Services, *Starting and Managing Business Improvement Districts* (New York: City of New York, 1996), p. 2.

14. Lawrence O. Houston, Jr., *BIDs—Business Improvement Districts* (Washington, D.C.: ULI–the Urban Land Institute and the International Downtown Association, 1997), p. 11.

15. Jackie Spinner, "Winning a Square-Foot Race—Fleeing High Rents, Agencies Revive Neighborhoods," *Washington Post,* June 15, 2001, p. E1.

16. Judith Schonbak, "Highlands Lures Downtown State Agency to Suburbs with Free Parking in $45.3 Million Lease," *GlobeSt.com,* February 14, 2001, http://www.globest.com/RMIKZBX66JC.html.

17. William Fulton, *Guide to California Planning* (Port Arena, CA: Solano Press Books, 1999), p. 22.

18. Peter Katz, "The New Urbanism in the New Millennium: A Postcard from the Future," in Jo Allen Gause, *ULI on the Future—Cities in the 21st Century* (Washington, D.C.: ULI–the Urban Land Institute, 2000), p. 55.

19. Geoffrey Booth, "The New Sensory Law—Sensory laws will shape the places in which we live and work," *Urban Land,* October 2000, p. 14.

20. Alexander Garvin, *The American City—What Works, What Doesn't* (New York: McGraw Hill, 1996), p. 445.

21. David J. O'Neill, *The Smart Growth Tool Kit* (Washington, D.C.: ULI–the Urban Land Institute, 2000), p. 15.

22. Altschuler, *Governance and Opportunity,* p. 309.

23. Andrew Cuomo, *The State of the Cities 2000* (Washington, D.C.: U.S. Department of Housing and Urban Development, 2000), p. A-1.

24. U.S. Department of Housing and Urban Development, *John J. Gunther Blue Ribbon Practices Categories,* June 19, 2001, http://www.hud.gov/ptw/categories.html.

25. U.S. Department of Housing and Urban Development, *Blue Ribbon Practices in Community Development,* June 19, 2001, http://www.hud.gov/ptw/docs/md01.html.

26. Ibid., http://www.hud.gov/ptw/docs/ny10.html.

27. Ibid., http://www.hud.gov/ptw/docs/ca5598.html.

28. Ibid., http://www.hud.gov/ptw/docs/nj0198.html.

29. Cuomo, *The State of Cities 2000,* p. A-1.

30. Altschuler, *Governance and Opportunity,* p. 105.

chapter 10

Developing a Strategic Plan

The world is awash with plans. There are master plans, comprehensive plans, infrastructure plans, development plans, policy plans, zoning plans, transportation plans, and on, and on. Plans can buy time and even look like a visionary solution to a pressing problem. Often, several plans purport to be solutions to the same problem but, on closer scrutiny, prove to be contradictory. In short, like many aging suburban business districts, the sum of the parts does not add up to a cohesive whole.

One thing, however, is certain. Unless a plan is implemented, it is not worth the paper it is written on—or the time and money invested in its preparation. To transform a suburban business district, just one plan is required—a strategic plan. A strategic plan should

- reduce complex problems to their essence;
- communicate the facts and analysis to all interested parties; and
- outline the steps that must be taken—by whom, at what cost, and in what sequence—to implement the plan.

The key to business district revitalization across the nation—whether in downtowns or in the suburbs—has been the recognition that successful business districts are large, multiuse real estate developments that need to be properly managed as a single entity even though their component parts are under separate ownership.

Business districts comprise many buildings and spaces between those buildings, which, if properly conceptualized, interconnect to create a sense of place, thereby creating real estate value through increased rents, retail sales, and growing capital value. The strategic plan is the effective management tool through which the place-making dividend is achieved and sustained.

Strategic Planning of Business Centers

Many central business district revitalization efforts have begun with a strategic planning process. One of the earliest central business district strategies was formulated for downtown Chattanooga in the mid-1980s. A relatively poor metropolitan area in the booming Sunbelt, Chattanooga, with its obsolete heavy-manufacturing base, was more akin to a struggling Rustbelt city. Yet, the city's private sector and civic leaders, nationally recognized for their progressive stance toward development, did not want the downtown to continue its downward spiral. Accordingly, the local leaders organized and paid for the development of a strategic plan for Chattanooga's central business district. The strategy was based on realistic market research, extensive community input, and an assessment of the strengths and weaknesses of the central business district. Equally important was the detailing of

the process by which the strategy would be brought to fruition.

Not only did the community leaders actively participate in creating and adopting Chattanooga's strategic plan, but they also allocated responsibility to individual community leaders to oversee and report on its implementation. The strategic plan addressed the following issues:

- organization of downtown merchants;
- creation of a free downtown shuttle;
- construction of new parking structures;
- development of festivals to draw the community back downtown;
- creation of new tourist attractions; and
- development of new high-density multi-family housing.

Given the city's then-weak economic condition, the most amazing aspect of the Chattanooga strategic plan was not its audacity but rather the speed of its successful implementation. It was thought at the time of the plan's adoption that plan implementation would require seven years. In fact, every item in the strategic plan was implemented within four years, and the city was well on its way to becoming the Southeast's poster child for successful downtown revitalization, a decade before the downtowns of Atlanta, Charlotte, and Orlando began their explosive growth. The one outcome the Chattanooga leaders failed to plan for was

Many suburban business districts have learned from downtown revitalization programs that mixed-use development like the Victoria complex in Rockville, Maryland, can bring life to a district outside normal working hours. The Victoria complex includes street-level retail uses with a floor of offices above and another three floors of residential apartments above the offices.

the amount of time they would have to spend showing visitors from other cities throughout the world how they made their plan a reality. The success of Chattanooga has been repeated throughout the United States in downtowns as

diverse as San Diego, Denver, Albuquerque, Boise, Portland, Seattle, Atlanta, Chicago, Cleveland, Orlando, Norfolk, and many others.

Practitioners of urban development now know how to revitalize downtowns. Of course, the recent successes in many downtowns are primarily attributable to a shift in market preference for a more urban lifestyle. In short, the driving force behind downtown revitalization is today's shifting demographics and the American people's changing needs and aspirations. However, it is not necessary to move downtown to secure the benefits of an urban lifestyle. The preparation of a strategic plan, and its effective implementation, can foster the transformation of suburban business districts into community assets that satisfy the needs of tenants and customers for urban-type living. Over time, many suburban business districts will evolve into urban-type places that provide urban-type services and experiences; after all, if they do not cater to the emerging market, the competition certainly will.

The first step is for the public, private, and civic leaders of suburban business districts to

Bollards, trees, custom-designed pole lighting, and distinctive paving add to the mix of textures, and carts and kiosks help provide the diversity that creates place at the Promenade at Westlake in California. A suburban business district can be transformed into a place through the implementation of a well-conceptualized strategic plan.

Compactness of form can make a suburban business district a more desirable living and working environment and more transit-friendly. Pictured is one of the office buildings and the Embassy Suites hotel served by the BART rapid transit system in Pleasant Hill, California.

recognize that a district can be transformed into a *place*. A suburban business district is a basic economic and market entity in need of a coherent strategy. Simply standing back and leaving everything to its own devices is not a strategic plan or, indeed, any type of plan. Suburban business districts that develop a strategic plan early on will secure a competitive advantage that will be reflected in increased market share, rental return, and capital value.

Critical Issues in a Strategic Plan

There is no one strategic plan that fits all suburban business districts. The unique circumstances of each suburban business district dictate the preparation of an individual plan that is tailored to tenants,' residents,' and customers' specific needs. However, all strategic plans for suburban business districts must address certain critical issues, including the following:

- character and form of development;
- employment;
- retail uses;
- residential product types;
- infrastructure;
- regulatory reform;
- neighborhood relations; and
- implementation.

Character and Form of Development

The most frequent criticism leveled at suburban business districts is that they do not possess a sense of place. This comment underscores the fact that it is only the compact suburban business district that has critical mass—a town center that is pedestrian-friendly and capable of supporting a range of community-building facilities. Compactness in form can make a district a more desirable living and working environment because a sufficient concentration of human activity can cost effectively support a choice in transportation options.

It is, of course, unrealistic to assume that dispersed and even fragmented suburban business districts will develop the higher development densities of a downtown or compact suburban business district across their entire area. Such an eventuality is neither desirable nor achievable in any reasonable time frame, if ever. However, what is realistic and desirable is that they develop a town or village center that exhibits a variety of key characteristics. Specifically, the town or village center must be accessible by a wide range of transportation options, it must be pedestrian-friendly, it must cluster a variety of community uses around a village green or park, and it must be the focus of residential development within the district.

A critical mass of human activity concentrated in a town or village center can provide cost-effective options for transit provision. The choice of transportation mode, which includes automobiles, transit, cycling, and pedestrian movement, is critical not only for providing access to the district but also for efficient and enjoyable movement within it. In developing a suburban business district strategy, the first task is to determine the character of the district. For several aging suburban business districts, the introduction of more urban densities in a town center might be appropriate; others might decide to replicate urban densities within and beyond the town center. Urban densities start at a floor/area ratio of 2.5 but can go many times higher. The key to density is transportation and appropriate parking solutions.

The achievement of urban densities means that transit will assume a more important role in getting people to the suburban business district and moving them around once they are in the district. In Cumberland-Galleria, a suburban business district in Atlanta, the committed expansion of light-rail service to the suburban business district was the catalyst for the district's strategic planning process. Decisions about the main line's station locations and secondary cir-

culator lines will be pivotal to determining the district's evolving urban character.

Expansion of the bus lines serving a suburban business district can represent all or part of the district's transportation solution. Bus transit is best accommodated through the creation of a bus hub that maximizes convenience to the customer. In fact, a bus hub is far less expensive than light- or heavy-rail service, although bus service may require extensive promotion if it is to attract all potential customers. In any event, an expanded bus hub could even support a circulator system to connect various parts of the suburban business district, particularly given that fragmented or dispersed suburban business districts are not walkable. A system's success depends on its quality, frequency, price, and whether people enjoy using it.

Parking provision, configuration, and layout determine the form and character of suburban business districts. The vast majority of suburban parking is located on grade; although it is inexpensive to build (about $2 to $4 per square foot for pavement and planting), it consumes most of the land in a suburban business district. Mixed uses, however, require structured parking that is generally located above ground because of the prohibitive cost of constructing underground parking. With the hard construction cost for parking decks between $6,500 and $12,000 per space, or $19 to $35 per square foot, the financing of parking projects needs to be offset by additional income streams.

One of the best ways to defray some of the additional capital cost of structured parking is to develop it as part of a "multimodal transit center" that combines a transit station on the first floor of the structure with parking above. As a focal point for pedestrians, transit centers properly located within the suburban business district generate retail customers for shop-lined pedestrian linkages connecting the transit center to residential buildings, offices, and entertainment venues. Federal transportation grants are available for building multimodal transit centers; under the grant provisions, the federal government covers 80 percent of the cost and local governments, 20 percent. Downtown Chattanooga funded two new parking decks and its

Geoffrey Booth

200

Carillon Point, a 31-acre mixed-use town center in Kirkland, Washington, combines the natural beauty of its location with retail, office, and residential uses. Each part of the town center is walkable and alive with human activity.

The public esplanade along the waterfront, which is a major feature of the Carillon Point town center, creates public outlooks across the lake and forms an essential part of the pedestrian linkages that provide circulation throughout the project.

circulator system by relying on the federal formula. Without federal assistance, the most likely way to justify the cost of parking decks is to include rent-paying uses on the facilities' ground floor or along their facades and to strike a balance among land cost, construction cost, and income stream. However, the income stream from parking is likely to be low in the initial years of the investment, with growth occurring over time.

In Kirkland, a suburban business district in the Seattle area of Washington, a mixed-use development employed decked parking to achieve the desired density even though early indications suggested that the market would not justify the cost of construction. However, the rents from this high-density, pedestrian-oriented project significantly exceeded initial projections, thereby offsetting the parking construction costs. Even better, the popularity of the development allowed the owner to charge for parking within a few years of the deck's construction, further benefiting project economics.

A pedestrian-oriented place is the product of urban design, improved transit, and structured parking. It is also the most important feature of a compact suburban business district. The pedestrian orientation is a differentiating factor in developing an area's urban character. Most pedestrians, however, will not walk any farther than 1,600 feet, or four typical street blocks (some believe 1,200 feet is the limit). A 1,600-foot circumference encompasses roughly 60 acres, and such a relatively small area must offer a diversity of uses—retail, office, hotel, and residential—to encourage the pedestrian to walk by preference rather than by necessity.

In view of the pedestrian's limited range and with far more land than could be redeveloped as a dense, pedestrian-oriented place, each suburban business district needs to decide what part of the district can reasonably achieve critical mass. The most likely place to start is in the parking lot of a large community center or the regional mall, which usually anchors a suburban business district. Several malls have already become the focus of a suburban business district's town center; however, one of the best examples is Valencia Town Center (in California), which has been a major financial and community-building success.

The Valencia strategic plan provided for a main street to be built from the nearby arterial road to one of the major mall entrances, thereby linking hotel, office, residential, and street-level retail uses. Before its construction, this main street had been part of a large parking lot that surrounded the mall on all four sides and segregated it from the community. Provision of a main street gave the mall an attractive point of entry, connected it to surrounding development, and created a pedestrian environment and critical mass of development. Valencia Town Center demonstrates how conventional mall development and the community can benefit from the access provided by traditional main street retailing.

Another example is the Reston Town Center (in the Washington, D.C., area), which developed an urban character in a main street configuration that has been critical to the creation of the town center's place-making dividend. Once an urban area has been established, it can grow block by block, enhancing the value of surrounding undeveloped land and thereby increasing investment returns.

Employment

There are three primary types of employment or business in any metropolitan area. For the suburban business district, identification of the dominant employment or business type within the district is crucial to the strategic plan. The three types of employment or business are

- export;
- region-serving; and
- local-serving.

Each plays a significantly different role in the metropolitan economy as well as in the growth of a suburban business district.

Export-Serving Employment

Export businesses and jobs

- create goods and services for export to other metropolitan areas, either domestically or abroad;
- generate new cash in the local economy, thereby permitting the purchase of other metropolitan areas' export goods;
- generate the wealth and demand for all other jobs in the metropolitan area, whether region- or local-serving;
- give local flavor to the metropolitan area; and
- ultimately provide the reason for the existence of the metropolitan area.

Export jobs represent about a third of the jobs in a metropolitan economy. By far the most important type of job, export jobs directly generate between two and three other region- or local-serving jobs. They are the highest-paying jobs on average and are responsible for the future economic growth of a region.

Each metropolitan area has a discrete collection of export businesses that tend to collocate or cluster together. Boston boasts a concentration of higher education, state government, high-tech, and tourism sectors. A high-tech cluster is an export business that produces hardware and software for sale worldwide. Higher education and tourism are less obvious export sectors in that the student or tourist must travel to Boston for the service after earning the money elsewhere to pay for such service. However, the money is spent on salaries, real estate, food, and other items in the Boston area. State government is also an export sector since the citizens of Massachusetts send their taxes to Boston every year. A large percentage of those funds stay in Boston and are not returned to the county or city of origin. The various clusters of export businesses give Boston its unique flavor and personality as well as provide a major source of economic growth. The same could be said about any metropolitan area in the United States and its unique cluster of export businesses.

The fact that export industries tend to cluster together is crucial to a metropolitan area's future economic development. Even during the industrial era, industry tended to cluster as in the case of steel production in Pittsburgh, port

activities in New York, and movie making in Los Angeles. Environmental and geographic reasons dictated these concentrations. However, in the knowledge economy, which has emerged in the postindustrial economy, the reasons for clustering tend to be related to a company's ability to attract employees. With respect to the nation's many high-tech clusters, the catalytic effect and draw of research universities and national laboratories spurred the development of high-tech corridors in San Francisco (Stanford University, University of California at Berkeley, and Lawrence-Livermore National Laboratories), Albuquerque (University of New Mexico and Sandia National Laboratories), and the Research Triangle (University of North Carolina, North Carolina State University, and Duke University).

Region-Serving Employment

Region-serving businesses and jobs such as bakeries, law firms, banks, wholesale food distribution, regional medical services, and real estate development provide goods and services to the metropolitan area as a whole. They represent about a sixth of the jobs in a metropolitan area

Rockville Town Center in Maryland is a suburban business district that relies heavily on its office employment and community services functions, but it is seeking to round out its mix of uses with entertainment, multi-family residential development, and hotel and retail uses.

Geoffrey Booth

203

Gregg Logan, Robert Charles Lesser & Co.

and on average pay the second-highest wages. They depend on the health of the export sector and share one characteristic with export jobs. They tend to cluster in the central business district or suburban business districts of metropolitan areas.

Local-Serving Employment

Local-serving businesses and jobs provide goods and services to the metropolitan area in direct proportion to the density of population and jobs. These jobs fall under the headings of retailing, medical and local professional services, real estate brokerages, teaching, and police and fire services. They represent about half the total jobs in a metropolitan area and on average pay the lowest wages.

Using an Understanding of Employment to Focus the Strategic Plan

The employment component of a strategic plan must be based on a profile of the suburban business district's export and region-serving businesses and jobs. These jobs underpin local real estate values and are the reason for the existence of the suburban business district. Understanding likely job growth is critical to the quality of the strategic plan and its prospects for early implementation. If the prospects for the existing business base are not in keeping with the expectations of suburban business district leaders, it

is important to identify the export and region-serving businesses that could reasonably be attracted to the district. Attracting new businesses not already in the metropolitan area can, however, pose a major challenge. Therefore, it is often advisable to start with the expansion of existing business clusters in a suburban business district and attempt to increase their market share.

Retail Uses

The retail strategy for a suburban business district falls into two categories: region-serving and local-serving. Region-serving retail uses include regional malls, power centers, main street retailing, and every other type of retailing that draws from three miles and beyond. Many suburban business districts began as regional malls and effectively pioneered the metropolitan edge. Examples include Tysons Corner Center (Washington, D.C., metropolitan area), Perimeter Mall (Atlanta), King of Prussia (Philadelphia), South Coast Plaza (Los Angeles), and the Galleria (Houston).

The nation's changing demographic composition has forced retailers to embrace new merchandising concepts. First came power centers and the reinvention of regional malls. More recently, the demand for main street open-air retailing has led to the development of a wider range of shopping experiences. Valencia Town Center and Reston Town Center, with their extended hours of operation, pedestrian orientation, and critical mass of activity, provide the best examples of today's new approach to retailing—an approach that is an essential component of any suburban business district's strategic plan.

Local-serving retail, such as grocery store–anchored neighborhood centers, is often absent from suburban business districts. In fact, over the past 30 years, region-serving retail uses and office-based employment have expanded in suburban business districts, vesting the districts with a nine-to-five persona. Encouraging the introduction of local-serving retailing for everyday needs can broaden the appeal of the suburban business district, particularly in support of a strategic plan's residential component. Bethesda Place in Bethesda, Maryland, a mixed-use multifamily residential, office, and retail complex linked to the county offices and the Bethesda multimodal transit center, includes a 30,000-square-foot Safeway supermarket and four levels of below-ground parking. The presence of the grocery store has been a major driver of subsequent multifamily housing development in this suburban business district.

Residential Product Types

Another missing ingredient in the land use mix of suburban business districts is rental and for-sale housing. Given that housing makes up about three-quarters of the private sector real estate market, the absence of housing constitutes a significant opportunity to add real estate value to the suburban business district, especially given that upper-middle- and upper-income households—often empty-nester households—are demanding pedestrian-oriented residential environments that offer services and employment opportunities within a comfortable walking distance of home. In fact, consumer preferences for high-density living open up a range of opportunities for recycling surface parking lots into residential development sites. However,

owing to their preoccupation with commercial uses, many civic leaders and developers have been blind to the magnitude of the demand for and profitability of residential development. Some developers have incorrectly assumed that the value of residential uses cannot compete with the value of commercial uses. Nonetheless, as central business districts have shown over the past decade, residential developers often pay as much as and in some cases more for land than commercial users. Moreover, provision of choice in transportation mode is a potent factor in driving residential growth in suburban business districts.

Infrastructure

In fragmented and dispersed suburban business districts, issues related to hard infrastructure usually revolve around transportation, particularly automobile transportation. Accordingly, many suburban business districts form transportation management associations (TMAs) to manage the existing roadway infrastructure and to lobby for or raise additional funds for future improvements. The major need for hard infrastructure improvements comes as suburban business districts change from a fragmented to a compact configuration. Changes in form are

The demand for high-density living being driven by America's changing demographic profile opens up a range of opportunities for redeveloping surface parking lots into residential communities within suburban business districts like this one at Pleasant Hill in California.

Geoffrey Booth

205

significant and often call for the expansion of bus service, including the development of multimodal centers, and the possible introduction of light- or heavy-rail service. Other improvements might include traffic calming along existing thoroughfares by narrowing streets, building more streets to decrease block sizes, adding on-street parking, converting one-way to two-way streets, or creating tighter curb radii. Investment in place-making assets such as street beautification, parkland provision, and pedestrian linkages often accompany the hard infrastructure upgrades for suburban business districts.

These are all expensive improvements. As already noted, some of the funding is available from the U.S. Department of Transportation; in fact, up to 25 percent of federal transportation spending now goes to nonhighway projects. At the same time, state and regional transportation agencies are weighting their spending more toward nonhighway projects. In the Atlanta metropolitan area, future transportation spending is estimated to be 50 percent for highways and 50 percent for transit. Another way to pay for hard infrastructure improvements is from the increased revenues associated with more productive—and therefore taxable—uses of land within the suburban business district. Narrow streets mean more land available for building rent-paying and tax-paying real estate, and increased densities result in higher property values and tax revenues. Enhanced tax collections can

be pledged to repay the public bonds that fund needed improvements. Shaker Heights in Cleveland, Ohio, undertook the development of several acres of city-owned land that involved road narrowing and density increases. The development generated upfront cash and ongoing incremental increases in taxes, both of which helped finance the project.

The issue of transit infrastructure demands attention. Strategic plans for central business districts often call for a shuttle bus system to foster interconnectivity. Even a dispersed development such as the White Flint suburban business district that forms part of Rockville Pike in Montgomery County, Maryland, provides a free shuttle bus service that operates on less than five-minute headways to promote interconnection of its scattered land uses.

Parking is another major issue that needs to be addressed by the strategic plan. The creation of compact suburban business districts requires the development of structured parking so that areas currently used for surface parking can be released for higher and better uses. In Arizona Center in downtown Phoenix, the city initiated the development of parking structures and then, as part of the entitlement process, required all future developments to buy a share of the structures rather than provide parking on their own sites. The experience in Phoenix demonstrates that the increased cost of structured parking cannot necessarily be passed on to consumers, at least in the initial years. As a result, developers need to exercise creativity in the financing of parking facilities.

And, to the extent possible, facilities must accommodate shared use, both day and night. Structured parking that helps create an urban character can eventually become paid parking, which will help amortize the cost of the structures. This was the case in the Kirkland, Washington, suburban business district project called Carillon Point. The project pro forma assumed that the parking structure would produce no revenue. Within three years, however, the owner capitalized on the overwhelming demand for parking and began to charge a fee.

As the density of development in a suburban business district increases, the district's success

A strategic plan for dispersed and fragmented suburban business districts is likely to include the provision of a free bus shuttle to promote interconnection of scattered land uses. This free bus shuttle operates on less than five-minute headways in the White Flint suburban business district in Maryland.

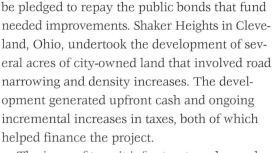

as a pedestrian-oriented, urban-type environment will require a greater focus on issues such as cleanliness, security, education, culture, sports, historic sites, connections to nature, and other soft infrastructure amenities. With more and more pedestrians taking advantage of walking opportunities, more trash accumulates and needs to be collected and removed. When people start thinking about living in a suburban business district, schools become a consideration. When households live at higher densities, a plan for walkable connections to nature is a necessity. Two major soft infrastructure issues that have arisen in the strategic planning process for the Cumberland-Galleria suburban business district are the connection of the district to the adjoining national park (which involves access across a freeway) and the development of a performing arts center.

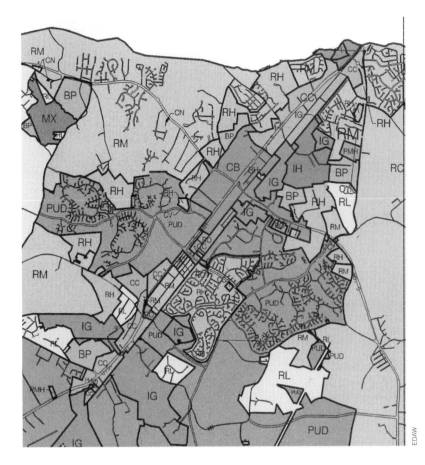

Regulatory Reform

It is essential to review all regulatory instruments. The entitlement process and the day-to-day management and operation of a suburban business district need to work together to ensure that they foster rather than frustrate the timely implementation of the strategic plan. Most zoning laws and regulatory regimes are woefully outdated and do not accord with a community's contemporary needs. In fact, since zoning's inception, many communities have simply copied zoning ordinances from other jurisdictions without reference to local circumstances. Moreover, with the U.S. Supreme Court's landmark decision in *Village of Euclid* v. *Ambler Realty Co.* in 1926, the separation of uses became and remains an accepted tenet of zoning. The separation of uses is the antithesis of what many strategic plans seek to achieve. Similarly, density provisions, building setbacks, parking standards, fire regulations, sidewalk dining provisions, and policing and enforcement practices have failed to keep pace with the times.

In the preparation of Albuquerque's new downtown development code, the city repealed the existing regulatory regime and replaced it with a modern code that promotes rather than prohibits place-making and community-building

investments. The new code encourages the transition between the public and private domains and encourages a pedestrian-friendly environment, shared use of parking, and a greater choice of transportation options.

Neighborhood Relations

The successful implementation of a strategic plan depends on a high level of community ownership, support, and resolve. During the development of a strategic plan, all interested parties must be encouraged to articulate their concerns and aspirations; the strategic plan must then address these issues. Failure to respond to local concerns jeopardizes implementation of the plan. When political leaders realize that the plan has earned widespread public support, they find it in their best interest to work toward its implementation.

Development density and congestion will likely be the issues of greatest concern. A common misconception holds that increased development density results in increased congestion.

Most zoning plans seek to segregate rather than integrate uses and therefore constitute a major legal barrier to the transformation of suburban business districts and the encouragement of pedestrian- and transit-friendly mixed-use development. The delays to development incurred in removing or modifying these zoning plans have ensured that many innovative projects are stillborn.

In fact, spreading development at low densities across a wide geographic area means that more vehicle miles are traveled, that more land is taken up with roads and parking, and that the provision of a safe, reliable, and convenient public transit system becomes cost-prohibitive. In addition, the segregation of housing from community facilities results in a sense of social isolation among residents.

Indeed, the integration of housing into suburban business districts can do much to build community. With the associated increase in density, existing residents realize an appreciation in real estate values and benefit from easy access to community facilities and a greater choice in transportation options. Such is the experience of Ansley Park in Atlanta; the Country Club Plaza area in Kansas City; and Bethesda in Maryland. In the recent case of the Cumberland-Galleria suburban business district in Atlanta, neighborhood groups supported an increase in residential mix and density where it was accompanied by local traffic management and parking programs.

Implementation

The successful implementation of a strategic plan depends on three essential ingredients.

- Implementation measures and actions must be clear and specific.
- The individuals, agencies, or groups responsible for each measure's implementation must be identified, with a program specified for achieving each measure.
- The strategic plan must embrace partnership, cooperation, and coordination.

In all circumstances, it is essential to secure community ownership, support, and resolve to make the suburban business district's strategic plan a reality.

The lead agency or individual responsible for coordinating implementation of the strategic plan will vary with local political circumstances, funding sources, and community preferences. In some cases, the responsible party will be

- the mayor or county executive, e.g., Mayor Al Larson, village of Schaumburg, Illinois;

- a public sector redevelopment agency, e.g., the City of San Jose Redevelopment Agency;
- a nonprofit development corporation, e.g., River Valley Partners in Chattanooga;
- a chartered public agency, e.g., Centre City Development Corporation in San Diego;
- a business or community improvement district, e.g., the Uptown Houston District in Houston; or
- a community association or organization, e.g., the Cumberland Transportation Network in Atlanta.

It is essential for the lead agency to gain the backing and maintain the support of all parties involved in the implementation of the strategic plan. Where this support is secured, the use of the power of eminent domain becomes an implementation tool of last resort.

Developing a Suburban Business District Strategic Plan

There are those who say that the fragmented ownership of the real estate assets within a suburban business district and the complexity of local community politics render impossible any attempt to prepare a strategic plan. Without doubt, great skill and leadership are prerequisites to successful plan preparation—and implementation. However, several situations can galvanize a unity of purpose and the determination to act. These catalytic events can arise from the opportunities presented by a major infrastructure investment, as was the case in Arlington County, Virginia, with the construction of Metro rail, and in the suburban business district of Cumberland-Galleria, with the proposed construction of MARTA's light-rail connection. Other events may be the redevelopment of a competitive suburban business district or the decline of real estate values, as occurred in many American downtown areas during the 20th century.

Organization and Funding

The first step in developing the strategic plan is to identify and empower the organization that

figure 10.1 The Eight Stages in Developing a Strategic Plan for a Suburban Business District

Stage	Action
One	Strategic plan steering committee established.
Two	Committee formulates budget and appoints consultant team.
Three	Consultant team undertakes research and interviews before preparation of the briefing book.
Four	Committee convenes for first full-day meeting to work through the briefing book.
Five	Committee convenes for second full-day meeting to review issues and to begin developing solutions; allocates policy and implementation responsibilities to task forces of committee members.
Six	Committee meets to hear reports from its task forces, resolve the content of the strategic plan that it subsequently adopts, and fine-tune task force implementation responsibilities.
Seven	Consultant team documents and copies strategic plan to all task force leaders and relevant agencies and groups.
Eight	Task forces undertake their work; the steering committee meets periodically to monitor progress and fine-tune the strategic plan.

Source: Christopher Leinberger, Robert Charles Lesser & Co.

will take responsibility for plan preparation. The organization or agency responsible for plan development may differ from that responsible for plan implementation; however, continuity is ensured when the two organizations are one and the same. In any event, the responsible organization could be the chamber of commerce, the transportation management organization, the business improvement district, or a property owners' organization. Figure 10.1 summarizes the eight stages in developing a strategic plan for a suburban business district.

The process begins when a committed group of key property owners and employers in the suburban business district come together and decide that a strategic plan is needed. In partnership with city or county government, the group forms the steering committee that will guide the development of the strategic plan and appoint and manage the consultant team responsible for undertaking the planning effort. The group's first order of business is to determine how the strategic planning process will be funded. In most cases, the committee will engage outside consultants who charge fees on the order of $150,000 to $300,000, depending on the depth of the required urban planning expertise. The cost could be much greater if detailed land planning is required and new development codes are to be developed.

The Briefing Book

Once the parties agree to the nature of the strategic planning effort, the next step is to assemble background information for compilation into a briefing book that will ground the strategic plan in market reality. The most important information to include is market research into already existing real estate product types and types likely to locate in the suburban business district. Product types will probably include various office uses, a range of retail establishments, hotels, rental and for-sale housing, and community amenities such as performing arts centers, convention centers, and sports venues. If the market lacks comparables for any of these product types, it might be necessary to conduct consumer research to assess the demand for the product(s). In addition, the briefing book should identify the various export and region-serving businesses and jobs in the suburban business district as well as the likely future of those businesses and jobs. Similarly, the briefing book might include an analysis of the possible new businesses and jobs that could logically be attracted to the suburban business district.

Based on the above data, the briefing book should assess the strengths and weaknesses of the suburban business district from the perspective of various constituencies: tenants, govern-

The Power of a ULI Advisory Services Panel in Downtown San Jose

Under the chairmanship of development industry leaders such as Smedes York, past chair of ULI and president of York Properties, Inc., ULI has convened over 400 ULI Advisory Services panels since 1947 to give independent advice on how to develop, finance, and implement strategic plans for local communities in the United States, Europe, and Asia. In June 2000, the City of San Jose Redevelopment Agency asked a ULI Advisory Services panel for advice on how to attract and retain retail uses in San Jose's business district (San Jose is one of the largest suburban business districts in the San Francisco Bay Area). The panel found that San Jose had a solid foundation on which to conceptualize and implement a retail strategy. Investments in an extensive range of civic, cultural, entertainment, and streetscape projects—an expanded convention center and ancillary hotels, the Tech Museum, the Children's Discovery Museum, the Museum of Art, the Arena, the Plaza de Caesar Chavez, and the installation of mature trees along First and Second streets—left San Jose well positioned for major retail development. But the disconnected nature of these various projects and spaces motivated predominantly single-purpose trips. In essence, the city boasted many freestanding projects but no memorable sense of place.

Although San Jose residents were time-poor, they were also income-rich. Yet, San Jose's business district offered them nothing like the menu of entertainment, retail, and residential experiences they demanded —just a collection of disconnected activities. After investing their time in coming to this suburban business district, would-be customers were leaving the area with money still in their pockets and a sense of frustration over the need to travel to Los Gatos, Willow Glen, Valley Fair, or San Fran-

The compact suburban business district of San Jose in California is walkable and boasts an extensive range of community and cultural facilities, San Jose State University, and a significant office population, but it lacks retail uses that would act as glue in the town center. A ULI Advisory Services panel was asked to address this problem and devise a strategic plan, which is currently being implemented in partnership by the Redevelopment Agency of the City of San Jose and the Palladium Company.

cisco to acquire merchandise, experiences, and memories.

As a critical first step in developing its strategic plan and recommendations, the ULI panel identified the need for San Jose's development agency to

- identify and package the retail space that can be offered to the market;
- set the strategic direction of the retail mix and identify target retailers by relying on the district's strong food, beverage, and entertainment retailers as the foundation for attracting a more diverse and complete retail mix;
- understand and match available space to the needs of targeted retailers;
- create new retail space to attract the right balance of national brand retailers and local San Jose retailers;
- provide and manage the parking areas and structures required to facilitate a pleasant shopping experience;
- provide for the management of the suburban business district real estate asset

in a manner similar to shopping center management;
- where cost-effective, provide for the retention and improvement of the retail skills of existing retailers;
- encourage the incubation of new retailers from within area communities so that the city can leverage its ethnic diversity into a rich retail mix;
- involve the community in harnessing its energy and resources to reconstruct and reinvest in San Jose;
- develop a marketing program; and
- establish a partnership among the redevelopment agency, the city, the community, and the private sector.

In accordance with the ULI Advisory Services panel's recommendations, the city initiated a Request for Qualifications process that resulted in the appointment of the Palladium Company as preferred developer. ●

Source: ULI Advisory Services Program.

ment officials, neighborhoods, property owners, and outside financial sources. Interviews, focus groups, or survey research are useful tools for gathering information on constituencies' needs and concerns. In addition, an assessment of the current condition of the hard and soft infrastructure is needed, along with an identification of required infrastructure improvements. Finally, the consultant team needs to prepare a fiscal analysis to compare existing and projected impacts of the suburban business district on government revenues and costs. As the strategic plan is developed, the model can test the plan's impact on government revenues and costs, helping to sell the strategic plan and providing a strong financial base from which to attract potential funding for strategic plan implementation.

A briefing book typically represents the work of the 20 to 30 members of the strategic plan steering committee. It is vital that all committee members play an active role in the planning process. They must represent every constituency of the suburban business district, including groups interviewed for the briefing book, tenants, government officials, neighborhood activists, property owners, outside financial sources, and any other group deemed crucial to the future of the suburban business district. These individuals should have the respect of their respective constituencies. Furthermore, fair and even representation of interests will guard against charges that decisions were made "behind closed doors," thereby helping to ensure the strategic plan's legitimacy. Finally, because committee participants are likely to be senior decision makers whose time is limited, the briefing book needs to be complete and concise.

The strategy formulation process can be accomplished in two to three full-day meetings of the steering committee with a month's interval between each meeting. It is crucial to keep the process short to respect the time constraints faced by participants and to encourage their continuing involvement.

The First Meeting

The goal of the first full-day meeting is for the total group of 20 to 30 participants to review and

understand the contents of the briefing book. Maintaining the involvement of the full group ensures efficiency and fosters trust building among participants, many of whom either do not know each other or who have previously met only on opposite sides of the negotiating table. The development of respect, understanding, and trust is a vital function of the first meeting.

The Second Meeting

The second meeting should focus on various issues outlined earlier in this chapter and discussed in the next chapter, such as the character of the suburban business district and its employment base, the role to be played by residential development, hard and soft infrastructure needs, and so on. Those issues that the committee decides to focus on comprise the core of the strategic plan. Participants should then specify the steps that will bring the strategic plan to fruition, including the designation of task forces to address particular initiatives, say, roadway improvements or code reform. Individuals from the steering committee should be encouraged to serve as the liaison between each task force and the larger committee. Finally, the steering committee should specify work items and deadlines for the first few steps in the implementation process.

It is vital that the briefing book for a strategic plan for a suburban business district contain an inventory of physical assets and that the process involve the best people from the local community to formulate, lead, and implement the strategic plan.

Securing the Competitive Edge: Development of the Strategic Plan for Cumberland-Galleria

The Cumberland-Galleria strategic planning process (Blueprint Cumberland) is a work in progress dedicated to preparing and implementing one of the nation's first strategic plans for transforming an aging suburban business district. Located in northwest Atlanta at the interchanges of two interstate highways and U.S. Route 41, Cumberland-Galleria is a large fragmented suburban business district that accounts for 22 million square feet of office space (18 percent of the Atlanta region's total) and 12 million square feet of retail space in several different projects. The ten-square-mile suburban business district provides homes for 30,000 residents and jobs for 65,000 workers. It is only 55 percent built-out and has the potential, subject to transit provision, to double in size. The Atlanta Regional Transportation Plan prepared by the Atlanta Regional Commission includes a $2 billion budget for construction of a light-rail transit system connecting the suburban business district to MARTA's existing Art's Center Station by 2010. Blueprint Cumberland is designed to spur the implementation of the light-rail project, the Cumberland connector that will increase transit access throughout the suburban

Office development in the Cumberland-Galleria suburban business district, in the Atlanta metropolitan area, consists of dispersed pods of development that are difficult to interconnect through pedestrian and transit networks. These pods have not been integrated with retail, entertainment, or multifamily residential development; rather, they are ad hoc projects that depend solely on automobile access.

business district, and to locate all transit facilities to promote the creation of interconnected, pedestrian-friendly real estate development and community-building opportunities within the suburban business district. The predominantly standalone development projects that currently comprise the suburban business district have not been undertaken in accordance with a master plan for the suburban business district but rather as individual developments that were largely geographically proximate but rarely interconnected. Figure 10.2 shows in schematic form the metropolitan Atlanta area and the location of the Cumberland-Galleria suburban business district.

With little residential development within the district's core, commuter traffic is significant as congestion continues to grow less tolerable. Further, activity in the suburban business district is largely limited to weekdays between 9:00 a.m. and 5:00 p.m. Since 1990, the jobs-to-housing ratio has become progressively more imbalanced, placing an increasing strain on the capacity of the district's road infrastructure. Atlanta's MARTA transit system does not serve the district. With an urban form that is not pedestrian-friendly, Cumberland-Galleria

is forced to rely on limited transportation options: the automobile and bus service operated by Cobb County.

Real Estate Values under Pressure

The Cumberland-Galleria office market is performing moderately well as of mid-2001, with an average vacancy rate of 10.9 percent (the Atlanta region's average) and rental rates holding at $20 to $21 per square foot for pre–1990 buildings and $23 per square foot for post–1990 buildings. However, Cumberland-Galleria's market share relative to Atlanta's other business centers has been shrinking. The April 2001 sale of the 900,000-square-foot Atlanta Financial Center for $154 million, or $171 per square foot, could make it difficult to sell the 407,000-square-foot Cumberland Center II for the asking price of $75 million, or $184 per square foot, which was the price reportedly paid for this office development in 1994.

Cumberland, the 1.2 million-square-foot shopping mall that triggered the development of the suburban business district, depends significantly on the daytime office market. Its sales per square foot of $379 in 2000 were significantly less than

figure10.2 Cumberland-Galleria's Location

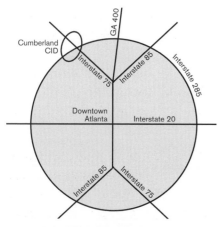

Source: Gregg Logan, Robert Charles Lesser & Co.

its competitors' sales, the suburban business centers of Perimeter (Perimeter Mall —at $455 per square foot) and Buckhead (Lenox Square—at $620 per square foot— and Phipps Plaza—at $584 per square foot). Once considered a premier mall, Cumberland, which is isolated from the surrounding suburban business district by its surface parking lots, has gradually lost its prestige and is now physically outdated.

Similarly, most retail space in the Cumberland-Galleria suburban business district is outdated. It generally takes the form of older strip centers and big-box retail facilities, all of which are experiencing difficulty in retaining tenants. Consequently, retail rents range from $16 to $30 per square foot. In contrast, two developments, Parkway Point (which offers deck parking) and Vinings Jubilee (which is pedestrian-friendly), are both located within the suburban business district, are laid out in a town center, village, or more urban-type setting, and are achieving higher rents.

The Impetus for the Strategic Plan

The average Atlanta commuter travels 36.5 miles a day, one of the longest average commutes in any U.S. city. The length of the commute, when combined with Atlanta's explosive population growth, translates into serious traffic congestion and deteriorating air quality. Given that the Clean Air Act states that no transportation activity can be funded in any state unless that activity conforms to the state's clean air plan, Atlanta faced the prospect of the federal government's withholding transportation funding. In addition to the federal government's response, a coalition of environmental organizations initiated a range of legal actions to block new road construction. On June 6, 2000, the U.S. District Court for the Northern District of Georgia refused to grant a preliminary injunction to halt about $400 million of fed-

erally funded highway projects in Atlanta, but the ruling judge did promise to render a final decision on the injunction before the end of summer 2001. The interpretation of the provisions of the federal legislation and the consequent impact on transportation funding have had and are likely to continue having a major impact on Atlanta as well as on its suburban business districts, which rely on the automobile as the predominant mode of customer and employee access. However, suburban business districts that are prepared to address their traffic problems and provide a premium level of access will reap the benefits of competitive positioning in the regional market.

In particular, in 1987, the Cumberland-Galleria suburban business district established Georgia's first community improvement district (CID) when a group of property owners voluntarily taxed themselves to raise seed money for transportation projects. The funds enabled the CID to complete the design work for various transportation projects that would be developed when federal and state funds became available for construction. To date, the CID has leveraged $400 million in local, state, and federal funds for transportation improvements. It also founded Georgia's first transportation management association (TMA), the Cumberland Transportation Network. The CID used its understanding of federal, state, and local government agencies and funding programs to focus resources on the Cumberland-Galleria suburban business district.

Pursuant to the Transportation Equity Act for the 21st Century (TEA-21), the Atlanta Regional Commission set out to develop transportation plans and programs for metropolitan Atlanta. Over the past five years, the commission, which serves as Atlanta's metropolitan planning organization, has made available $5 million for suburban business district planning under

its Livable Centers Initiative. It will follow this program with a $350 million program, commencing in 2003, to implement suburban business district improvement projects. The projects are required to be consistent with the commission's regional development plan, which promotes compact, integrated, and walkable town center developments that contain a mix of higher-density office, retail, restaurant, entertainment, and residential uses. To support the cost-effective provision of transit, the plan is geared to achieving a critical mass of human activity in suburban business districts' town centers.

The Cumberland-Galleria CID recognized the Livable Centers Initiative as an opportunity to prepare a strategic plan to guide the future development of the Cumberland-Galleria suburban business district. It applied for and secured a grant under the Livable Centers Initiative, which it leveraged to engage Robert Charles Lesser & Co. and Mayes, Sudderth & Etheredge (transportation consultants) to prepare the Blueprint Cumberland Strategic Plan.

Blueprint Cumberland Strategic Plan

The strategic planning process for Cumberland-Galleria involves the following three stages, of which the first two have been completed and the third is underway:

- Stage 1—Preparation and discussion of the briefing book, including issues and initiatives;
- Stage 2—Strategic plan formulation; and
- Stage 3—Review, adoption, and implementation of the Blueprint Cumberland Strategic Plan.

A stakeholders' steering committee, consisting of senior representatives of the Cumberland-Galleria suburban business district and the surrounding community, continued on next page

continued on next page

Key:
1. Riverwood
2. Wildwood
3. Overlook
4. Paces West
5. Cumberland Office Park
6. Atlanta Galleria
7. Platinum Tower
8. 1000 Parkwood
9. 1300 Parkwood
10. City View Center - Phase 1
11. One Riverside
12. Paces Summit
13. Interstate North Office Park
14. 3333 Riverwood
15. Cumberland Center
16. The Forum
17. One Overton Park
18. Cresent

Gregg Logan, Robert Charles Lesser & Co.

This map extracted from the Blueprint Cumberland briefing book shows the dispersed nature of major office development within the suburban business district. A similar pattern was evident for retail and multifamily residential development. This presents a major challenge for cost-effective public transit provision and the construction of effective pedestrian linkages. Merely rezoning the land for higher-density development and waiting for infill development to occur was not an option given the wide area covered by the Cumberland-Galleria suburban business district. While no scale is shown on this plan, the distance from the intersection of Windy Hill Road and I-75 to the intersection of I-75 and I-285 is about one mile.

committee's deliberations will culminate in the adoption of the Cumberland Blueprint Strategy Plan in the latter half of 2001.

The Briefing Book

The briefing book contained a situation analysis of the Cumberland-Galleria suburban business district and presented summary data and findings from reviews of the following:

- real estate and economic performance and trends;
- demographic trends;
- transportation systems, traffic congestion, and the need to provide freedom of choice in mode of transportation;
- land use trends, development form, density, mix of uses, and interconnections particularly in and around transit stops;
- the need for public open space and plazas linked with one another to provide pedestrian routes and to convey a sense of place;
- existing zoning provisions that limit pedestrianization and undercut the cost-effective provision of transportation options;
- domination of the streetscape by large surface parking lots that compromise the aesthetic character of the district and limit interconnectivity between properties;
- the need to create a consistent "fabric" given that freeways and major roads have bisected the area and carved it into subareas;
- the dominance of large office uses whose future is uncertain because of obsolete retail facilities, lack of a focal point, and transportation/mobility issues;
- older strip development and an outdated mall that has been losing market share to regional competitors;
- a lack of nighttime retail uses leading to a perceived crime problem;

came together to prepare a strategic plan. The steering committee met on December 13, 2000, to discuss the findings outlined in the briefing book and to begin development of the Blueprint Cumberland Strategic Plan. The consensus that emerged

from that first meeting guided the formulation of the Cumberland-Galleria suburban business district plan that evolved during the committee's second round of meetings, which commenced in first-quarter 2001. Now, at the third stage of the process, the

- residential stock largely in the form of outdated, suburban-style rental apartments that fail to attract more affluent and diverse renters;
- perception of the business district as a lower-income area due to an abundance of older apartments even though new single-family homes nearby sell for close to $1 million (on average);
- lack of neighborhood retail and service uses necessary to support a growing residential development; and
- perception of poor-quality schools.

The Briefing Book Overview of Performance

The lead indicators shown in Figure 10.3 are drawn from the Cumberland-Galleria briefing book and illustrate the comparative performance of the suburban business district vis-à-vis its competitors in the Atlanta metropolitan region. To redress the growing imbalance between employment and households, the Cumberland-Galleria will need to increase the offering of multifamily residential development within the suburban business district.

The Office Market Fair Share Index

The fair share growth index was developed by Robert Charles Lesser & Co. It is a ratio of the percentage of space absorbed by a suburban business district divided by the percentage of occupied space within the same suburban business district. A fair share growth index below 1 indicates slower growth relative to occupied space, and a fair share growth index above 1 indicates a faster rate of growth, or an emerging area relative to other suburban business districts. In 1992, Cumberland-Galleria had a fair share growth index of 1.11. Perimeter North had an index of 1.29 and North Fulton, 2.4. By way of comparison, the briefing book reported the

continued on next page

figure 10.3 Cumberland-Galleria Lead Indicators

Retail Performance Indicator

Cumberland Mall's Performance in Relation to Other Atlanta Malls	Area of Mall (square feet)	Sales per Square Foot (dollars)
Lenox Square	1,565,000	620
Phipps Plaza	824,856	584
Perimeter Mall	1,430,924	455
Gwinnett Place	1,240,000	415
North Point	1,500,000	392
Town Center	1,275,000	395
Cumberland Mall	1,198,440	379
Southlake	1,020,000	348
Northlake	1,000,000	285

The Relationship of Employment to Households

Relationship of Employment to Households in Selected Atlanta Suburban Business Districts	1990 Employment-to-Households Ratio	1999 Employment-to-Households Ratio
Cumberland-Galleria	4.61	6.01
Town Center	4.06	4.51
Buckhead/Lenox	3.22	6.38
Perimeter Center	7.17	7.18
North Point	1.69	1.90
Atlanta metropolitan region	1.54	1.60

Fair Share Indexes, Third-Quarter 2000

Suburban Business District	Percentage of Existing Office Space	Percentage of Vacant Office Space	Fair Share Index
Midtown	9.0	7.2	0.80
Buckhead	10.0	4.9	0.49
Cumberland-Galleria	18.3	17.7	0.97
Perimeter	18.3	18.7	1.02
North Fulton	9.6	12.2	1.27
Northeast I-85	9.4	15.6	1.66
Northlake	9.0	6.1	0.68
South Atlanta	2.4	5.2	2.17

Riverside in Atlanta is a mixed-use development by Post Properties that includes residential, retail, and office space. More than 57 percent of this 85-acre riverfront site is dedicated open space. Located within the Cumberland-Galleria suburban business district, the project has a sense of place that is a model for the future.

urban business district falls into four major subareas as follows:

- northeast (east of I-75, north of I-285, including the Powers Ferry corridor);
- northwest (west of I-75, north of I-285, including the Circle 75 area);
- southwest (south of I-285, from the mall east across I-75, including Overton Park); and
- far south (extending along Cumberland Boulevard southwest across Paces Ferry to Atlanta Road).

fair share indexes for third-quarter 2000, included in Figure 10.3.

Developing Consensus on the Strategic Plan's Provisions

With the development of the strategic plan, a vision for Cumberland emerged. That vision is more urban in nature compared with what exists today. It is characterized by decreased setbacks; increased residential densities; greater integration of land uses (including vertically mixed-use properties); greater emphasis on pedestrian access, aesthetics, and mobility; decreased emphasis on the automobile; and a desire for a public sphere typified by active spaces, including public gathering places.

The stakeholders agreed that the vision must vary by quadrant, given that the sub-

The vision for new housing development in the Cumberland area pictures market-rate attached rental and for-sale product. In view of the abundance of moderately priced rental product already in the area, the development of new moderately priced housing is not appropriate. In the future, however, moderately priced for-sale product could be created through conversion of some of the existing rental product to condominium ownership.

The steering committee also agreed that the most urbanized areas (southwest and northwest quadrants), including the area around the mall, should develop as a connected pedestrian-friendly, transit-accessible development with floor/area ratios greater than 1. Such development

The Third Meeting

If funds are available for land planning, the third meeting should focus on the physical changes proposed by the strategic plan and how those changes may affect the suburban business district's layout, transportation options, and parking arrangements. The physical implications of the strategic plan should be put into a presentation-quality format, possibly including architectural renderings, for later communication of the strategy to the various constituencies.

Whether or not the third meeting deals with land use issues, it should not occur until representatives of the affected constituencies have had an opportunity to review the work completed by the several task forces. Thus, the third meeting provides an opportunity to modify the strategic plan. The full committee of 20 or 30 then adopts the strategic plan for implementation. From time to time thereafter, the committee should meet to update the plan (if necessary) but certainly to monitor its implementation.

would consist of either mid- or high-rise product with some or no setback from sidewalks and structured or underground parking (or possibly significant off-site parking and a higher percentage of mass transit commuters). The steering committee also decided that the southwest quadrant needs a greater pedestrian orientation while the northwest quadrant needs a pedestrian core with automobile-oriented "satellites" to the core.

Under these scenarios, the suburban business district will remain automobile-dependent, though with increased attention to its pedestrian character. The development of a light-rail transit (LRT) system and circulator that would serve the Cumberland CID study area is a critical component of the vision for the area. Stakeholders now recognize the importance of implementing policies that foster higher-intensity mixed-use and multiuse developments around future transit stations. Developing two major stations along a trunk line connecting with MARTA at locations where existing development is most intense *and* where future development would be intensely urban is central to realizing the vision for transit-oriented development.

One major proposal involves the construction of main street retail connection between Cobb-Galleria and Cumberland Mall (focusing on the Cumberland Mall parking area) that will become the retail center of the suburban business district and create the much-needed sense of place that the district currently lacks. Parking decks will be "wrapped" with retail and residential uses. The provision of parking around new transit facilities is proposed as part of joint developments with Cobb County Transit and Georgia Regional Transportation Authority (GRTA).

The stakeholders concluded that the existing zoning regime could pose a significant obstacle to achieving an urban character for the area, particularly those zoning provisions that govern setbacks and the development of interconnected mixed-use projects. However, the examination of Cobb County's UVC (urban village commercial) and PVC (planned village community) zoning districts that is now underway will help the steering committee understand the two zoning districts' capacity to accommodate desired development, perhaps leading the way to needed zoning reforms.

Lessons Learned

The Cumberland strategic planning process has served two important purposes —to craft the actual plan and to create a network of stakeholders who will drive and ensure plan implementation. The consul-

tant team enhanced the briefing book by undertaking interviews with individual members of the steering committee and representatives of relevant government agencies and the community. The issue of increasing density to create critical mass, a sense of place, and transit efficiencies has been particularly challenging as the notion of increasing density to decrease congestion is not widely understood.

The concept of a place-making dividend is proving powerful in focusing the steering committee's vision. To realize the vision for the Cumberland CID, groups of committee members have taken on a variety of tasks associated with implementation of the major components of the Blueprint Cumberland Strategic Plan. Over the coming months, the groups will convene to identify specific projects that will take the Cumberland-Galleria suburban business district from its current status to the steering committee's collective vision. The strategic plan will play a major role in the coordination of public and private sector funds and programs to effect the transformation of the Cumberland-Galleria suburban business district.

Source: Christopher Leinberger and Gregg Logan, Robert Charles Lesser & Co.

The Value of Common Sense and Consensus

A consensus strategy is the only strategy with any reasonable prospect for effective and timely implementation. After all, strategic planning is a process based on common sense, good will, and mutual understanding. Ultimately, the success of a strategic plan hinges on the depth of its conceptualization and the implementation of place-making and community-building initia-

tives relevant to the needs and circumstances of a given suburban business district. In addition, the commitment to and timely manner of plan implementation are crucial to a plan's ability to enhance real estate values. Chattanooga and Albuquerque offer outstanding examples of two communities that undertook successful strategic planning efforts that transformed their business districts; indeed, they stand as models for transforming America's suburban business districts.

chapter 11

Creating Place, Not Just Space— Capturing the Place-Making Dividend

Major demographic changes in America's population are creating new but as yet unsatisfied demands and opportunities. The real estate capital markets are looking for safe havens secured by strong market demand. Traffic congestion, fiscal constraints, and political opposition to significant road expansion programs are pointing to fundamental shifts in residential, office, and retail location and commuting patterns. Americans traveling extensively overseas and with more disposable income than in any preceding generation are demanding far more from their living, working, and shopping environments. New approaches to governance and city planning are fostering the emergence of fresh approaches to development opportunities as residential neighborhoods are closing their hearts and minds to suburban expansion in their own backyards.

These development trends offer the potential to transform America's more than 200 suburban business districts into more vibrant, pedestrian-friendly live-work-shop places. Currently, such places are in short supply as most suburban business districts encompass a variety of free-standing uses with little or no integration among them, a transportation system that is automobile-oriented and often hostile to pedestrians, and an absence of civic identity that translates into no sense of place. The transformation of suburban business districts demands a new form of community building that relies on both the vertical and horizontal integration of office, retail, residential, and community uses through the creation of places that Americans find so special and irresistible that they reward them with repeat visitation, personal investment, and residential choice.

ULI's Ten Principles

In late June 2001, the Urban Land Institute convened a task force of 17 planning and development experts under the chairmanship of ULI Trustee A. Eugene Kohn of Kohn Pedersen Fox in New York. Over two and one-half days, the task force was briefed on the research and analysis that formed the basis of this book, visited suburban business districts in the metropolitan Washington, D.C., area, and then devised ten principles to underpin strategic planning aimed at transforming suburban business districts.

1. Understand Your Position in the Market

The essential foundation of any strategic plan for transforming a suburban business district is an understanding of the demographic and market trends influencing that district and its associated opportunities. It is vital to understand the suburban business district's position and potential in the market vis à vis other competing districts in the region. The existence of too many competing districts within the region can lead to a surplus of retail space, lease restrictions, and low rents that frustrate rather than facilitate the transformation of suburban business districts. Indeed, an oversupply of development entitlements can similarly undermine the effective transformation of suburban business districts. To identify unsatisfied opportunities for investment and growth, both development interests and state and local governments must understand and evaluate trends in multifamily residential, retail, office, civic, cultural, and community development on the basis of local market circumstances.

A clear and concise evaluation of potential public revenue sources and the strength of the local tax base is essential. On the basis of fiscal assets and liabilities, the strategic plan can set forth priorities for both the private and public sectors that have a realistic prospect of achievement. Such an honest and lucid analysis of market potential also acts as the investment prospectus that can attract the attention and capital of investors. Suburban business districts that decisively transform their develop-

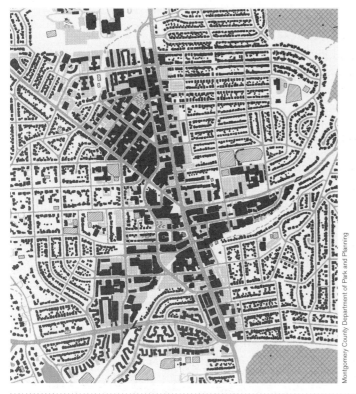

The map on the left shows the compact suburban business district of Bethesda, Maryland. The map on the right shows the fragmented suburban business district of Rock Spring Park and Montgomery Mall in Montgomery County, Maryland. As both maps are at the same scale, the distance between buildings, the plat, and the amount of land consumed by surface parking graphically displays how the fine grid creates a compact, connected, and pedestrian- and transit-friendly suburban business district.

ment configuration, density, and use mix to become pedestrian- and transit-friendly will reap dividends in the form of enhanced real estate value, community building, and tax base. The precise strategy for each suburban business district will necessarily vary with local circumstances and needs.

2. Build Community Support

Community building involves the mobilization of public and private capital to create assets that engender community use, pride, and value. Laying the foundation for successful community building requires the activation and growth of community support through stakeholder consensus. The transformation of suburban business districts relies on a three-way partnership that brings together the private sector, government, and the broader community. Community outreach must be ingrained in the process of transformation from the outset. Understanding builds trust, ownership builds commitment, and

achievement builds pride. Many community-building projects have failed or wasted precious time and financial resources either in litigation or in regaining community support because the essential communication channels were not in place from project inception. The three-way partnership should be built on a firm foundation of shared goals and, at the very least, include a fair and open process that allows all interested parties to be heard before decisions are made and implemented.

The use of the Internet, architectural renderings and virtual computer models, public meetings, community workshops, community advisory groups, stakeholder meetings, local press briefings, design charrettes, and/or public/private partnerships combine traditional with more innovative techniques to tap community advice, understanding, and support. These instruments should facilitate an explicit process of decision making that enables the transformation of the suburban business district to proceed step by step to an outcome welcomed by a majority of the stakeholders. The process should have a finite time frame and focus on outcomes. Caution needs to be exercised to ensure that the process is not subverted by parties with a vested interest in delaying the transformation of the suburban business district.

Citizen opposition to development, often termed NIMBY-ism (not in my back yard), will be less likely to be an issue in suburban business districts for the simple reason that districts generally lack a residential component. Nonetheless, community concern with traffic congestion and other issues makes it essential that the planning, regulatory, and marketing tools for the transformation of suburban business districts are visual and accurately simulate the real-life impact of development proposals if such proposals are to gain citizen support. The communication process between developer and government needs to be of a high standard, particularly as government agencies may need to play a financial role in support of a project. The process should explicitly identify who is responsible for making what decisions while the communication process should focus on transparency and the building of trust and understanding among all stakeholders. Finally, local government support is

absolutely crucial in that land use is most frequently a matter of local government control. Without an entitlement, there is no right to develop, no potential income stream, and therefore no bankable development project.

3. Develop a Vision and a Plan

Armed with a proper understanding of market potential and community and government

In the Anaheim district around Disneyland in southern California, a pedestrian-unfriendly space was transformed into a pedestrian-friendly space. Pictured are the before-and-after photographs that show the significance of the transformation.

needs and aspirations, a development vision can be shaped of what is feasible and then a strategic plan can be devised to enable realization of the vision. While the vision needs to be tempered with realism, it should nonetheless be bold and innovative, drawing on the history, character, and strengths of the community of which it is a part. A transformed suburban business district should become a community center that offers a range of live-work-shop opportunities and is seamlessly integrated into the surrounding community through strong pedestrian interconnections.

The strategic plan that guides implementation of the vision must have community support and draw on expert professional advice. It must also be financially robust. Business districts comprise many buildings, and the spaces between those buildings, if properly conceptualized and redesigned, can interconnect to create a sense of place. It is the sense of place that the community recognizes and rewards, thereby creating real estate value through increased rents, retail sales, and growing capital value. The strategic plan is the management tool through which the place-making dividend is achieved and sustained. Unless a strategic plan is implemented, it is not worth the paper it is written on—or the time and money invested in its preparation.

4. Stress Results over Regulations

An essential part of the transformation of suburban business districts is the move from the segregation of land uses through zoning to the creation of mixed-use and integrated development through place making. The regulatory tools applied during the 20th century to mandate and control place making have been woefully inadequate and in most cases counterproductive in vesting suburban business districts with a sense of place. In concentrating on legally

In the proposed downtown Kendall development in Miami, Dade County, Florida, the banks of Snapper Creek are to be transformed through the use of infill development. The photographs of the existing development and the proposed redevelopment capture the extent of the planned transformation.

prescriptive and exclusionary zoning codes, we have come to rely on a flawed mechanism to convey the vision of the places we wish to create. Black-letter law and legal terminology do not evoke the full power of the visual sense, and they certainly do not trigger the companion senses of sound, smell, taste, or touch. The literal interpretation of the law, with its limited and limiting vocabulary and legal style, fails to evoke a sense of place or capture the imagination in the way good writing or a film can.

The advent of "sensory law" and visioning processes is one approach that can equip us with new tools to aid the regulatory process to "virtually" create places so we can experience them *before* we approve and construct them. Sensory law can permit us to use our senses to assess the quality of a proposed project and its contribution to place making. Using this approach, the district plan, in digital form, can use real-time interactive design models synchronized with sound to evoke a three-dimensional sense of place. Through a thorough process of consultation and the creation of a development vision, the land use entitlement process for suburban business districts could move from inflexible zoning codes to strategic plans that allow greater flexibility and encourage the district and its component developments to be progressively modified to meet ever-changing community needs and aspirations. As Eugene Kohn said during the ULI task force's deliberations, "Land use controls should allow projects to be modified to meet changing community needs without necessarily triggering a new entitlement process."

At its inception, nearly every best-practice example in this book contravened and required amendment to the zoning code before it became reality. The amendment process involved lengthy and expensive delays to what were inherently risky projects. Scarce funds lost to regulatory amendment or a lengthy entitlement process can significantly erode a project's financial feasibility and bankability. Orenco Station in Hillsboro, Oregon, provides an instructive example of flexible regulatory performance standards and design guidelines as does the Place Making Code developed and pioneered

by the Gold Coast City Council in Australia as part of its sensory law project. It is likely that the best results will be achieved where the community, government, and private sector work together through public/private partnerships such as were used at CityPlace in West Palm Beach, Florida, and downtown San Diego.

5. Break Up the Superblocks and Optimize Connectivity

The transformation of a suburban business district from a collection of geographically proximate but segregated real estate projects into integrated places allows customers and clients to patronize various establishments in that district more easily. No longer forced into their cars to move from one establishment to another, patrons and clients can park their car once for the duration of their stay, thereby reducing the amount of space otherwise needed for on-site parking at each establishment. At the same time, the reduced number of vehicle trips within the suburban business district translates into lower levels of congestion and permits a reduction in the width and capacity of internal roads; as a result, the district can develop into a place. Achieving the integration of uses demands a pedestrian-friendly, fine-grid development that engages and does not intimidate the pedestrian; instead, it offers interconnectivity and easy walking access between uses. Achieving this transformation in suburban business districts will require strong political leadership and, often, the catalytic investment of public funds to

- break up superblock plats;
- create improved pedestrian linkages;
- provide or enhance public open space;
- establish community uses;
- develop structured parking;
- create public/private partnerships;
- establish special taxing districts and tax-increment financing mechanisms; and
- provide public transit before demand exists to support it.

As Carol Willis alluded to in her book *Form Follows Finance,* the value of real estate derives from its intensity and interconnection of use. The essence of community is human connection and a sense of belonging—an identifiable place and an active public realm.

Initially, both tenants and investors found standalone real estate projects in suburban business districts simple to understand and easy to access. As discrete packages, the investment markets found them simple to finance and digest. Further, with the growing number of comparable developments, appraisers could readily determine a project's capital value. Increasingly, standalone projects reflect a compartmentalization of community life.

Improved interconnectivity, however, can be achieved through better signage and way-finding to encourage intradistrict movement, improved road layouts and circulation patterns, the provision of shuttle bus service, and the strategic location of parking areas and sidewalk connections. The integration of development, the provision and management of shared parking, the creation of mixed uses along pedestrian linkages, and the increase in density around transit stations can be effective tools to break the cycle of traffic congestion while creating more pedestrian- and community-friendly living environments.

6. Embrace Mixed Uses

Mixed uses create critical mass and a sense of place by affording the community a wider range of goods, services, and experiences at one location, thereby increasing connectivity and choice and reducing trip generation rates. The diversification of uses within projects hedges a district's income stream and makes for proper and balanced risk management of property investments. Not surprisingly, after a half-century of segregation of uses, property investors and financiers are learning today's lessons even as consumers grow more discerning about the environments in which they want to live. Mixed uses can play a critical role in the transformation of suburban business districts. Mixed uses provide us with choice. It is for this reason that most suburban business districts would benefit from the addition of multifamily

housing, increased development densities to support transit, and the development of a mix of uses on infill parcels, voids, and open parking lots to create more pedestrian-friendly environments.

To create and reinforce a sense of community in a suburban business district requires a critical mass of mixed uses—a rule of thumb suggests a minimum of 200,000 square feet of retail uses and 2,000 dwelling units within a ten-minute walk. Office uses feed retail operations by supplying customers for stores and restaurants both during the day and after work. Retail uses within a ten-minute walk of employment places or residences reinforce amenities—restaurants, bookstores, clothing stores, gift shops, and coffee bars—that permit and encourage employees and residents to go out to lunch or run errands without relying on their cars. The addition of theaters, museums, art galleries, libraries, post offices, and town halls, where properly integrated into suburban business districts, attracts significant pedestrian traffic that supports a range of other uses.

7. Honor the Human Scale— Create a Pedestrian-Friendly Place

The creation of a live-work-shop environment with a sense of place is both a community need and aspiration. Thomas Lee got it right in his opening remarks at ULI's first Place Making Conference in Chicago in May 1999. "Place making is the very essence of real estate development. As people choose one place over another, the place of choice attracts a higher valuation and sells at a premium. Desired places are ones that appeal to all the senses—sight, sound, smell, taste, and touch. It is a rich mix of aesthetic design, the activities available in that place, the quality of what is being provided, and its price. Successful place making is therefore about meeting the demand from the local community. It is not a formulaic real estate product or the latest fad. Therefore, developers should exercise a high level of conceptualization and market matching in their place-making activities."

In transforming suburban business districts, decision makers need to think like a pedestrian.

The successful transformation of a district demands a strong focus on improving the public domain and the design and activity within the streetscape, specifically as related to

- the length and width of the public domain or street;
- the volume and speed of vehicles;
- lighting, finishes, and street furniture;
- the range of available activities;
- the scale of development, human comfort, and sense of belonging;
- the ability to engage the place and navigate easily within it;
- the animation and continuity of pedestrian-friendly street-level activities;
- the incorporation of art, architecture, and community icons;
- the provision of on-street parking and ease of access to off-street parking garages;
- the creation of pedestrian linkages lined with interesting and enticing activities;
- the provision of transportation choice;
- the maintenance of clean, safe, and diversified streets where people of all ages and races, visitors and residents, come together to celebrate community life;

- the provision of public parks and community celebration places that are alive with civic and cultural events; and
- the interest and stimulation created by the passing parade down the street.

Besides allowing people to perform essential functions such as employment and shopping, places should be enjoyable, entertaining, and educational. Success in place making lies in configuring spaces and structures and the interconnections between them in a way that facilitates and encourages human activity and interaction —an environment that people want to be a part of because it has been designed, built, and main-

In its Santana Row development in San Jose, California, Federal Realty Investment Trust is replacing an obsolete strip mall with a pedestrian-friendly, tree-lined shopping street and mixed-use development that honor the human scale.

tained with the goal of satisfying human needs and aspirations from the mundane to the spiritual. A successful place appeals to the senses, engaging visitors and inhabitants alike in a voyage of discovery of enticing sights, sounds, and scents.

8. Think Transit—Think Density

With the increasing public awareness of the cost of traffic congestion, suburban business districts that offer a choice of transportation options and more than a 9:00-to-5:00 range of activities—and thus promote travel at other than peak hours—will enjoy a competitive advantage.

Jones Lang LaSalle's Frank Mann reports, "Access to mass transportation and rich cultural activities are the two pluses of in-town property that aren't found in outlying counties. Culture and transportation add value because they attract a young workforce which my clients seek." Similarly, Terry Holzheimer's comparative study of the Arlington and Fairfax, Virginia, office markets found that a significant percentage of office tenants willingly pay a rental premium for locating in transit-linked offices—a factor that will become more critical as employers are forced to compete for a reduced labor supply that is demanding greater transportation choice.

Increased development density, especially around transit stations, offers the potential to make the suburban business district more compact by reducing the space between buildings and, in turn, permitting better integration and pedestrian interconnections. Increased density supports the cost-effective provision of a wider range of uses and transportation systems. According to Professor Edward Glaeser of Harvard University, "The future of the city depends on the continued advantages of density. . . . The dominant urban form of the future, almost unquestionably, will be the edge city [the subur-

Using the existing street to accommodate transit can provide the suburban business district with a freedom of choice in transportation mode and create a more pedestrian-friendly place. A typical suburban commercial street (top) and its proposed new form (above) show how dramatically suburban business districts can be transformed.

ban business district as defined by ULI] with its moderate density levels." Indeed, Arlington County, Virginia, by increasing density of development around its Metro rail stations, has consolidated its tax base and protected the balance of the county from more intense development.

With available options such as pedestrian connections, transit, and bicycle use, vehicle trips and required parking areas are reduced along with the level of traffic congestion. Multifamily housing integrated into the suburban business district further promotes transportation choice. More balanced government transportation spending should enhance the accessibility of existing community and real estate assets rather than providing, as it has to date, the means to abandon existing congested locations for greener pastures at the urban fringe and beyond. Those suburban business districts that fail to balance automobile access with improved pedestrian and transit access will put their future patronage, attractiveness, and capital value at risk.

9. Create a Public/Private Partnership

In most cases, the successful transformation of a suburban business district depends on the ability of the public and private sectors to cooperate under a partnership arrangement that engenders community support, minimizes project risk, and delivers place-making dividends to all stakeholders. The place-making dividend accrues to both the developer and the community. Therefore, it is only fair that both should invest in its creation by way of a partnership that leverages the investments of both. Business improvement districts (BID) or redevelopment agencies can establish the public/private management entities that can use tax-increment financing (TIF) or special tax levies to fund capital and recurrent expenditures in the catalytic transformation of a suburban business district. The Bethesda Urban Partnership, a BID, now manages and promotes the Bethesda, Maryland, suburban business district through the provision of local transit services, a program of special events, and development. The county government provides library services, public park improvements, and garages for shared parking.

Public Financing Tools

- Tax-increment financing
- Tax abatements
- Parking bonds
- Land leases
- Low-income housing tax credits
- Transit-oriented development funding–Transportation Equity Act for the 21st Century (TEA-21) funds
- Loans and grants

In Uptown Houston, the suburban business district has used TIF to break up the superblock plat and provide better pedestrian interconnectivity within the suburban business district. This program has been pivotal to the transformation process and would not have occurred without a public/private partnership. The realization of the strategic plan cannot rely solely on developer levies or a zoning and entitlement process that often works against the transformation process. To harness government processes and structures in furtherance of desired development outcomes, a community must understand and endorse a clear vision and act to bring it to fruition. A concise strategic plan is an essential prerequisite to those vital public/private partnerships that embrace government as a strategic partner. To be most effective, the strategic plan must become the vehicle for coordinating the policies, programs, and fiscal priorities of each level of government so as to transform suburban business districts into new live-workshop places.

10. Share and Manage Parking

Where each development stands alone, it must necessarily provide its own on-site parking. Devoting large portions of a development site to surface parking lots encourages patrons to rely on the automobile and, at the same time, prevents integrated, pedestrian-friendly development and ensures that the development density is so low as to preclude cost-effective transit provision. The predominant driver of development form and configuration becomes parking. It is therefore vital in the transformation of suburban business districts that the place—not the parking facility—becomes the destination. According to one estimate, for every car in San Diego, there are currently five parking spaces provided throughout the city, which means that accommodating the projected 1 million increase in population over the next 20 years will demand the provision of an additional 685,000 parking spaces—37 square miles of surface area. In these circumstances, it becomes virtually impossible to go from one building to another without driving.

One solution is increased use of parking structures and improved parking design and placement, which can reduce the land area devoted to parking and allow buildings to be closer and more integrated with each other. The strategic location, design, and programming of parking structures can also create or enhance attractive, well-traveled pedestrian linkages that can reduce demand for car movement and thus parking spaces. Moreover, the use of ground-level space in parking structures for retail and service uses can create a more attractive streetscape and pedestrian environment, encouraging more pedestrian trips. On-street parking can be used effectively to provide attractive and functional parking arrangements in retail areas.

Another solution is to allow and plan for shared parking within mixed-use areas. When properly managed, shared parking can reduce the maximum number of parking spaces required, as different users can park in the same space for different purposes at different times of the day and week, thus reducing the effects of peak demand from a single land use. Mixed-use environments can also reduce demand for parking by increasing pedestrian trips. For example, a restaurant/delicatessen within walking distance of lunchtime office workers will require fewer parking spaces than a restaurant that can be reached only by automobile. Office space located within easy walking distance of a hotel may require fewer visitor parking spaces than office space without such proximity, as business guests staying at the hotel will be able to walk to the office.

Parking nonetheless involves an opportunity cost, which is the forgone development potential of the land. However, free or low-cost parking is likely to remain a feature of suburban business districts. For this reason, local government funding or underwriting is often required to cover the difference in construction costs between surface parking lots and parking garages. Apart from the potential to charge nominal parking fees, costs can be defrayed by rent derived from using the ground floor of the parking garage for restaurants and shops. First-floor retail uses lining structured parking creates an active streetfront as in Walnut Creek, California. In Mizner Park in Boca Raton, Florida, the parking structure is separated from the street by a row of apartments.

In downtown Phoenix, the Arizona Center adopted an innovative parking policy and financial solution when the city developed the parking structures and then, as part of the entitlement process, required all future developments to buy a share of the structures rather than provide parking on their own sites. It is essential to provide no more parking than is required for the economic viability of the development and to require the incorporation of shared-parking provisions into strategic plans in place of mandatory zoning and parking codes. Where possible, tenants should be charged at least a nominal rent so that parking is recognized as a service with an attendant cost. The rental fee creates the basis for the parking structures' treatment and valuation as a real estate asset that can then be leveraged.

Carpe Diem—Seize the Day

Suburban business districts, if they are to realize their potential, must be transformed into more functional, more diverse, more interconnected, and more pedestrian-friendly places than they are today. These places are likely to be linked by improved transit service. They will place greater emphasis on improved pedestrian linkages and the achievement of place-making standards beyond the realm of traditional zoning provisions. Public agencies are likely to be called on to become full financial partners in the transformation of suburban business districts.

At the same time, the automobile, far from being abandoned as a mode of transportation, should be put in its proper place and become part of a balanced choice of transportation options. Limited government spending on infrastructure expansion and the proliferation of smart growth programs will severely curtail the practice of abandoning obsolete buildings for new greenfield development on the exurban fringe. Indeed, employers when faced with a tight labor market will compete for the best employees by touting the quality of life that distinguishes the areas in and around their place of employment.

To transform suburban business districts, the U.S. land use planning/regulatory and real estate community will need to shift its focus to the creation of *place*. This can happen only when a strong partnership between the community and the public and private sectors is developed, focusing on the implementation of a new vision to achieve a sense of place for the suburban business district.